Daniel W. Phil...
Editor

Ment...
in the Cri...

Mental Health Issues in the Criminal Justice System has
been co-published simultaneously as *Journal of Offender
Rehabilitation*, Volume 45, Numbers 1/2 2007.

Pre-publication
REVIEWS,
COMMENTARIES,
EVALUATIONS . . .

"TIMELY AND INFORMATIVE. . . .
The articles discuss the growing
nature of the problem, some of the
special challenges that offenders
with serious mental illness present
for the corrections system as well as
some programs and strategies to
more effectively deal with offenders
with a serious mental illness within
the criminal justice system."

Elizabeth Rehm Wachtel, PhD
*Associate Professor, Department
of Correctional and Juvenile Justice
Studies, Eastern Kentucky University*

More pre-publication
REVIEWS, COMMENTARIES, EVALUATIONS . . .

"READERS WILL BENEFIT FROM THE TIMELINESS AND BREADTH OF COVERAGE and also from the realistic nature of the focus; the focus is on problems and issues routinely faced in the field rather than celebrated, unusual cases. Particularly informative are the sections of the volume that address mental health issues in prison and jail settings as well as sections addressing successful community adjustment."

Kevin Minor, Professor and Chair
Correctional and Juvenile Justice Studies
College of Justice and Safety
Eastern Kentucky University

"A WELCOME ADDITION TO THE LITERATURE. . . . A COMPELLING SUMMARY of the data regarding the size, scope, and complexity of the issues. . . . Goes beyond reminding us of the system failures that led to the over-representation of people with mental illness in the criminal justice system and challenge us to confront that history by changing the way we serve people. The authors portray the diversity of subpopulations and offer guidance on managing the balance between therapeutic and safety concerns for both youth and adults. . . . A BOOK THAT SHOULD BE READ AND DISCUSSED by professionals in the fields of mental health, criminal justice and addiction. . . . Gets us closer to a shared understanding, a common vision, and the elements of a strategy that will result in more treatment, less incarceration, and more lives restored."

Margaret A. Pennington, MSSW
Director of Planning, Evaluation and Consultation Services, R.E.A.C.H. of Louisville, Inc.

"INSIGHTFUL AND POWER-FUL. . . . Phillips understands the challenges and needs that jails across America face regarding the mentally ill. . . . Honest and aware of the prevalence of mental illness in jails and prisons and what is happening to the mentally ill due to the lack of resources, medications, funding, successful diversion programs and therapeutic services and the need for services upon release. . . . A WONDERFUL AND IMPORTANT ACCOUNT OF MENTAL ILLNESS IN JAILS AND PRISONS and what is needed to assist this population in being successful."

Marilyn Rogan, BS
Captain of Central Booking Bureau
Clark County Detention Center
Las Vegas, Nevada

"A TIMELY AND INSIGHTFUL ANALYSIS of what can perhaps best be described as a crisis facing our jails and prisons. . . . This edited book's strengths lie in the breadth and depth of the chapters. Initial chapters identify the prevalence of mental health problems, while subsequent chapters provide direction for those who want to address these problems. What I liked most about this book is the balance of discussion of institutional and community programs. . . . Phillips and his contributing authors are to be commended for producing AN EXCELLENT COMPILATION that will be of value to policy makers, mental health professionals, and corrections personnel who are concerned with meeting the needs of offenders with mental health problems."

Ronald Roesch, PhD
Professor of Psychology, Director
Mental Health, Law, and Policy Institute
Simon Fraser University, BC, Canada

Mental Health Issues in the Criminal Justice System

Mental Health Issues in the Criminal Justice System has been co-published simultaneously as *Journal of Offender Rehabilitation*, Volume 45, Numbers 1/2 2007.

Monographic Separates from the *Journal of Offender Rehabilitation*®

For additional information on these and other Haworth Press titles, including descriptions, tables of contents, reviews, and prices, use the Quicksearch catalog at http://www.HaworthPress.com.

The *Journal of Offender Rehabilitation*® is the successor title to the *Journal of Offender Counseling, Services & Rehabilitation,** which changed title after Vol. 15, No. 2, 1990. The *Journal of Offender Rehabilitation*®, under its new title, begins with Vol. 16, Nos. 1/2, 1990.

Mental Health Issues in the Criminal Justice System, edited by Daniel W. Phillips III, PhD (Vol. 45, No. 1/2, 2007). *"Timely and informative. . . . The articles discuss the growing nature of the problem, some of the special challenges that offenders with serious mental illness present for the corrections system as well as some programs and strategies to more effectively deal with offenders with a serious mental illness within the criminal justice system." (Elizabeth Rehm Wachtel, PhD, Associate Professor, Department of Correctional and Juvenile Justice Studies, Eastern Kentucky University)*

Women Who Perpetrate Relationship Violence: Moving Beyond Political Correctness, edited by Frederick P. Buttell, PhD, and Michelle Mohr Carney, PhD (Vol. 41, No. 4, 2005). *"The overview and review of the literature by Dutton and colleagues is quite good. There is a good discussion of clinical implications and a very thorough list of published work in this area." (Bonnie E. Carlson, PhD, Professor, School of Social Welfare, University at Albany, State University of New York)*

Rehabilitation Issues, Problems, and Prospects in Boot Camp, edited by Brent B. Benda, PhD, and Nathaniel J. Pallone, PhD (Vol. 40, No. 3/4, 2005). *"A well-researched, well-written, and well-presented collection of chapters by the leading experts on the subject. Required reading for policymakers and scholars interested in discovering what works (and what doesn't) in corrections. This book collects some of the best and most recent empirical research on boot camps, along with several excellent summaries of the extant research. It is timely, thought-provoking, and a major contribution to the literature on correctional treatment." (Craig Hemmens, JD, PhD, Chair and Professor, Department of Criminal Justice Administration, Boise State University)*

Treating Substance Abusers in Correctional Contexts: New Understandings, New Modalities, edited by Nathaniel J. Pallone, PhD (Vol. 37, No. 3/4, 2003). *"Intriguing and illuminating. . . . Includes qualitative and quantitative research on juvenile and adult-oriented programs in the United States, Britain, and Hong Kong. . . . Examines a multitude of issues relevant to substance abuse treatment in the criminal justice system. . . . Also includes several chapters examining the effectiveness of drug courts. . . . Provides some answers to the questions being asked about RSAT programs and highlights what may be the most intriguing and encouraging development in corrections in the past quarter-century. I highly recommend this book to anyone interested in substance abuse treatment programs." (Craig Hemmens, JD, PhD, Chair and Associate Professor, Department of Criminal Justice Administration, Boise State University)*

Transcendental Meditation® in Criminal Rehabilitation and Crime Prevention, edited by Charles N. Alexander, PhD, Kenneth G. Walton, PhD, David Orme-Johnson, PhD, Rachel S. Goodman, PhD, and Nathaniel J. Pallone, PhD (Vol. 36, No. 1/2/3/4, 2003). *"Makes a strong case that meditation can accelerate development in adult criminal populations, leading to reduced recidivism and other favorable outcomes. . . . Contains original research and reviews of over 25 studies that demonstrate the effectiveness of TM programs in criminal rehabilitation." (Juan Pascual-Leone, MD, PhD, Professor of Psychology, York University)*

Religion, the Community, and the Rehabilitation of Criminal Offenders, edited by Thomas P. O'Connor, BCL, BTheol, MS, and Nathaniel J. Pallone, PhD (Vol. 35, No. 3/4, 2002). *Examines the relationship between faith-based programs, religion, and offender rehabilitation.*

Drug Courts in Operation: Current Research, edited by James J. Hennessy, PhD, and Nathaniel J. Pallone, PhD (Vol. 33, No. 4, 2001). *"As one of the founders of the drug court movement, I can testify that Dr. Hennessy's book represents the highest level of sophistication in this field." (Michael O. Smith, MD, Director, Lincoln Recovery Center, Bronx, New York; Assistant Clinical Professor of Psychiatry, Cornell University Medical School)*

Family Empowerment as an Intervention Strategy in Juvenile Delinquency, edited by Richard Dembo, PhD, and Nathaniel J. Pallone, PhD (Vol. 33, No. 1, 2001). *"A hands-on book. . . . Provides detailed guidelines for counselors regarding implementation of the FEI curriculum . . . accurately describes the scope of counselor responsibilities and the nature of treatment interventions. Unique in its coverage of counselor competencies and training/supervision needs. Innovative and based on solid empirical evidence." (Roger H. Peters, PhD, Professor, University of South Florida, Tampa)*

Race, Ethnicity, Sexual Orientation, Violent Crime: The Realities and the Myths, edited by Nathaniel J. Pallone, PhD (Vol. 30, No. 1/2, 1999). *"A fascinating book which illuminates the complexity of race as it applies to the criminal justice system and the myths and political correctness that have shrouded the real truth. . . . I highly recommend this book for those who study causes of crime in minority populations." (Joseph R. Carlson, PhD, Associate Professor, University of Nebraska at Kearney)*

Sex Offender Treatment: Biological Dysfunction, Intrapsychic Conflict, Interpersonal Violence, edited by Eli Coleman, PhD, S. Margretta Dwyer, MA, and Nathaniel J. Pallone, PhD (Vol. 23, No. 3/4, 1996). *"Offers a review of current assessment and treatment theory while addressing critical issues such as standards of care, use of phallometry, and working with specialized populations such as exhibitionists and developmentally disabled clients. . . . A valuable addition to the reader's professional library." (Robert E. Freeman-Longo, MRC, LPC, Director, The Safer Society Press)*

The Psychobiology of Aggression: Engines, Measurement, Control, edited by Marc Hillbrand, PhD, and Nathaniel J. Pallone, PhD (Vol. 21, No. 3/4, 1995). *"A comprehensive sourcebook for the increasing dialogue between psychobiologists, neuropsychiatrists, and those interested in a full understanding of the dynamics and control of criminal aggression." (Criminal Justice Review)*

Young Victims, Young Offenders: Current Issues in Policy and Treatment, edited by Nathaniel J. Pallone, PhD (Vol. 21, No. 1/2, 1994). *"Extremely practical. . . . Aims to increase knowledge about the patterns of youthful offenders and give help in designing programs of prevention and rehabilitation." (S. Margretta Dwyer, Director of Sex Offender Treatment Program, Department of Family Practice, University of Minnesota)*

Sex Offender Treatment: Psychological and Medical Approaches, edited by Eli Coleman, PhD, S. Margretta Dwyer, and Nathaniel J. Pallone, PhD (Vol. 18, No. 3/4, 1992). *"Summarizes research worldwide on the various approaches to treating sex offenders for both researchers and clinicians." (SciTech Book News)*

The Clinical Treatment of the Criminal Offender in Outpatient Mental Health Settings: New and Emerging Perspectives,* edited by Sol Chaneles, PhD, and Nathaniel J. Pallone, PhD (Vol. 15, No. 1, 1990). *"The clinical professional concerned with the outpatient treatment of the criminal offender will find this book informative and useful." (Criminal Justice Review)*

Older Offenders: Current Trends,* edited by Sol Chaneles, PhD, and Cathleen Burnett, PhD (Vol. 13, No. 2, 1985). *"Broad in scope and should provide a fruitful beginning for future discussion and exploration." (Criminal Justice Review)*

Prisons and Prisoners: Historical Documents,* edited by Sol Chaneles, PhD (Vol. 10, No. 1/2, 1985). *"May help all of us . . . to gain some understanding as to why prisons have resisted change for over 300 years. . . . Very challenging and very disturbing." (Public Offender Counseling Association)*

Gender Issues, Sex Offenses, and Criminal Justice: Current Trends,* edited by Sol Chaneles, PhD (Vol. 9, No. 1/2, 1984). *"The contributions of the work will be readily apparent to any reader interested in an interdisciplinary approach to criminology and women's studies." (Criminal Justice Review)*

Current Trends in Correctional Education: Theory and Practice,* edited by Sol Chaneles, PhD (Vol. 7, No. 3/4, 1983). *"A laudable presentation of educational issues in relation to corrections." (International Journal of Offender Therapy and Comparative Criminology)*

Mental Health Issues
in the Criminal Justice System

Daniel W. Phillips III
Editor

Mental Health Issues in the Criminal Justice System has been co-published simultaneously as *Journal of Offender Rehabilitation*, Volume 45, Numbers 1/2 2007.

The Haworth Press

www.HaworthPress.com

Mental Health Issues in the Criminal Justice System has been co-published simultaneously as *Journal of Offender Rehabilitation*, Volume 45, Numbers 1/2 2007.

Library of Congress Cataloging-in-Publication Data

Mental health issues in the criminal justice system / Daniel W. Phillips III, editor.
     p. cm.
     "Mental Health Issues in the Criminal Justice System has been co-published simultaneously as Journal of Offender Rehabilitation, Volume 45, Numbers 1/2 2007."
     Includes bibliographical references and index.
     ISBN 978-0-7890-3769-5 (hard cover : alk. paper) – ISBN 978-0-7890-3770-1 (soft cover : alk. paper)
     1. Mentally ill offenders. 2. Criminal justice, Administration of. 3. Forensic psychiatry.
I. Phillips, Daniel W. II. Journal of Offender Rehabilitation.
  HV6133.M45 2008
  364.3'8–dc22

                             2008001734

The HAWORTH PRESS
Abstracting, Indexing & Outward Linking
PRINT *and* ELECTRONIC BOOKS & JOURNALS

This section provides you with a list of major indexing & abstracting services and other tools for bibliographic access. That is to say, each service began covering this periodical during the year noted in the right column. Most Websites which are listed below have indicated that they will either post, disseminate, compile, archive, cite or alert their own Website users with research-based content from this work. (This list is as current as the copyright date of this publication.)

Abstracting, Website/Indexing Coverage . . . . Year When Coverage Began

- **Academic Search Premier (EBSCO)**
  <http://search.ebscohost.com> **2006**
- **Expanded Academic ASAP (Thomson Gale)** **1999**
- **Expanded Academic ASAP–International (Thomson Gale)** **1999**
- **InfoTrac Custom (Thomson Gale)** **2006**
- **InfoTrac OneFile (Thomson Gale)** **1999**
- **MasterFILE Premier (EBSCO)**
  <http://search.ebscohost.com> **2006**
- **ProQuest Academic Research Library**
  <http://www.proquest.com> **2006**
- **Psychological Abstracts (PsycINFO)** <http://www.apa.org> . . . **1976**
- **Research Library (ProQuest)** <http://www.proquest.com> **2006**
- **Social Services Abstracts (ProQuest CSA)**
  <http://www.csa.com> **1991**
- **Social Work Abstracts (NASW)**
  <http://www.silverplatter.com/catalog/swab.htm> **1982**
- **Sociological Abstracts (ProQuest CSA)**
  <http://www.csa.com> **1991**
- *Academic Source Premier (EBSCO)* <http://search.ebscohost.com>. . **2007**
- *British Library Inside (The British Library)*
  <http://www.bl.uk/services/current/inside.html> **2006**
- *Cambridge Scientific Abstracts (now ProQuest CSA)*
  <http://www.csa.com> **2006**

(continued)

(continued)

(continued)

- *Social Sciences Index/Abstracts/Full Text (H.W. Wilson)*
  <http://www.hwwilson.com> 1999
- *Studies on Women and Gender Abstracts (Routledge, Taylor &*
  Francis Group) <http://www.tandf.co.uk/swa> 1998
- *SwetsWise <http://www.swets.com>* 2001
- *TOC Premier (EBSCO) <http://search.ebscohost.com>* 2007
- *Violence and Abuse Abstracts (Sage)* 1994
- *Wilson Web <http://vnweb.hwwilsonweb.com/hww/Journals>* 2005
- *Women, Girls & Criminal Justice Newsletter (Civic Research*
  Institute) 2002
- *zetoc (The British Library) <http://www.bl.uk>* 2004

Bibliographic Access

- *Cabell's Directory of Publishing Opportunities in Psychology*
  <http://www.cabells.com>
- *Magazines for Libraries (Katz)*
- *MediaFinder <http://www.mediafinder.com/>*
- *Ulrich's Periodicals Directory: The Global Source for Periodicals*
  Information Since 1932 <http://www.Bowkerlink.com>

Special Bibliographic Notes related to special journal issues (separates) and indexing/abstracting:

- indexing/abstracting services in this list will also cover material in any "separate" that is co-published simultaneously with Haworth's special thematic journal issue or DocuSerial. Indexing/abstracting usually covers material at the article/chapter level.
- monographic co-editions are intended for either non-subscribers or libraries which intend to purchase a second copy for their circulating collections.
- monographic co-editions are reported to all jobbers/wholesalers/approval plans. The source journal is listed as the "series" to assist the prevention of duplicate purchasing in the same manner utilized for books-in-series.
- to facilitate user/access services all indexing/abstracting services are encouraged to utilize the co-indexing entry note indicated at the bottom of the first page of each article/chapter/contribution.
- this is intended to assist a library user of any reference tool (whether print, electronic, online, or CD-ROM) to locate the monographic version if the library has purchased this version but not a subscription to the source journal.
- individual articles/chapters in any Haworth publication are also available through the Haworth Document Delivery Service (HDDS).

AS PART OF OUR CONTINUING COMMITMENT TO BETTER SERVE OUR LIBRARY PATRONS, WE ARE PROUD TO BE WORKING WITH THE FOLLOWING ELECTRONIC SERVICES:

AGGREGATOR SERVICES

- EBSCOhost
- Ingenta
- J-Gate
- Minerva
- OCLC FirstSearch
- Oxmill
- SwetsWise

LINK RESOLVER SERVICES

- 1Cate (Openly Informatics)
- ChemPort (American Chemical Society)
- CrossRef
- Gold Rush (Coalliance)
- LinkOut (PubMed)
- LINKplus (Atypon)
- LinkSolver (Ovid)
- LinkSource with A-to-Z (EBSCO)
- Resource Linker (Ulrich's)
- SerialsSolutions (ProQuest)
- SFX (Ex Libris)
- Sirsi Resolver (SirsiDynix)
- Tour (TDnet)
- Vlink (Extensity)
- WebBridge (Innovative Interfaces)

The Haworth Press
Phone: 800–429–6784 • Fax: 800–895–0582 • Web: www.HaworthPress.com

Mental Health Issues
in the Criminal Justice System

CONTENTS

ABOUT THE EDITOR

Daniel W. Phillips III, PhD, is Assistant Professor of Sociology and Criminal Justice at Lindsey Wilson College in Columbia, Kentucky. He teaches a wide variety of classes including Corrections, Research Methods, and Mental Health Issues in the Criminal Justice System. Dr. Phillips has just completed a chapter on "Correctional Suicide" for the textbook entitled *Prison and Jail Administration: Practice & Theory*, 2nd edition. His recent peer-reviewed journal publications have been in the *American Journal of Criminal Justice* concerning disulfiram and the *Journal of Correctional Health Care* concerning jailer attitudes toward detainees with mental illness. He has presented in the past at the American Jail Association, American Corrections Association, and the National Sheriffs' Association regarding jail mental health and suicide. Dr. Phillips currently serves as a manuscript reviewer for more than 20 peer-reviewed journals. He also serves as a grant reviewer for the Substance Abuse and Mental Health Services Administration (SAMHSA).

Mental Health Issues in the Criminal Justice System. Pp. xvii-xviii.
Available online at http://jor.haworthpress.com

Preface

At the time of this writing, it has not been two weeks since the "Virginia Tech shooting" claimed the lives of more than 30 people. This case was particularly tragic to myself and book contributor Keith Durkin as we were graduate students at Virginia Tech for several years during the 1990s. Since the shootings much has been learned about the solo mass murderer. He suffered from some form of mental illness and had been seen by mental health professionals. He had even been held for psychiatric observation and been legally deemed a danger to himself. The very next day following the shootings I had to give a presentation entitled "Mentally Ill People in the Criminal Justice." This presentation had been scheduled more than two months previous. At this presentation everyone in the room knew my personal connection to Virginia Tech and the title of the presentation. They expected to hear me speak about the Virginia Tech shooting, the mind of a mass murderer, and how such people can be picked from the crowd before they harm others. What could be more dramatic than 30 + people killed by an offender with mental illness, building doors chained to prevent escape, and 170 + rounds fired? I let the audience know that this case was not the typical intersection of mental health and criminal justice and that I would speak about primarily non-killers who suffer from a mental illness who are a part of the criminal justice system and need treatment. In subsequent days, many newspaper stories discussed the idea that if mentally ill people don't want treatment, they should be forced into it and that people who fit some kind of potential mass murderer "profile" should be held over for psychiatric observation. I was very frustrated and let more than one reporter know that we have an obligation to treat those persons with mental illness who are currently incarcerated before we embark on a witch-hunt to find potential mass murderers in our midst. The articles contained in this special edition speak more to typical mental health and criminal justice intersections, not to spectacular cases like Virginia Tech. In this edition there are articles about a jail mental health diversion program, a specific prison profile, a segregation unit, and juveniles. There are qualitative pieces written by a jailer, an ex-convict who now works in mental health, and a criminologist who has been an expert in death penalty cases involving mental health issues. One article focuses on atypical anti-psychotics and their cost while others focus on sexual predators. Co-occurring disorders are the topic of two separate articles. The journal edition ends with a review of a book concerning abused children. The article authors have produced great works. They have produced a great amount of work within a small amount of time. Editing was easy as the manuscripts were interesting and complete. It has been a pleasure interacting and working with the contributors!

I would like to personally thank the following people for reviewing manuscripts: Daniel Williamson, Jennifer Williamson, Jody Crane, Myra Ford, David Ludden, Gary Patton, Martin Wesley, Cyril Kendrick, and Jackie Sandifer. Their help was instrumental in completing this project.

Daniel W. Phillips III, PhD

Mental Health Issues in the Criminal Justice System. Pp. 1-17.
Available online at http://jor.haworthpress.com
© 2007 by The Haworth Press, Inc. All rights reserved.
doi:10.1300/J076v45n01_01

Mental Illness in Offender Populations: Prevalence, Duty and Implications

IRINA R. SODERSTROM

ABSTRACT Prisons are increasingly being filled with inmates who suffer from mental illness. This paper examines the prevalence of mental illness in American jails and prisons, the duty government and society has to provide appropriate mental health treatment, and the implications for inmate safety, costs, recidivism, and community reintegration if meaningful mental health treatment is not provided. Finally, some recommendations regarding required and desired components of correctional mental health programs are discussed. doi:10.1300/J076v45n01_01 *[Article copies available for a fee from The Haworth Document Delivery Service: 1-800-HAWORTH. E-mail address: <docdelivery@haworthpress.com> Website: <http://www.HaworthPress.com> © 2007 by The Haworth Press, Inc. All rights reserved.]*

KEYWORDS Mental illness, mentally ill offenders, jails, prisons, prevalence

INTRODUCTION

When popular culture portrays inmates, it usually depicts hardened men with calculating minds and predatory dispositions. In reality, our prisons are filled mostly with non-violent, property and drug offenders.

Many of these prisoners are poor, uneducated, elderly, female, disabled, physically or mentally ill; many are a combination of all of the above. It is the mentally ill offenders who are the most vulnerable to self-harm and victimization by other inmates (Ruddell, 2006). It is the mentally ill offenders who are the most likely to fall through the cracks of the treatment, habilitation, and rehabilitation components of the criminal justice system (Human Rights Watch, 2003).

On the popular televisions series *Law and Order* (as well as *Law and Order: Special Victims Unit*) almost weekly appearances are made by the forensic psychologist to assess the mental health of the defendant and to use that information to help the police obtain a conviction. Unfortunately, pop culture leaves the public with a dichotomous understanding of what happens to the mentally ill in the criminal justice system—either a defendant "gets off" with a Not Guilty by Reason of Insanity (NGRI) plea and is locked up in a mental hospital for an indeterminate amount of time, or a defendant is found fit to stand trial and from thenceforth will be treated as any other inmate in the system. Rarely is there an accurate portrayal of the gray area where a significant proportion of inmates fall, where even though the defendant is found fit to stand for trial, s/he is in need of lifelong treatment for a serious mental illness.

It is also interesting to note that pop culture (e.g., the television series *Prison Break* and *OZ*) typically portrays mental health staff as correctional staff that pays more attention to security issues than wellness. While sometimes this is true, it is the very nature of the therapeutic relationship that the mental health clinician be, at least to the extent possible, an advocate for the patient. This is particularly true since the deinstitutionalization of the public mental health system since the 1980s has resulted in correctional institutions becoming the "poor person's mental health facility" (Favier, 1998, p. 143). This trend is alarming given the fact that the correctional environment is conducive neither to positive mental health nor successful mental health treatment.

State and Federal legislators have been taking notice and action. In January, 2004 a Nebraska legislative committee was told that it needed to set standards for treating inmates with mental illness after an inmate who had failed to take his psychotropic medication was beaten to death by another inmate. Senator Ernie Chambers of Omaha presented his bill (LB1000) with the Judiciary Committee saying, "Because a significant number of inmates have psychological, mental, drug, alcohol, and other problems, it's necessary that the system recognize these problems and address them" (Managed Care Weekly Digest, 2004, p. 25). He added that in light of the Governor's plans to close two of Nebraska's State mental hospitals, "More people in need of mental nurturing will wind up, unfortunately, incarcerated. So the state should assume its responsibility toward these people when they fall into the state's hands" (Managed Care Weekly Digest, 2004, p. 26).

The purpose of this paper is to examine the prevalence of mental illness in American jails and prisons, the duty government and society has to provide appropriate mental health treatment, and the implications for inmate safety, costs, recidivism, and community reintegration if meaningful mental health treatment is not provided. Finally, some recommendations regarding required and desired components of correctional mental health programs are discussed.

PREVALENCE

The rate of mental illness among inmates is estimated to be two to three times higher than in the general community (Roskes & Feldman, 1999). There are several explanations for this phenomenon, including:

- Deinstitutionalization of state mental hospitals resulted in the mentally ill residing in communities rather than hospitals, thus, there are increased opportunities for them to behave in ways that come under the attention of police officers. This behavior is often a manifestation of their illness.
- Mentally ill offenders of minor crimes are often subjected to inappropriate arrest and incarceration.
- The more formal and rigid criteria now in place for civil commitment to a state mental facility.
- The lack of adequate support systems for mentally ill persons in the community.
- Released mentally ill offenders have difficulty gaining access to both community mental health treatment in general, as well as treatment that is appropriate to their specific needs (Lamb & Bachrach, 2001, p. 1042).

Erik Roskes (1999) presents some chilling statistics in reporting that most studies estimate that approximately 10-15% of the nearly 6 million offenders in U.S. jails and prisons and on probation and parole are mentally ill. These estimated 600,000 to 900,000 individuals are not the relatively small group of mentally ill offenders who are adjudicated NGRI under state and federal law (Roskes, 1999). In many cases they make society, in general, extremely uncomfortable. They are the poorest, often homeless, socially and psychologically, educationally and vocationally, challenged individuals in our communities.

The estimates of community corrections inmates with mental illness are more variable. Bureau of Justice Statistics were reported by Roskes, Cooksey, Feldman, Lipford, and Tambree (2005) indicating that approximately 16% (547,800) of individuals on probation are mentally ill. Across 15 states that collected this type of data, an average of 5% (range 1-11%) of parolees and 6% (range 3-23%) of probationers have a disabling mental illness. This diagnosis has been defined by the National Coalition for Mental Health and Substance Abuse Care in the Justice System as "adults having a disabling mental illness, which includes schizophrenia and/or an affective disorder" (Roskes et al., 2005, p. 230).

While diagnostic statistics are not available for all states, the Georgia Department of Corrections figures for their March 2001 mental health inmate caseload indicated the following diagnoses:

- Schizophrenia–28.74%
- Bipolar Disorder–8.31%
- Depression–38.15%
- Anxiety Disorder–8.49%
- Adjustment Disorder–3.17%
- Mental Retardation–0.43%
- Other Diagnoses–12.72% (Moore, 2003, p. 12-4)

There is no reason to believe that other states would not report similar statistics.

This problem is not unique to America, as research outlines the alarming increase in mentally ill offenders in other countries as well. For example, a survey of 13,250 adults in British households and prisons screened respondents for psychosis, followed by a diagnostic interview for those with positive results (Brugha, Singleton, Bebbington, Farrell, Jenkins, Coid, Fryeres, Melzer, & Lewis, 2005). The findings indicated that the estimated prevalence of psychiatric morbidity was over 10 times greater in the prison sample than the community sample–52 per 1,000 vs. 4.5 per 1,000, respectively. The consistent conclusion drawn from these types of studies is that the prevalence of mental illness is much higher in correctional populations than in community populations indicating a dire need for increased awareness and resources directed at treatment and prevention.

Unfortunately, mental illness appears to discriminate across demographic groupings of inmates. What follows is a brief discussion of the prevalence statistics for various subgroups of offenders, namely, females, minorities, elderly, substance addicted, developmentally disabled, administratively segregated, and maximum- and supermaximum-security inmates.

Female Offenders

Catherine Lewis (2005) summarizes a number of studies regarding the epidemiology of psychiatric disorders in female offenders. The studies indicate that an estimated 1/3 to 2/3 of all women entering correctional facilities need mental health services, and are extremely likely to have the co-morbid diagnoses of substance abuse and Axis I or Axis II mental illness as indicated in the DSM-IV. Even the low end of this estimate (33.3%) is more than twice the high end of the overall inmate prevalence rate of 15%. This high rate of mental illness among female offenders is particularly alarming given the fact that the female incarceration rate has been increasing even faster than the rate for males over the past 10 years.

Harrison and Beck (2004) reported the following after a review of prison inmates: "Since 1995, the total number of male prisoners has increased 29%, whereas the number of female prisoners has increased 48%" (p. 10). A Bureau of Justice Statistics (BJS) special report on medical problems of inmates in 1997 revealed that 16.1% of state female offenders, and 9.7% of federal female offenders had a mental condition; this compares to 9.6% and 4.4% of male offenders, respectively (Maruschak & Beck, 2001). Clearly, mental illness is significantly more prevalent in female offender populations.

Minority Offenders

For decades minorities have been overrepresented in the correctional system. Harrison and Beck (2006) report that in midyear 2005, 12% of black males ages 25-29 were in the prison system, compared to 3.7% of Hispanic male counterparts, and 1.7% of white male counterparts. It is difficult to find similar ethnicity statistics for the prevalence of mental illness among offenders. However, the *News and Notes* section of the Journal of Psychiatric Services (1999) reported that 23% of white inmates in state prisons and local jails are mentally ill, compared to 14% of black inmates and 11% of Hispanics. Thus, while minority populations are overrepresented in the general inmate population, a larger proportion of white inmates are identified as being mentally ill.

Elderly Offenders

The Bureau of Justice Statistics (Maruschak & Beck, 2001) reported that 11.7% of state inmates ages 45 and older, and 5.9% of federal inmates 45 and older, had a mental condition; this compares to 7.8% of state inmates 24 and younger, and 4.0% of federal inmates 24 and younger. The fact that there is a higher prevalence of mental illness among elderly inmates than younger inmates is compounded by the fact that there has been a steady growth in the elderly inmate population. This growth is due to the combined effect of more offenders being incarcerated coupled with them serving longer sentences due to mandatory minimum sentences and three-strikes legislation. Thus, the general population is older as well. As Frederick Maue (2001) pointed out, as this increasing inmate population ages, their medical and mental health needs will increase.

Substance Abusing Offenders

Substance use and abuse is extremely high among correctional populations. A study by Conklin, Lincoln, and Tuthill (2000) indicted that over 60% of male and female offenders had used alcohol during the three months prior to incarceration, and 1/3 of those reported using it on a daily basis. This study also found that 2/3 of newly admitted inmates had used drugs (excluding nicotine and alcohol) at some point in their life, and of those reporting use, 80% had used them during the three months prior to incarceration.

This high rate of substance use/abuse is evident among mentally ill inmates as well. Abram and Teplin (1991) found that over half of the inmates with current severe mental disorders had a co-occurring substance use at the time of their arrest, but this estimate goes up as high as 90% when the co-morbid criterion is a substance use disorder at some point during their lifetime (Roskes et al., 2005).

It is important to recognize that many inmates who have co-occurring disorders of substance use/abuse and mental illness are likely to fall through the treatment cracks of the correctional system. Shabo (2001) discusses how most drug courts exclude from eligibility persons with serious mental illness, while simultaneously, mental health agencies refuse treatment to the mentally ill who use or are addicted to alcohol and/or drugs. He goes as far as to say, "the institutional unwillingness to treat persons with both diagnoses is undoubtedly a significant reason why mentally ill persons find themselves criminalized and institutionalized under the criminal justice system" (Shabo, 2001, p. 7).

Developmentally Disabled Offenders

McDermott, Hardison, and Mackenzie (2005) suggest that the prevalence studies on inmates with developmental disabilities are replete with methodological problems including differences in assessment criteria and definition. For example, they provide estimates from 1% to 3% for mental retardation in the U.S. population, while state and federal prison estimates range from .5% to 30%. They go on to state, "One significant problem that has hampered the development of appropriate approaches with these individuals is the confusion and/or lack of distinction in the legal system between mental illness and mental retardation or developmental disabilities" (McDermott et al., 2005, p. 191).

Regardless of the specific prevalence rate, most studies indicate that inmates with mental retardation and developmental disabilities are overrepresented in correctional systems. Furthermore, research (McDermott et al., 2005) has shown that this special group of inmates is more likely to have trouble understanding their rights upon arrest, to be interrogated, to waive their *Miranda* rights, and ultimately to be convicted and incarcerated. Furthermore, since probation and parole are granted more often to offenders who are educated and have a stable work history, developmentally disabled inmates are less likely to receive a community sanction (Santamour & West, 1982).

Administrative Segregation, Maximum- and Super-Maximum Security Inmates

It has been estimated that 20,000 inmates are housed in segregation units on any given day and that the mentally ill are overrepresented in that subpopulation (Cohen & Gerbasi, 2005). In the 2003 Human Rights Watch report on U.S. prisons and offenders with mental illnesses, a rather gloomy forecast is painted:

> Our research suggests that few prisons accommodate their mental health needs. Security staff typically view mentally ill prisoners as difficult and disruptive, and place them in barren high-security solitary confinement units. The lack of human interaction and the

limited stimulus of twenty-four-hour-a-day life in small, sometimes windowless segregation cells, coupled with the absence of adequate mental health services, dramatically aggravates the suffering of the mentally ill. . . . The penal network is thus not only serving as a warehouse for the mentally ill, but, by relying on extremely restrictive housing for mentally ill prisoners, it is acting as an incubator for worse illness and psychiatric breakdowns. (p. 3)

Gary Beven (2005) concurs in stating that, "Prolonged isolation of inmates in segregation poses an inherent risk of psychological deterioration that cannot be ignored but that becomes difficult to address effectively when it occurs" (p. 209). In fact, two of the 14 characteristics of a segregation facility that provides effective mental health care are (1) that acutely mentally ill inmates with active psychosis are rarely placed in administrative segregation; and (2) that inmates with mental illnesses are not transferred to supermax facilities (Beven, 2005).

In summary, these prevalence statistics suggest that a number of special inmate populations have significant mental health needs that only compound the problems already associated with their demographic group membership. In particular, inmates who are female, white, elderly, have substance abuse disorders, have developmental disabilities, or are incarcerated in a segregation housing unit, are all more likely to exhibit mental illness than their counterparts.

DUTY TO PROVIDE MENTAL HEALTH SERVICES

It is important for society to realize that incompatibility of the prison (i.e., security) environment does not negate the rights of offenders to receive appropriate medical care, including mental health services. Nor does it negate the duty of the state and federal governments to uphold those rights. This statement is supported by a number of constitutional amendments and Supreme Court cases.

The Eighth Amendment, which prohibits cruel and unusual punishment, is made applicable to the states through the Fourteenth Amendment specifying due process procedures. In *Estell v. Gamble* (1976) the U.S. Supreme Court recognized that an inmate must rely on prison authorities to treat his medical needs, and that prison officials who show a *deliberate indifference* to do so violate the inmate's constitutional rights (Cohen & Gerbasi, 2005). In *Farmer v. Brennan* (1974) the U.S. Supreme Court defined the term *deliberate indifference* to be more than simple negligence, but something less than purposely causing harm (Cohen & Gerbasi, 2005).

However, it was not until *Bowring v. Godwin* (1976) that the *Estelle v. Gamble* requirements were extended to psychiatric care. Cohen and Gerbasi (2005) provided the following quote from the Court's decision:

> We see no underlying distinction between the right to medical care for physical ills and its psychological or psychiatric counterpart. Modern science has rejected the notion that mental or emotional disturbances are the products of afflicted souls, hence beyond the purview of counseling, medication and therapy. (p. 264)

Obviously, the primary goals of corrections must be security and public safety. The security needs, however, do not negate the duty of the government to provide physical and mental health treatment to the charges in their care. As Gary Beven (2005) stated, "Irrespective of a prisoner's security needs or prior egregious behavior, the community standard of care for treatment of mental illness should be followed" (p. 218). Unfortunately, the community standard of care may not be much better than the correctional standard, given the fact that so many of the mentally ill in society are homeless, without treatment, and increasingly ending up in the correctional system.

The American Correctional Association (ACA) issued a policy statement in June, 1996 which stated that mental health treatment should be provided to inmates and detainees. Kenneth Faiver (1998) states that:

> Competent treatment for serious mental illness should be provided to inmates and detainees in order to reduce the unnecessary extremes of human suffering that can be caused by untreated mental illness. Though inmates (not detainees) are sentenced to prison or jail as punishment, the terror that can accompany hallucinations or delusions, the profound grief that can accompany a suicidal depression, and other symptoms of mental illness go far beyond the expectations of a civilized society and serve no reasonable purpose. Mental health professionals have a duty to provide such treatment in correctional settings. (p. 145)

Thus, mandates from the U.S. Constitution, the U.S. Supreme Court, and the accrediting body of the U.S. correctional system (ACA), are clear with respect to the duty of American society to provide appropriate mental health treatment to inmates.

IMPLICATIONS AND RECOMMENDATIONS

There are a number of long-term implications for society if correctional systems do not embrace the mandate to provide appropriate mental health care for mentally ill inmates. These implications have to do with inmate safety, correctional and mental health staff, costs, recidivism and public safety.

Inmate Safety

The most serious concern for inmate safety when mental illnesses are left untreated is increased risk of suicide. Lindsay Hayes (1989) has reported that suicide is the leading cause of death in jails with more than 400 inmates committing suicide each year. In her chapter on suicide prevention in correctional facilities, Hayes (2005) summarizes a 2000 BJS study reporting that "suicide ranks third, behind natural causes and AIDS, as the leading cause of death in prisons" (p. 73). She goes on to document that most research on the causes of prison suicide has determined that the vast majority of victims had histories of suicide attempts and mental illness.

Fortunately, a number of states (e.g., Texas and New York) have developed effective suicide prevention programs. These programs are based on the following principles (Felthous, 1994): screening, psychological support, close observation, removal of dangerous items, clear and consistent procedures, diagnosis, treatment, and transfer to the hospital if needed. Hayes (2005, pp. 82-85) presents nine guiding principles for suicide prevention, three of which appear to be crucial: Promote and maintain communication among correctional, medical, and mental health staff; Avoid creating barriers that discourage an inmate from accessing mental health services; and Create and maintain sound suicide prevention programming.

Thus, it is recommended that corrections officials develop policies and mental health treatment programs in accordance with the guidelines put forth by Hayes (2005), the American Correctional Association (Favier, 1998), and the American Psychiatric Association (2000). The lack of such policies and programming can only lead to dire consequences for inmate safety.

It is also recommended that inmates with mental illness be housed in the least restrictive housing unit possible, with particular effort placed on not placing mentally ill inmates in segregation units, and not transferring them to maximum- and supermax-security facilities. Beven

(2005, p. 217) supports this recommendation, stating: "At present, it is considered a best practice that inmates with serious mental illness, or those with a psychological disposition prone to behavioral decay under severe stress, be precluded from transfer to such facilities unless adequate mental health resources are available." Support for this recommendation can be found in a study conducted in April of 2006 that found mentally ill inmates ". . . are at a higher risk of personal victimization" (Ruddell, 2006, p. 119).

Correctional and Mental Health Staff

Kenneth Applelbaum (2005) discusses the impediments to practicing psychiatry in the correctional setting. He states that, "Correctional officers have the authority to enforce rules, regimentation, and sanctions. Unlike health care providers, who typically seek negotiated compliance from their patients, correctional officers have an authoritarian relationship with inmates. These disparate ideologies sometimes lead to conflict between officers and clinicians" (Applebaum, 2005, p. 25; internal citations omitted).

Thus, it is recommended that corrections officials adopt a policy of *cross-training* staff, whereby security staff and mental health staff are trained beside each other, as well as train each other, so that they understand and appreciate the functions of both professional roles (Roskes et al., 2005). This should serve to break down walls of communication and other barriers related to the security vs. treatment dichotomy of professional goals.

Costs

Society has been paying a heavy price for locking up lawbreakers in increasing numbers and for longer periods of time. Moore (2003) reports that the average annual operating expenditures per inmate nationwide were $20,100 (that figure does not include capital expenditures). For the 16 states who report correctional mental health expenditures, the percentage of their annual state department of corrections budgets that were spent on inmates' mental health care averaged 17% (individual state figures range from 5.4% [Minnesota] to 42.7% [Michigan]), with another approximate 12% spent on medical and dental care. For comparative purposes, in 1995 the average U.S. citizen spent $1,807/ year on his/her own health care, states spent on average $2,386/year on each inmate's health care. In total, states spend $2.5 billion/year on health care of inmates (Moore, 2003). When you multiply these figures times the 1,512,823 persons incarcerated in U.S. prisons and jails (year 2005 figure), you are talking about a considerable amount of money.

Chaiken, Thompson, and Shoemaker (2005) discuss how quality mental health programming in prisons can lead to lower prison operating costs as well as public safety: "Successful mental health programs focus on treating serious mental illness and reducing patients' destructive, disruptive, assaultive, and self-injurious behavior, thereby increasing staff and public safety as well as reducing the cost of incarcerating mentally ill inmates" (p. 112). They go on to discuss the features that in combination, or in total, make up a successful correctional mental health program including: appropriate pharmacological treatment, individual psychotherapy, group and recreational therapy, cognitive-behavioral therapy, dialectical behavioral therapy, therapeutic communities, behavioral incentive programs, and residential community corrections centers (Chaiken et al., 2005, pp. 118-128).

While providing additional and enhanced mental health treatment and programming in our prisons will only add to the high costs mentioned previously, the Human Rights Watch (2003) report on U.S. prisons and offenders with mental illness sums it up best:

> No one doubts that a treatment-oriented milieu for mentally ill prisoners who are disruptive must be labor-intensive–and hence expensive. Yet until the expense is undertaken, the vicious cycle of segregation and decompensation and short-term hospitalization will continue until the prisoners are ultimately released, at least as sick as they were upon entry into the criminal justice system, from prison back into the community. (p. 163)

Clearly, the cost of not effectively treating mentally ill offenders will increase the likelihood of recidivism and ultimately return to prison.

Recidivism and Community Reintegration

It has been reported that mentally ill persons have a 67% greater chance of being arrested than those who are not mentally ill (Teplin, 2000). Further, the recidivism rate for mentally ill offenders is much higher than the rate for offenders without a mental illness (Roskes, 2005). For example, a study by Ditton (1999) reported that 49% of federal inmates with a mental illness had three or more probations, incarcerations, or arrests, as compared to 28% of federal inmates without a mental illness. Yet, incarcerated mental health services are provided to only an approximate 17% of prison inmates and 11% of jail inmates (Ditton, 1999). However, despite these low percentages, "many inmates with mental disorders receive their first comprehensive treatment services during their incarcerations" (Applebaum, 2005, p. 26).

In an article discussing the need for post-release aftercare for mentally ill offenders, Jay Pomerantz (2003) discusses the fact that mentally ill persons tend to spend a short time in jail rather than a long time in prison. Clearly, jails have an important role to play in identifying, diagnosing, referring and providing treatment for mentally ill offenders, but before jails can fulfill that role, continuum-of-care coordination must be in place:

> The key point is that correctional institutions are reservoirs of physical and mental illness, which constantly spill back into the community. If these diseases are to be treated properly, transmission interrupted, and the health of the general public optimized, then effective treatment and education must be provided in the jail system. These conditions are public health problems that demand effective management and close coordination among correctional health, community health, public health, and mental health facilities. (Pomerantz, 2003, p. 21)

Thus, it is imperative that jail and prison officials embrace the treatment mandate before them. Unfortunately, "the criminal justice system has largely taken the place of the state hospitals in becoming the system that can't say no" (Lamb & Bachrach, 2001, p. 1042). Society must honor its duty to provide meaningful mental health treatment for inmates with mental disorders. Additionally, services must be provided to address substance disorders, developmental disorders, and educational and vocational deficiencies. Fortunately, the limited research on prison-based programming suggests its effectiveness. For example, Pomerantz (2003) summarizes a 1999 report on drug offenders who completed a prison-based substance treatment program and work-release program. The participants were 70% less likely to be rearrested than non-participants.

Before we rely on the correctional system to handle this significant public health problem, it is in the interest of offender community reintegration goals and public safety that the mentally ill be diverted from the criminal justice system altogether and subsequently provided necessary mental health services. Diversion options can include things like using pre-booking and post-booking diversion opportunities, mental health courts, and less severe and community-based sentences (e.g., probation, parole, and supervised release) (Roskes et al., 2005). However, Roskes and colleagues (2005) warned that diversion programs are of little service to mentally ill offenders if they are not accompanied by access to mental health treatment, stating, "absent improvements in the mental health and social service system to which people are diverted, jail diversion programs have only limited impact on the lives of people with mental illness" (p. 241).

In fact, a jail diversion effectiveness study conducted by Steadman, Deane, Morrissey, Westcott, Salasin, and Shapiro (1999) reported that there are two core elements necessary for a diversion program to be successful: "aggressive linkage to an array of community services, especially those for co-occurring mental health and substance use disorders; and nontraditional case managers" (p. 1623). They define nontraditional case managers as "staff that were hired less for their academic credentials and more for their experience *across* criminal justice, mental health, and substance abuse systems" (Steadman et al., 1999, p. 1621).

CONCLUSION

The prevalence of persons with mental illness in our correctional systems is significant and ever-increasing. Particularly affected subpopulations of offenders include females, whites, elderly, developmentally disabled, substance disordered, administratively segregated, and maximum- and supermax-offenders. There are several factors that have contributed to this phenomenon, with deinstitutionalization of state mental hospitals over the past four decades being the primary cause.

While the therapeutic nature of mental health service delivery is often at odds with the security and public safety goals of corrections, it should be recognized that the point of incarceration is an opportunity to identify, diagnose, and begin to treat the mentally ill. Cross-training of correctional and mental health staff can facilitate the communication and cooperation necessary between the staff roles.

More importantly, mentally ill offenders have a constitutional right to treatment and American society has a duty to provide it. It will be expensive, but that is not sufficient reason to withhold such care. Fortunately, the limited evidence available suggests that prison-based programming is effective at reducing recidivism; thus, the costs of treating mentally ill offenders may actually result in long-run cost savings for taxpayers if the treatment prevents future incarcerations. Successful community reintegration is a goal for all offenders and it is realistic to believe that this goal is obtainable for a significant proportion of mentally ill offenders as well.

Finally, corrections officials need to embrace the treatment mandate before them by adopting and implementing meaningful mental health treatment policies and programs in their facilities. Components of quality mental health treatment programs are specified by ACA and the APA Guidelines. Another excellent source of guidelines can be found in the Appendix of the book edited by Charles L. Scott, M.D., and Joan B. Gerbasi, J.D., M.D. (2005), entitled, *Handbook of Correctional Mental Health*. Key features of these guidelines are that they focus on diverting mentally ill offenders from the criminal justice system whenever possible; cross-training correctional and clinical staff; adopting meaningful treatment policies and programs aimed at appropriately medicating, habilitating and rehabilitating mentally ill offenders; providing co-occurring substance disorder treatment; maximizing access to care; providing aftercare services; and engaging in outcome-based program evaluation research.

REFERENCES

Abram, K.M., & Teplin, L.A. (1991). Co-occurring disorders among mentally ill jail detainees: Implications for public policy. *American Psychologist, 46*, 1036-1045.

American Psychiatric Association (2000). *Psychiatric services in jails and prisons*, 2nd Ed. Washington, DC: American Psychiatric Association.

Applebaum, K.L. (2005). Practicing psychiatry in a correctional culture. In C.L. Scott, & J.B. Gerbasi (Eds.), *Handbook of correctional mental health*. Arlington, VA: American Psychiatric Publishing, Inc.

Beven, G.E. (2005). Offenders with mental illnesses in maximum- and supermaximum-security settings. In C.L. Scott, & J.B. Gerbasi (Eds.), *Handbook of correctional mental health*. Arlington, VA: American Psychiatric Publishing, Inc.

Bowring v Godwin, 551 F.2d 44 (4th Cir. 1977).

Brugha, T., Singleton, N., Bebbington, P., Farrell, M., Jenkins, R., Coid, J., Fryers, T., Melzer, D., & Lewis, G. (2005). Psychosis in the community and in prisons: A report from the British National Survey of Psychiatric Morbidity. *American Journal of Psychiatry, 162*, 774-780.

Chaiken, S.B., Thompson, C.R., & Shoemaker, W.E. (2005). Mental health interventions in correctional settings. In C.L. Scott, & J.B. Gerbasi (Eds.), *Handbook of correctional mental health*. Arlington, VA: American Psychiatric Publishing, Inc.

Cohen, F., & Gerbasi, J.B. (2005). Legal issues regarding the provision of mental health care in correctional settings. In C.L. Scott, & J.B. Gerbasi (Eds.), *Handbook of correctional mental health*. Arlington, VA: American Psychiatric Publishing, Inc.

Conklin, T.J., Lincoln, T., & Tuthill, R.W. (2000). Self-reported health and prior health behaviors of newly admitted correction inmates. *American Journal of Public Health, 90*, 1939-1941.

Ditton, P.M. (1999). *Mental health and treatment of inmates and probationers (NCJ 174463)*. Washington, DC: Office of Justice Programs, Bureau of Justice Statistics, U.S. Department of Justice. Retrieved October 20, 2005, from http://www.ojp. usdoj.gov/bsj/pub/pdf/mhtip.pdf.

Estelle v Gamble, 426 U.S. 97 (1976).

Faiver, K.L. (1998). *Health care management issues in corrections*. Lanham, MD: American Correctional Association.

Farmer v Brennan, 511 U.S. 825 (1994).

Felthous, A. (1994). Preventing jailhouse suicides. *Bulletin of the American Academy of Psychiatry Law, 22*, 447-488.

Harrison, P.M., & Beck, A.J. (2004). *Prisoners in 2003 (NCJ 203947)*. Washington, DC: Office of Justice Programs, Bureau of Justice Statistics, U.S. Department of Justice.

Harrison, P.M., & Beck, A.J. (2006). *Prison and jail inmates at midyear 2005 (NCJ 213133)*. Washington, DC: Office of Justice Programs, Bureau of Justice Statistics, U.S. Department of Justice.

Hayes, L. (1989). National study of jail suicides: Seven years later. *Psychiatric Quarterly, 60*, 7-29

Hayes, L. (2005). Suicide prevention in correctional facilities. In C.L. Scott, & J.B. Gerbasi (Eds.), *Handbook of correctional mental health*. Arlington, VA: American Psychiatric Publishing, Inc.

Human Rights Watch (2003). *Ill-equipped: U.S. prisons and offenders with mental illness*. New York: Human Rights Watch.

Lamb, H., & Bachrach, L.L. (2001). Some perspectives on deinstitutionalization. *Psychiatric Services, 52*(8), 1039-1045.

Lewis, C.F. (2005). Female offenders in correctional settings. In C.L. Scott, & J.B. Gerbasi (Eds.), *Handbook of correctional mental health*. Arlington, VA: American Psychiatric Publishing, Inc.

Managed Care Weekly Digest (2004). Mental health standards needed for prisons, Nebraska Senator says. *Managed Care Weekly Digest*, February 16, 2004.

Maruschak, L.M., & Beck, A.J. (2001). *Medical problems of inmates, 1997 (NCJ 181644)*. Washington, DC: Office of Justice Programs, Bureau of Justice Statistics, U.S. Department of Justice.

Maue, F.R. (2001). An overview of correctional mental health issues. *Corrections Today, 63*(4), 8.

McDermott, B.E., Hardison, K.A., & MacKenzie, C. (2005). Individuals with developmental disabilities in correctional settings. In C.L. Scott, & J.B. Gerbasi (Eds.), *Handbook of correctional mental health*. Arlington, VA: American Psychiatric Publishing, Inc.

Metzner, J.L. (2002). Class action litigation in correctional psychiatry. *Journal of the American Academy of Psychiatry Law, 30*, 19-29.

Moore, J. (2003). *Management and administration of correctional health care*. Kingston, NJ: Civic Research Institute.

Pomerantz, J.M. (2003). Treatment of mentally ill in prisons and jails: Follow-up care needed. *Drug Benefit Trends, 15*(6), 20-21.

Psychiatric Services New and Notes (1999). More than a quarter million inmates in U.S. prisons and jails are mentally ill, Justice Department report finds. *Psychiatric Services, 50*(9), 1243.

Roskes, E. (1999). Offenders with mental disorders: A call to action. *Psychiatric Services, 50*(12), 1596.

Roskes, E., & Feldman, R. (1999). A collaborative community based treatment program for offenders with mental illness. *Psychiatric Services, 50,* 1614-1619.

Roskes, E., Cooksey, C., Feldman, R., Lipford, S., & Tambree, J. (2005). Management of offenders with mental illnesses in outpatient settings. In C.L. Scott, & J.B. Gerbasi (Eds.), *Handbook of correctional mental health.* Arlington, VA: American Psychiatric Publishing, Inc.

Ruddell, R. (2006). Jail interventions for inmates with mental illnesses [Electronic version]. *Journal of Correctional Health Care, 12,* 118-131.

Santamour, M.B., & West, B. (1982). The mentally retarded offender: Presentation of the facts and a discussion of the issues. In M.B. Santamour, & P.S. Watson (Eds.), *The retarded offender.* New York: Praeger.

Scott, C.L., & Gerbasi, J.B. (Eds.) (2005). *Handbook of correctional mental health.* Arlington, VA: American Psychiatric Publishing, Inc.

Shabo, H.E. (2001). *Social costs: Criminal justice and mental health system gaps which contribute to the criminalization of mentally disordered persons.* Supervising Judge, Mental Health Departments, Superior Court of California, Los Angeles County, Santa Barbara, CA: Transcript of speech given on November 3, 2001.

Steadman, H.J., Deane, M.W., Morrissey, J.P., Westcott, M.L., Salasin, S., & Shapiro, S. (1999). A SAMHSA research initiative assessing the effectiveness of jail diversion programs for mentally ill persons. *Psychiatric Services, 50*(12), 1620-1623.

Teplin, L. (2000). Keeping the peace: Police discretion and mentally ill persons [Electronic version]. *National Institute of Justice Journal,* July, 8-15.

AUTHOR'S NOTE

Irina R. Soderstrom PhD, is affiliated with Eastern Kentucky University, Richmond, KY 40475.

doi:10.1300/J076v45n01_01

Mental Health Issues in the Criminal Justice System. Pp. 19-31.
Available online at http://jor.haworthpress.com
© 2007 by The Haworth Press, Inc. All rights reserved.
doi:10.1300/J076v45n01_02

Jail Diversion: Addressing the Needs of Offenders with Mental Illness and Co-Occurring Disorders

SCOTT MIRE
CRAIG J. FORSYTH
ROBERT HANSER

ABSTRACT The primary purpose of this research is to illuminate three critical components related to the success of jail diversion programs. First, prior to diversion there is the need to identify those offenders most open to therapeutic services. Second, for those offenders diverted, there must be a proper match between the offender and the mental health professional who provides therapeutic services. Third, quality mental health services must have therapists that are routinely involved in the offender's clinical progress from intake to program completion. Suggestions are offered which may serve to forward the evolution of jail diversion implementation and enhance success rates. doi:10.1300/J076v45n01_02 *[Article copies available for a fee from The Haworth Document Delivery Service: 1-800-HAWORTH. E-mail address: <docdelivery@ haworthpress.com> Website: <http://www.HaworthPress.com> © 2007 by The Haworth Press, Inc. All rights reserved.]*

KEYWORDS Jail diversion, resistance to treatment, therapeutic alliance

INTRODUCTION

Throughout the last 15 to 20 years, law enforcement organizations have increasingly looked to new programs aimed at serving offenders with mental illness (Reuland, 2004; The Sentencing Project, 2002). These new programs have evolved primarily in response to the increasing numbers of people with mental illness coming into contact with police, often the same individuals, repeatedly and sometimes with tragic consequences (Reuland & Cheney, 2005; The Sentencing Project, 2002). To simply incarcerate non-violent offenders suffering from mental illness or co-occurring disorders without attending to the underlying psychological and emotional problems has proven costly and does little to reduce rates of recidivism (Champion, 2002; The Sentencing Project, 2002). In fact, there is a wide body of literature that demonstrates that jail and prison environments can make matters substantially worse for the mentally ill (Bartol & Bartol, 2005; Cordess, Davidson, Morris, & Norton, 2005). At the forefront of these new programs is a comprehensive and theoretically driven approach called jail diversion. Jail diversion programs are, most commonly, aimed at diverting individuals suffering from mental illness or co-occurring disorders away from jails and prisons and into the care of community health organizations better able to serve their needs (The Sentencing Project, 2002).

As stated by Massaro (2005), "The criminal justice and mental health service systems appear to meet very different societal needs, yet they overlap in two significant ways. First, they both seek to maintain the safety of the people in the community; second, both systems work with the same individuals" (p. 1). The first postulate by Massaro (2005) is obvious–safety and security of members of a community are always paramount. The second postulate is not so obvious but may be of equal significance. If both service providers, law enforcement and mental health organizations, are dealing with the same clientele it makes sense to collaborate and consult the expertise of each entity in order to provide a more beneficial service (The Sentencing Project, 2002).

LITERATURE REVIEW

An estimated 11 million people are booked into U.S. jails throughout the course of a year (Stephan, 2001). Of these 11 million offenders, approximately 800,000 suffer from serious mental illness and 72 percent of these suffer from co-occurring substance use disorders. Similarly, the U.S. Department of Justice reports that approximately 16 percent of inmates are diagnosed with severe mental illness (Faust, 2003). This sentiment was recently echoed by a local Sheriff in Louisiana. The Sheriff indicated that at any given point approximately 15 percent of his jail's population suffers from some type of mental illness (personal communication, 2006).

Regarding substance use disorders, Teplin (1994) collected data over a two-week period from male detainees entering the Cook County Department of Corrections (Chicago, IL). At the time of intake 29.1 percent of male detainees had a substance use disorder. Male detainees reported a slightly higher percentage of alcohol addiction (19.1%) than drug addiction (15.3%). Data collected during the same time span for female detainees show that 53.3 percent had a substance use disorder at the time of intake. In addition, among female detainees the prevalence of drug addiction (43.6%) was almost double the rate of alcohol addiction (22.1%) (National Gains Center for People with Co-Occurring Disorders in the Justice System, 2001).

Finally, when considering the prevalence rates of offenders suffering from co-occurring disorders, mental illness and substance use, the numbers are staggering (LASACT, 2004; SAMHSA, 2004; The Sentencing Project, 2002). Similar to the figure mentioned above, Hoff, Rosencheck, Baranosky, Buchanan, and Zonana (1999) report that up to 75 percent of offenders diagnosed with a psychiatric disorder also have symptoms of drug or alcohol abuse. For criminal justice practitioners the prevalence rates of offenders suffering from mental illness and co-occurring disorders demand attention.

Current Jail Diversion Programs

In essence, there are two types of jail diversion programs currently implemented in various jurisdictions throughout the country: Pre-booking jail diversion and Post-booking jail diversion (The Sentencing Project, 2002). It is not meant to be implied that these two variations of jail diversion are the only two in operation. However, the literature indicates that they are certainly the most frequently employed diversion programs (National Institute of Mental Health, 1995; The Sentencing Project, 2002).

Pre-booking jail diversion consists of diverting the offender at the moment of police contact. In pre-booking diversion programs the offender is assessed in the field and, if found to be within the parameters of diversion eligibility, is immediately processed into a community health organization in lieu of jail. Pre-booking diversion programs require highly trained officers to be able to recognize the possibility of some offenders suffering from mental illness or co-occurring disorders (Massaro, 2004).

In addition, pre-booking diversion programs must have the capacity of being highly mobile. For pre-booking diversion to function effectively, street officers must be trained in the identification of mental illness and substance use disorders (Kerle, 1999; The Sentencing Project, 2002). It is rarely the case, however, where a department is able to train all of its street officers in the detection of mental illness and substance abuse (Kerle, 1999). Therefore, most departments participating in a pre-booking diversion program have a special unit of officers, trained to deal with and identify offenders suffering from mental illness, who are dispatched to appropriately respond to and guide the offender into community care organizations. Some law enforcement agencies contract with mental health providers who are sent directly to the scene of an incident when it is suspected that an offender may be suffering from mental illness.

Pre-booking diversion programs have enormous potential. If properly implemented, a pre-booking diversion program may be the most efficient and effective method for dealing with offenders suffering from mental illness (The Sentencing Project, 2002). From a practical standpoint, however, there are a few issues that make pre-booking diversion programs difficult to implement and sustain. First, pre-booking diversion programs demand highly trained first responders able to identify and conceptualize basic characteristics of mental illness. For some smaller, rural agencies this degree of specialized training is difficult to achieve and maintain due to limited resources. Second, although seldom mentioned as a relevant characteristic, is the issue of liability. With pre-booking diversion programs the issue of liability is more pronounced, especially when police officers are responsible for detecting mental illness. A mistake in classification that leads to injury may leave the department vulnerable to lawsuit.

A post-booking diversion program is one that screens offenders at the time of intake or arraignment (Massaro, 2004). The offenders have been placed under arrest and initial charges are filed by arresting officers. Once processed into the facility those offenders who meet the initial criteria, usually charges of nonviolent misdemeanors, are assessed to determine eligibility in relation to mental illness and co-occurring disorders. Offenders diagnosed with mental illness and/or co-occurring disorders are then invited to participate in the diversion program in lieu of spending time in jail. Additionally, divertees who choose to participate in the diversion program and successfully complete program criteria usually have the initial charges dropped or significantly reduced.

Once offenders have been initially screened and assessed, and choose to enroll in the diversion program they are typically assigned to a caseworker. It is the caseworker's responsibility to determine what types of services are most relevant, based on the offender's needs, and then identify providers within the community that are able to deliver appropriate services. This nexus between the offender, caseworker, and mental health provider is arguably the most critical component related to the success of a jail diversion program.

Preliminary Results

To date, the most comprehensive literature assessing the effectiveness of jail diversion programs for persons with serious mental illness and co-occurring substance use disorders is provided by Steadman and Naples (2005). Data analyzed was produced by six different jail diversion programs currently operating throughout the United States. Three of the diversion programs diverted offenders pre-booking while the remaining three were post-booking.

Overall, results were mostly positive, however, only marginally. Variables measured included demographics and living arrangements; mental health and treatment history; substance abuse and treatment history; health problems; social support; employment and finances; and criminal justice involvement and violence. The data were gathered over a 12 month period at three different points from both diverted and non-diverted offenders.

In essence, based on the most current assessment data, jail diversion programs are not fully achieving several of the most basic goals. First, there is not a significant increase in public safety. Second, recidivism rates for diverted and non-diverted offenders are mostly the same. Third, the amount of days spent in the community by both diverted (303) and non-diverted offenders (245) is comparable (Steadman & Naples, 2005). Finally, when comparing psychological symptomatology among diverted and non-diverted participants, there were no significant differences between the two groups. For practical purposes these numbers reflect results that are not much better than chance.

DISCUSSION

Specifically, this article is intended to illuminate three critical components that may serve to enhance success rates among jail diversion programs:

1. Offenders must be psychometrically assessed for resistance to treatment.
2. There must be a proper match between offender and service provider.
3. Quality mental health services must include treatment specialists who are routinely involved from intake all the way through program completion.

Currently, the literature suggests that few jail diversion programs assess an offender's openness to receiving mental health services. "Traditionally, very little attention has been given to identifying offenders who were receptive to counseling and those who were not" (Shearer & Ogan, 2002, p. 72). It is critical to understand that not everyone is open to receiving mental health services. In essence, if we are not assessing offenders regarding their openness to the constructs of jail diversion, our ability to be successful is limited *a priori* to the percentage of offenders open to receiving mental health services. It is not sufficient to utilize the jail diversion recruitment process to gauge an offender's willingness to participate in or receive mental health services. The important distinction that must resonate is that some offenders may be very willing to enroll in jail diversion (in order to have charges dropped or reduced) but not open to receiving mental health services.

It is likely that jail diversion programs would be well-served by incorporating an instrument able to measure treatment resistance among offenders. Completion of the instrument would be the first requirement of all offenders eligible for diversion. One effective instrument aimed at measuring similar concepts is the Correctional Treatment Resistance Scale (Shearer, 1999). Thus far, the scale has proved to be reliable and valid with sound psychometric properties (Shearer & Ogan, 2002). Jail diversion programs should consider further investigation of this scale's utility and the possible adoption and implementation of the Correctional Treatment Resistance Scale (Shearer, 1999) or some other similar instrument that is able to capture an offender's perceptions of openness to receiving mental health services. Three reasons for implementing a treatment resistance scale are:

1. It provides a preliminary screening instrument to identify offenders who are less likely to benefit from treatment programs so that they can be matched to more appropriate interventions (e.g., educational and consciousness-raising programs).

2. It provides an instrument to identify offenders who can benefit the most from treatment programs and from more therapeutic treatment planning (Shearer & Ogan, 2002).
3. It will improve overall treatment prognoses of offenders processed through any such system, thereby lowering costs while simultaneously maintaining public safety.

The second component critical to the success of jail diversion is the proper match between the offender and service provider. There must be a positive therapeutic alliance forged between the offender and service provider. The therapeutic alliance is typically characterized as a collaboration between the therapist and client regarding goals and outcomes that are the targets of intervention (Hintikka, Laukkanen, Marttunen, & Lehtonen, 2006). The personalities of those involved must be amenable to the successful formation of a positive and nurturing environment; one that includes empathy, trust, autonomy and freedom, among others. Likewise, there is a specific need for careful attention to therapeutic alliances when considering transference issues among offenders with co-occurring and/or personality disorders (Williams, Haigh, & Fowler, 2005). Transference, the client's underlying perception of the therapist, can often be interrelated with client resistance, making the choice in mental health providers all the more important (Williams, Haigh, & Fowler, 2005). There is overwhelming support and agreement throughout the various helping professions that a critical factor affecting the success of therapy is the therapeutic alliance, regardless of theoretical technique (Meissner, 1996; Buck & Alexander, 2006; Williams, Haigh, & Fowler, 2005). It needs to be noted, however, that in order for the alliance to be established, the service provider must possess sufficient knowledge to deal with wide-ranging complexities of offenders in the criminal justice system suffering from mental illness and co-occurring disorders (Ashford, Sales, & Reid, 2001; Kerle, 1999; LASACT, 2002; Wallenstein, 1999; Williams, Haigh, & Fowler, 2005). This is particularly true when one considers that it is the dual diagnosed population that is most likely to drop out of treatment and is the most likely to recidivate (LASACT, 2004; The Sentencing Project, 2002).

Based on this information, jail diversion programs should consider using an instrument able to measure the degree to which a therapeutic alliance has been established between an offender and service provider. One such instrument is the Working Alliance Inventory Scale (WAI; Horvath, 1982). The WAI is a 36 item self-report measure consisting of three subscales: (1) Task agreement–the level of agreement between the therapist and client on techniques and procedures used to accomplish goals; (2) Goals agreement–level of agreement between the therapist and client on what is to be accomplished; (3) Bond component–measures the bond or relationship formed between the therapist and client (Horvath, 1982). Furthermore, the WAI has been utilized in a wide array of settings and consistently found to be reliable and valid (Hintikka et al., 2006; Knaevelsrud & Andreas, 2006).

The third component identified in the literature is the quality of health care services received by offenders who have been diverted. Steadman and Naples (2005) clearly assert their concern that some offenders participating in diversion may not be receiving quality health care services. In addition, "offenders with co-occurring disorders represent one of the most challenging groups encountered in the criminal justice system" (Chandler, Peters, & Juliano-Bult, 2004, p. 432). Managing the mental health needs of offenders with co-occurring disorders involves a multitude of systems, institutions and agencies that often have different missions, structures, and resources (Chandler et al., 2004; LASACT, 2002; The Sentencing Project, 2002).

In essence, providing quality health care services for offenders suffering from mental illness and/or co-occurring disorders is difficult (Wallenstein, 1999). The literature does contain empirical support, however, for a variety of programs and strategies currently operating (Kerle, 1999; Wallenstein, 1999). As cited by Chandler et al. (2005) some of these programs include:

- specialized screening and assessment for co-occurring disorders
- staged interventions
- pharmacological interventions
- motivational interventions
- cognitive-behavioral strategies
- modified therapeutic communities
- assertive community treatment
- comprehensive integrated treatment
- housing and employment services

Our assertion, similar to Chandler et al. (2005), is that mental health services for offenders can help to reduce recidivism and provide a better quality of life in general. The above mental health programs and strategies have been shown to work. Success is even more likely when these programs have integrated casework oversight that is comprehensive in nature.

Thus, providing quality mental health services to offenders with co-occurring disorders will require the provision of different treatment services during different stages of treatment (Chandler et al., 2005; LASACT, 2004). For this reason, quality mental health services should include an integrated dual disorder case management program that includes mental health and addiction treatment programs, as well as collaborative integrated programs (LASACT, 2004). Programs should be designed to: (1) engage clients, (2) accommodate various levels of severity and disability, (3) accommodate various levels of motivation and compliance, and (4) accommodate patients in different phases of treatment (LASACT, 2004). Different levels of care, ranging from more to less intense treatment, should be available since this is reflective of any individualized treatment orientation.

Quality mental health services are also achieved when there is a sense of continuity of care that is delivered to the offender (LASACT, 2004). When treating offenders with mental health issues, it is critical to develop treatment continuity over a long-term duration (LASACT, 2004). Burnout among correctional treatment specialists within a variety of different sites or locations may lead to frequent turnover among service providers (LASACT, 2004). This may result in the offender experiencing a series of disjointed therapeutic professional relationships, with none of these having sufficient emotional depth and/or clinical knowledge of the individual offender's treatment concerns. This serves to undermine likely treatment effectiveness and impairs any sense of in-depth rapport that is characteristic of a true therapeutic alliance between the offender-client and the treatment professional (Hintikka et al., 2006; Williams, Haigh, & Fowler, 2005). For this reason, treatment should include an integrated dual disorder case management program that ensures longevity among those treatment staff who are involved with offenders who are most at-risk of relapse and/or recidivism (LASACT, 2004; Williams et al., 2005).

Based on the literature, and as previously noted, the nexus between the caseworker, offender, and mental health provider is paramount (Ashford et al., 2001; LASACT, 2004). Once an offender has been properly screened and assessed, the caseworker must appropriately match the offender with mental health providers. This component of jail diversion can not be left to chance. The caseworker must be intimately familiar with all mental health providers available to the jail diversion program. Strengths and weaknesses of each provider must be known. The caseworker should be familiar with the psychological and emotional constructs measured by each of the instruments administered to the offenders participating in diversion. The caseworker's knowledge of these constructs (trauma, quality of life issues, depression, anxiety, substance use, etc. . . .) allows her/him to locate mental health providers who specialize in working with one or more of the disorders deemed critical by jail diversion programs.

The caseworker must also be actively involved in the progress of each offender. At a minimum, weekly or bi-weekly contacts must be made with each offender to assess progress and adjust services if necessary. The caseworker's caseload should be kept sufficiently small to allow for much if not all contact with the offender to be carried out in person. Personal contact allows for more in-depth observation and communication which should lead to better assessment of services being provided.

CONCLUSION

Jail diversion is a theoretically sound concept that was created and implemented based on the literature. Nothing in the literature suggests that jail diversion cannot be successful. In fact, the opposite is true. The totality of the literature suggests that jail diversion should be successful and should result in better safety for communities, money saved via reduced recidivism, and better qualities of life for offenders.

The concept of jail diversion and its implementation has evolved quickly in recent years. For example, we know that there needs to be communication between all stakeholders; we know there needs to be comprehensive representation of all relevant professionals and disciplines. Currently, the literature suggests that the stage of jail diversion programs most in need of scrutiny is the point at which we diagnose an offender as suffering from mental illness and/or co-occurring disorders. The stages prior to diagnoses are mostly settled.

Further assessment beyond mental illness/co-occurring disorders is necessary. Specifically, we need to assess the offender's openness/resistance to treatment. This is a critical decision point that drives future actions and placement of the offender. Not assessing this construct allows chance to immediately enter the equation negatively impacting program results. The next decision point is the appropriate matching of offenders with available mental health services. We must ensure that the therapeutic alliance has been established and that it continues to flourish throughout the duration of provided services. Finally, we must ensure that a quality mental health service is being provided. This is primarily accomplished through the intense oversight of knowledgeable and informed caseworkers.

Future research needs to focus on methods that ensure these three postulates are operationalized. A valid and reliable instrument must be adopted or created that is able to quantify an offender's openness to treatment. A scientifically driven and documentable method of matching offenders with providers should be developed in addition to psychometrically measuring the strength of the therapeutic alliance. And, jail diversion success would be greatly enhanced through the creation of a quantifiable, real-time method of measuring the quality of service rendered. In essence, the literature suggests that we immediately bring to bear resources and enhanced methods aimed at improving jail diversion success. Failure to do so may prove catastrophic concerning the issue of program sustainability.

REFERENCES

Ashford, J., Sales, B.D., & Reid, W.H. (2001). *Treating adult and juvenile offenders with special needs.* Washington, DC: American Psychological Association.

Bartol, C.R., & Bartol, A.M. (2005). *Criminal behavior: A psychological approach* (7th ed.). Upper Saddle River, NJ: Prentice Hall.

Buck, P.W., & Alexander, L.B. (2006). Neglected voices: Consumers with serious mental illness speak about intensive case management. *Administration and Policy in Mental Health and Mental Health Services Research, 33*(4), 470-481.

Champion, D. (2002). *Probation, parole, and community corrections* (4th ed.). Upper Saddle River, NJ: Prentice Hall.

Chandler, R.K., Peters, R.H., Field, G., & Juliano-Bult, D. (2004). Challenges in implementing evidence-based treatment practices for co-occurring disorders in the criminal justice system. *Behavioral Sciences and the Law, 22*, 431-448.

Cordess, C., Davidson, K., Morris, M., & Norton, K. (2005). 'Cluster B' antisocial disorders. In G.O. Gabbard, J.S. Beck, & J. Holmes (Eds.), *Oxford Textbook of Psychotherapy.* New York: Oxford University Press.

Faust, T.N. (2003). Shift the responsibility of untreated mental illness out of the criminal justice system. *Corrections Today, 65*(2), 6-7.

Hintikka, U., Laukkanen, E., Marttunen, M., & Lehtonen, J. (2006). Good working alliance and psychotherapy are associated with positive changes in cognitive performance among adolescent psychiatric inpatients. *Bulletin of the Menninger Clinic, 70*(4), 316-335.

Hoff, R.A., Rosenheck, R.A., Baranosky, M.V., Buchanan, J., & Zonana, H. (1999). Diversion from jail of detainees with substance abuse: The interaction with dual diagnosis. *The American Journal on Addictions, 8*, 201-210.

Kerle, K. (1999). Short-term institutions at the local level. In P.M. Carlson, & J.S. Garrett (Eds.), *Prison and Jail Administration: Practice and Theory.* Gaithersberg, MD: Aspen Publishers, Inc.

Knaevelsrud, C., & Maercker, A. (2006). Does the quality of the working alliance predict treatment outcome in online psychotherapy for traumatized patients? *Journal of Medical Internet Research, 8*, 4.

LASACT (2004). *Assessment and treatment of co-occuring disorders: Alcohol, other drug abuse and mental illness.* Baton Rouge, LA: Louisiana Association of Substance Abuse Counselors and Trainers.

Massaro, J. (2005). *Overview of the mental health service system for criminal justice professionals.* Delmar, NY: GAINS Technical Assistance and Policy Analysis Center for Jail Diversion.

Massaro, J. (2004). *Working with people with mental illness involved in the criminal Justice system: What mental health service providers need to know* (2nd ed.). Delmar, NY: Technical Assistance and Policy Analysis Center for Jail Diversion.

Meissner, W.W. (1996). *The therapeutic alliance.* Yale University Press.

National GAINS Center for People with Co-Occurring Disorders in the Justice System (2001). *The prevalence of co-occurring mental illness and substance use disorders in jails.* Fact Sheet Series, Delmar, NY.

National Institute of Mental Health (1995). *Jail diversion: Creating alternatives for persons with mental illness* [Brochure]. Delmar, NY: Author.

Reuland, M. (2004). *A guide to implementing police-based diversion programs for people with mental illness.* Delmar, NY: Technical Assistance and Policy Analysis Center for Jail Diversion.

Reuland, M., & Cheney, J. (2005). *Enhancing success of police-based diversion programs for people with mental illness.* Delmar, NY: GAINS Technical Assistance and Policy Analysis Center for Jail Diversion.

SAMHSA (2004). *The DASIS report–admissions with co-occurring disorders: 1995-2001.* Washington, DC: U.S. Department of Health and Human Services. Retrieved from: http://www.oas.samhsa.gov/2k4/dualTX/dualTX.cfm.

Shearer, R.A. (1999). Resistance to counseling by offenders who abuse substances. *Annals of the American Psychotherapy Association, 2*, 7.

Shearer, R.A., & Ogan, G.D. (2002). Measuring treatment resistance in offender counseling. *Journal of Addictions & Offender Counseling, 22*, 72-82.

Steadman, H.J., & Naples, M. (2005). Assessing the effectiveness of jail diversion programs for persons with serious mental illness and co-occurring substance use disorders. *Behavioral Sciences and the Law, 23*, 163-170.

Stephan, J.J. (2001). *Census of jails, 1999, NCJ186633.* Washington, DC: Government Printing office.

Teplin, L.A. (1994). Psychiatric and substance abuse disorders among male urban jail detainees. *American Journal of Public Health, 84*, 2.

The Sentencing Project (2002). *Mentally ill offenders in the criminal justice system: An analysis and prescription.* Washington, DC: The Sentencing Project.

Wallenstein, A. (1999). Intake and release in evolving jail practice. In P.M. Carlson, & J.S. Garrett (Eds.), *Prison and Jail Administration: Practice and Theory.* Gaithersberg, MD: Aspen Publishers, Inc.

Williams, P., Haigh, R., & Fowler, D. (2005). 'Cluster A' personality disorders. In G.O. Gabbard, J.S. Beck, & J. Holmes (Eds.), *Oxford Textbook of Psychotherapy.* New York: Oxford University Press.

AUTHORS' NOTES

Scott Mire, PhD, is Assistant Professor of Criminal Justice at the University of Louisiana at Lafayette. He is currently serving as the lead evaluator of a jail diversion program being implemented in Lafayette, LA.

Craig J. Forsyth, PhD, is Professor/Department Head of Criminal Justice at the University of Louisiana at Lafayette. He is currently serving as an evaluator of a jail diversion program being implemented in Lafayette, LA.

Robert Hanser, PhD, is Assistant Professor of Criminal Justice and is Director, Institute of Law Enforcement at the University of Louisiana at Monroe.

Address correspondence to Scott Mire via e-mail (smm6281@louisiana.edu).

doi:10.1300/J076v45n01_02

Mental Health Issues in the Criminal Justice System. Pp. 33-46.
Available online at http://jor.haworthpress.com
doi:10.1300/J076v45n01_03

Protecting Prisoners from Harmful Research: Is "Being Heard" Enough?

ALAN MOBLEY
STUART HENRY
DENA PLEMMONS

ABSTRACT Improving the conditions under which incarcerated populations give "informed consent" is a desirable goal given prisoners' lack of autonomy; part of the Institutional Review Board's (IRB) procedures is the inclusion of representative voices from the prisoner population as a mechanism to reduce harms. The most recent review of the ethics of research on prisoners by the Institute of Medicine recommends an expanded role for prisoner involvement, outlining a collaborative research approach involving prisoners as active participants in *all* aspects of the research, including design, planning and implementation, not just at the IRB stage.

In this paper, we briefly outline the existing state of IRB protections for prisoners selected for research, and focus on the effectiveness of prisoner representatives in this process. We suggest that there are weaknesses within the existing system such that representation may provide little more than ideological legitimation for the process. Moreover, we argue that while the Institute of Medicine's recommendations mark a major improvement in protection vis-à-vis prisoner representation, it does not go far enough in articulating the process whereby the voices of prisoners, their advocates or their representatives are included in the different stages of the process. In short, we question whether "being heard" is enough. We suggest that research needs to be conducted to more extensively map the scope of this issue and to raise some critical questions in order to improve the effectiveness of the ethical considerations for research on prisoners, as well as the IRB process and any post-IRB oversight, in protecting this vulnerable population. doi:10.1300/J076v45n01_03 *[Article copies available for a fee from The Haworth Document Delivery Service: 1-800-HAWORTH. E-mail address: <docdelivery@haworthpress.com> Website: <http://www.HaworthPress.com> © 2007 by The Haworth Press, Inc. All rights reserved.]*

KEYWORDS Prisoner populations, research, informed consent, Institutional Review Boards

INTRODUCTION

In 1974, Congress established the National Commission for the Protection of Human Subjects (NCPHS) and, since their initial recommendations in 1976, there have been established further recommendations for a series of protections for prisoners against research that might increase the risk of physical or psychological harm for this vulnerable, stable, routinized and accessible population. Improving the conditions under which incarcerated populations give "informed consent" is a desirable goal given prisoners' lack of autonomy. In their efforts to craft prisoner protections into the Institutional Review Board's (IRB) procedures, direction was given to include representative voices from the prisoner population. The point of such representation was to take into account the views of those subjected to research *before* any possible negative impact on this group. In the most recent review of the ethics of research on prisoners by the Institute of Medicine for the Department of Health and Human Services (DHHS), an expanded role for prisoner involvement is recommended (Gostin, Vanchieri, & Pope, 2006). The report recommends a collaborative research approach involving prisoners, together with other stakeholders, as active participants in *all* aspects of the research, including design, planning and implementation, not just at the IRB stage, and also in an enhanced oversight role "throughout the course of the study" by a prison research subject advocate (PRSA) who is not employed by the facility (Gostin, Vanchieri, & Pope, 2006, p. 12).

In this paper, we briefly outline the existing state of IRB protections for prisoners selected for research, and focus on the effectiveness of prisoner representatives in this process. Informed by first-hand, retrospective participant observation by one of the authors (Mobley), we suggest that there are weaknesses within the existing system of controls such that representation may provide little more than ideological legitimation for the process, and that this alone may not be enough to improve protection for prisoners. Moreover, we argue that while the Institute of Medicine's recommendations mark a major improvement in protection vis-a-vis prisoner representation, it does not go far enough in articulating the process whereby the voices of prisoners, their advocates or their representatives are included in the different stages of the process. In particular we argue that expanding opportunities to be heard is not the same as prescribing a mechanism whereby their voice is incorporated into the decision-making process. In short, we question whether "being heard" is enough. We suggest that research needs to be conducted to more extensively map the scope of this issue and to raise some critical questions in order to improve the effectiveness of the ethical considerations for research on prisoners, as well as the IRB process and any post-IRB oversight, in protecting this vulnerable population.

We begin by outlining the nature of the general concern for protecting the vulnerable population of prisoners, and then consider the situation of coercion in which prisoners exist, before considering the recommended improvements to the process. We conclude with suggestions about the kind of research that may lead to improvements in the protections currently in place.

PRISONERS AS VULNERABLE POPULATIONS

According to federal regulations, IRBs are designed to protect the subjects of research from unnecessary risk and harm. In this spirit:

> IRBs give special consideration to protecting the welfare of particularly vulnerable subjects, such as children, prisoners, pregnant women, mentally disabled persons, or economically or educationally disadvantaged persons [Federal Policy §___.111]. . . The DHHS regulations set forth specific provisions on research involving fetuses, pregnant women, and human in vitro fertilization [45 CFR 46 Subpart B]; prisoners [45 CFR 46 Subpart C]; and children [45 CFR 46 Subpart D]. In general, these special regulations allow IRBs to approve research that is of minimal risk or that will benefit the subjects directly. Investigations involving these subjects that present significantly greater than minimal risk without direct benefit to them must be reviewed and approved by the Secretary of

Health and Human Services, in consultation with appropriate experts. (IRB Guidebook, 2006)

These subparts make it clear that each of these vulnerable populations need additional protections beyond those articulated in the general federal regulations–questions of autonomy and "free" and voluntary consent become somewhat more complicated with these populations. As noted, prisoners are considered vulnerable subjects. In order to understand the need for additional protection of prisoners, beyond that needed to protect non-prisoners, it helps to consider the definition of *prisoner* used by the Federal Policy governing IRBs [45 CFR 46.303(c)]: "any individual involuntarily confined in a penal institution," including persons: "(1) sentenced under a criminal or civil statute; (2) detained pending arraignment, trial, or sentencing; and (3) detained in other facilities (e.g., for drug detoxification or treatment of alcoholism) under statutes or commitment procedures providing such alternatives to criminal prosecution or incarceration in a penal isnstitution." Such persons are, relative to non-prisoner populations, in various states of deprivation, not least in relation to freedom: to associate with others, to move to non-routinized spaces, to earn income, to receive treatment. Indeed, as Goffman (1957; 1961) described it, prisons are total institutions in which every aspect of one's daily life is controlled, regulated, and micro-managed by the organization. Therefore, research that offers to relieve the inmate of the deprivations deriving from their subordination in a total institution can be seen as an exploitative incentive, since the prisoners' desire to mitigate their deprivation stems from the uniqueness of their confinement.

In a 2005 report of the Secretary's Advisory Committee on Human Research Protection, it was recommended that "additional circumstances in which liberty is so restricted that informed consent cannot be said to be voluntary (e.g., community correctional settings and halfway houses, probation and parole)" be added to the category (Dubler & Barnes, 2005). This expanded definition was echoed in the 2006 Institute of Medicine report which recommended extending the reach of human subjects protection for prisoners to include "all settings, whether a correctional institution or a community setting, in which a person's liberty is restricted by the criminal justice system" (Gostin, Vanchieri, & Pope, 2006, pp. 4-5); this also included those on parole or probation. In other words, the protected category of prisoners should be expanded from the roughly 2 million persons actually in prison or jails to include the additional 5 million subjected to other forms of supervision.

There are additional factors that amplify the vulnerability of prisoners beyond the conditions of their incarceration. This is because, rather than being representative of the population as a whole, prisoners have among them a disproportionate number of persons who would qualify as a vulnerable population in their own right. These include a disproportionate number of "decisionally impaired persons," being those "who have a diminished capacity for judgment and reasoning due to a psychiatric, organic, developmental, or other disorder that affects cognitive or emotional functions," and those "under the influence of or dependent on drugs or alcohol" (Deighton, 2006), as well as economically or educationally disadvantaged groups, who "may speak and understand English but are unable to read" (Deighton, 2006). Indeed, 40 percent of prisoners are defined as functionally illiterate (Henry, 2005, p. 46).

An extreme reaction to these problems of vulnerability might be to refuse any and all research on prisoners on the grounds that, as a class, prisoners are too vulnerable. However, such a policy would add additional deprivations, since prisoners would not then be afforded the opportunities that research might provide. At present, in order to protect prisoners as a class, and prisoners as individuals, from the exploitative effects of incentives that have the capacity to diminish the exercise of true voluntary choice over whether to participate in research, and from research on them for no other reason than because they are captive subjects, DHHS limits the kinds of research in which prisoners can be involved. Only four kinds of research are allowed and each has to do with prisoners' situation of incarceration. These include studies of: (1) causes, effects and processes of incarceration; (2) prison as an institution or prisoners as incarcerated persons; (3) conditions affecting prisoners as a class; and (4) therapies likely to benefit prisoners (IRB Guidebook, 2006)

However, Dubler and Sidel (1989) are concerned with the comparative level of risk that prisoners might be subject to as a result of deciding to participate. They distinguish between risks to which prisoners are subject and risks that would be accepted by non-prisoner volunteers. They see those risks to which prisoners are subject stemming from several sources including: (1) prison authorities, (2) parole boards, (3) prison officers, (4) fellow prisoners, and (5) researchers and/or their funding agencies. Moreover, rather than comparing the risks to which prisoners should be exposed to those normally encountered by other prisoners, a position that some have argued is sufficient, Dubler and Sidel (1989, pp. 199-200) argue that minimal risk is desirable, that is, risk compared to that normally encountered in the daily lives of healthy persons who are not prisoners, taking into account the additional hazards such as the impossibility of confidentiality.

This new ethos on protecting prisoners is found in Dubler and Sidel's (1989, p. 204) statement originally written in connection with AIDS research in which they state:

> Inmates as a group need to be *protected* from research designs that can acquire the data through other routes and may present risks to inmates as a class. They need to be *provided with access* to clinical trials of new and innovative therapies that present the possibility of direct benefit to the subjects. They must be presented with the opportunity for informed choice when appropriate, despite recognition that the systematic deprivations and inherent coerciveness of the institutions . . . compromise the consent process.

This position was acknowledged in the Institute of Medicine's 2006 report which recommended a fundamental shift from the present categorical basis for review (which was seen as too restrictive in that it denied potential benefits of research) to a "risk-benefit framework" that weighed the "risks and benefits" for the individual human subject (Gostin, Vanchieri, & Pope, 2006, p. 8). The authors state that "ethically permissible research must offer benefits to prisoners that outweigh the risks" and risks "cannot be allowed among prisoners unless there is an associated benefit . . . in the absence of benefit, either to the prisoner-subject or to the prisoners as a class, the research should be conducted in other settings" (Gostin, Vanchieri, & Pope, 2006, p. 123). In other words, a compromise "moderate protectionism" position is sought in which prisoners are permitted to be research subjects, provided there are adequate controls and conditions on their participation and provided they are not denied the advantages of participation simply because there are risks of harm.

As part of the process of controls and the facilitation of benefits, prisoner representatives have been seen as needing to occupy an increasing role within both the review process and, importantly, in the design, planning, implementation, and oversight of research on prisoners. At present, however, they are only required to be involved in the IRB process.

THE ROLE, FUNCTION AND CHALLENGES OF PRISONER REPRESENTATIVES

Under current law Subpart C [45 CFR 46.303(c)] of the law on Human Research Protections, "at least one member of an IRB [reviewing a protocol which involves prisoners] must be a prisoner or a 'prisoner representative with appropriate background and experience to serve in that capacity.' " However, in multi-site studies this fails to take into account the diversity of prisoner services in a variety of prison contexts (Subpart C, Section 46.304 (a) and (b); See Dubler & Barnes, 2005). This law also states: "In the absence of choosing someone who is a prisoner or has been a prisoner, the IRB should choose a prisoner representative who has a close working knowledge, understanding and appreciation of prison conditions from the perspective of the prisoner" (OHRP, 2004). The common interpretation of this rubric is seen in the following example from the University of Washington:

> When a committee reviews research that involves prisoners, a prisoner advocate must be present. The prisoner advocate is an ad hoc member with voting privileges on applications involving prisoners. The advocate is drawn from a roster of local individuals with appropriate background and expertise to serve in this capacity. (University of Washington, 2006)

Dubler and Barnes (2005), on behalf of the Secretary's Advisory Committee on Human Research Protections, state, "The three primary considerations for a prisoner representative should be:

–Empathy for prisoners, sharing concerns that prisoners would have about a study

–Particular knowledge of correctional settings, including some awareness of local conditions in which the study will be conducted

–Independence from prison administration and other outside influences."

They argue that "some sources of representatives might include:

–Family members of prisoners

–Former prisoners

–People in recovery from substance addiction who have had experience as inmates in the correctional settings

–Service providers who assist the correctional population, including in the release process."

Moreover, they claim "the burden of protecting prisoners in research should rest not only on the IRB, but also on investigators, who because of their presence in the correctional settings will have more awareness of actual circumstances than an IRB" (see Dubler & Barnes, 2005). Importantly, the committee points out that "expedited review of protocols that fall under Subpart C would not necessarily include the input of the prisoner representative, thus frustrating the purpose of having such a representative in the first place" (Dubler & Barnes, 2005). In its 2006 Report, the Institute of Medicine addresses these concerns, discussed in more detail below.

THE EXPANDED ROLE OF PRISONER REPRESENTATION: IS IT ENOUGH TO BE HEARD?

The DHSS-sponsored, 2006 Institute of Medicine report, *Ethical Considerations in Research Involving Prisoners*, published by the National Academy of Sciences, makes a series of wide-ranging recommendations for improving the protection and opportunity for benefits of prisoners, some of which have been summarized above. Here we are particularly concerned with those recommendations that address the role of the prisoners in the process of their own protection. The Institute of Medicine Report addresses this issue in three ways. First, in developing their new ethical framework they assert that informed consent is too narrow a criteria on which to consider research ethics and regulation, arguing instead that attention should be paid to "risks and benefits analysis" (Gostin, Vanchieri, & Pope, 2006, p. 118). Second, they argue

> One can simultaneously believe that the piling on of more rules and oversight bodies at some point becomes counterproductive and that human subjects are presently inadequately protected. Indeed, many modern ethicists seem to hope for a reawakening of scientific conscience rather than additional fortifications of the citadel of regulations. (Gostin, Vanchieri, & Pope, 2006, p. 120)

Third, the committee advocates enhancing ways that promote researchers to act virtuously in order to protect their vulnerable subjects. Moreover, the committee advocates that, to be ethical, research needs to recognize diverse settings, meaning that prisons or other forms of restrictive detention each have a unique culture and history and that these require localized knowledge. As such these settings can only be understood through "close cooperation and communication with all relevant parties" (Gostin, Vanchieri, & Pope, 2006, p. 114). However, drawing on Eckenwiler's (2001) caution that socioeconomic differences between researchers and subjects prevent the former from understanding the risk undertaken by the latter, the committee developed the concept of "collaborative responsibility" in which "investigators should find ways to obtain input from prisoners and other stakeholders on the design and conduct of any research protocol involving prisoners" (Gostin, Vanchieri, & Pope, 2006, p. 129. For an elegant description of this kind of partnership in the field of public/community health, see Baker, Homan, Schonoff, & Kreuter, 1999). This ranges from collaboration with prisoners in constructing the research question, in protocol development and in recruitment and enrollment in the study, because "if prisoners have a voice in how subjects are enrolled, they can help protect themselves from inappropriate recruitment practices that infringe on their autonomy . . . or unfairly distribute risks and benefits within the prison population" (Gostin, Vanchieri, & Pope, 2006, p. 130). This illustration of the Institute of Medicine's recommendations about the inclusion of the human subject at every level of the research process is instructive, not just for its genuine awareness of the value of incorporating the subject's definition of the situation and assessment of his or her own risk, but also for the naivety with which it fails to follow through with identifying the problems and the politics of the very incorporation of the research subject into the research process. Nowhere is this better illustrated than in the following statement that "the human research participants protection program (HRPPP) can ask if all relevant people were consulted and determine that the process was transparent and fair. *As long as all parties are consulted fully and fairly, given an opportunity to be heard, the goal is met*" (Gostin, Vanchieri, & Pope, 2006, p. 130; our emphasis). As we shall argue below, this is precisely the problem; expanding opportunities to be heard, laudable in itself, is not the same as prescribing a mechanism whereby their voice is incorporated into the decision, and this report consistently fails to articulate how precisely that would occur. Similar problems emerge in the committee's discussions on the IRB process and their proposal for enhanced oversight.

In the IRB process a critical concern becomes who reviews the research proposals involving prisoners; under current law this research must be reviewed by an independent research committee and

> the committee should include at least one prisoner representative who has experience with the prison setting, but is not an employee of the setting. This person should have particular knowledge of the correctional setting and should be able to represent the interests of the prisoners. The prisoner representative, who is a voting member on the committee, could be a person who works with prisoners (e.g., an attorney, a service provider, or a chaplain who is not an employee of the correctional institution or agency), a family member of an inmate, or an ex-offender. (Gostin, Vanchieri, & Pope, 2006, p. 141)

Two critical factors govern the role of the prisoner representative: that they (1) "have sufficient opportunity to be heard, independent of the people who work in the prison" and (2) "have the independence to freely express prisoner concerns, even when they may come in conflict with the institutional issues" (Gostin, Vanchieri, & Pope, 2006, p. 141). In order to accomplish this, it is necessary to provide training particularly to familiarize the representative with the research process and with human subjects' protections. Further, the Institute of Medicine report states that to enhance the insight of researchers about a particular correctional setting and to develop appropriate procedures, "it may be desirable for researchers to convene a prison advisory group . . . composed of current prisoners who can inform the researchers about unique factors to consider in their particular institution" (Gostin, Vanchieri, & Pope, 2006, pp. 146-47). Again, while the expanded inclusion of prisoners is laudable, the failure to document how their views are to be incorporated, and to invest faith in the belief that the researcher will somehow be sensitive to this, seems to be seriously problematic. This all but ensures that the prisoner representative remains but a token presence in satisfaction of the requirements, with no real structural process in place to embody his or her unique and valuable contributions.

Finally, the Institute of Medicine report recommends a level of oversight post IRB review and approval to involve monitoring by a Prison Research Subject Advocate (PRSA). This role is designed "to provide assurance, via ongoing onsite monitoring, such that research subjects within a specific facility or program are protected" (Gostin, Vanchieri, & Pope, 2006, p. 154). Again, there is no explanation of how the PRSA's observations, view and voice are translated into the research process in such a way that they have an impact on that process.

REPRESENTATION, LEGITIMACY AND EFFICACY: IS REPRESENTATION ENOUGH?

The central question we are asking here, then, is whether having a formal position, as a prisoner representative, regardless of the institutionally prescribed role in the process, is effective as a means of protection from exploitation, harm or elevated risk for harm. This question arises because incorporating prisoner advocates into the research design and implementation process, the IRB process, and the extended oversight process, while each a major advance over their omission, might function to include the *symbolic* voice of prisoners, but to exclude the *content* of their substantive contribution. This is because prisoner experiential knowledge might be discounted relative to the apparently more objective knowledge of those skilled in the knowledge of research design, research implementation, or the other IRB or oversight committee members. However, the experiential knowledge of the prisoner representative might be cognizant of a variety of informal practices that are contrary to the IRB members' assumptions about, for instance, prison security and confidentiality. For example, situations where the research expert might consider risk to be low would be compromised through informal practices such as collusion between guards and treatment staff, guards and certain prisoners, and insecure record keeping practices. In the discussion between IRB members these issues may range from "not being a risk," "being a manageable risk" to being a "tremendous risk." When some members of the IRB committee hold views expressed as "it's not our job to be protecting criminals," the issue of moving from a discussion to a vote on a particular proposal begs the question of the relative weight afforded to the prisoner representative's views. Rather than being given the benefit of the doubt, or even being given privileged voice, human subject inclusion as one voice among many, in a research design, or in an IRB committee, may render the prisoner voice neutralized at best, and marginalized at worst; relying on the ethical awareness of committees, however elaborate the research collaboration process, is too unreliable. Without a mechanism for the inclusion of the heard voice into the actual research process, such that the outcome is substantially affected by his/her input, all attempts to include the human subject's voice may be negated.

IMPLICATIONS FOR POLICY
AND THE NEED FOR RESEARCH

The implications of the previous discussion lead to a number of policy-related questions, the most compelling of which include: (1) How far does the existing representation, even at multiple stages in the process, provide protection? (2) Does the current deliberative practice and process effectively undermine the representative's substantive contribution? (3) How can the representation of the subjective voice be better incorporated into the deliberative process? Depending upon the outcome of this research, subsequent study might address: the structural and process changes that might be necessary to increase the level of protection for prisoner research subjects; and the reduction or elimination of barriers to subjective representation to avoid compromising the researcher's original proposal. In order to address the first three questions it would be helpful to launch a series of exploratory research projects to establish whether the concerns discussed here have any foundation.

An appropriate design for addressing these policy questions would involve a series of ethnographic studies of the decision-making process in IRB deliberations on prisoner projects. Researchers with ethnographic training, such as anthropologists, or sociologists with training in qualitative methods, specifically participant-observation, should be able to participate in and document the deliberative process. A second level of research would involve qualitative semi-structured interviews with persons who have served on IRBs considering prisoner research. A third level might involve interviews with convict criminologists who have both served time in prison and been trained in research methods. Finally, interviews might be conducted with prisoner-representatives who have served on these boards across the country.

To date, there have been four ethnographic studies of the deliberative process of IRBs, with data available for two of those (in the remaining two cases, analysis is continuing) (Stark, 2006; Lane, 2005), and one of the authors (Plemmons) has begun preliminary work in this area, as well. Among other things, these studies looked at the process of including the voices of the lay or community members of the IRBs and how successful that process was/was able to be. This kind of ethnographic design would be necessary here in order to look at *how* those who are the designated prisoner representatives are being heard in the deliberative process of IRB meetings, and how (or if) what is heard is incorporated into or influences the decisions which are reached about specific research protocols. Moreover, should the Institute of Medicine's recommendations to incorporate prisoner representatives into the design and planning stages of research proposals be implemented, then a similar series of studies should be implemented there also.

Ultimately, as mentioned above, there may be a role in the future for prisoner councils or other forms of prisoner participation such as prisoner forums, consultative councils, inmate committees, representative councils, etc., in the research review process similar to the kinds that exist and are being encouraged in Europe (Bishop, 2006), since this process alone may empower prisoners to become further protected through working together in a communal context involving their own governance. However, the fundamental issue here is that representation without having the research subject's voice make a difference is, at best, another turn of the ideological screw, regardless of the representation advocate's good intentions.

Recent corrections innovations and the proposed expansion of many existing programs for "special populations" combined with the call for evidence-based corrections and adherence to correctional best practices indicate that the need for corrections research is intensifying. As the field of corrections research begins this renaissance, we believe that it is not only timely to address issues related to the research process, but critical that we move toward maximizing the ethical basis on which such research proceeds. To do so requires research on that process to ensure that it achieves the maximum protection for those who are its subjects.

REFERENCES

Baker, E.A., Homan, S., Schonhoff, R., & Kreuter, M. (1999). Principles of practice for academic/practice/community research partnerships. *American Journal of Preventive Medicine, 16*, 86-93.

Bishop, N. (2006). Prisoner participation in prison management. *Penal Field: The New French Journal of Criminology, 3*, http://champpenal.revues.org/document 487.html

Deighton, B. (2006). *SJMHS Institutional Review Board(s): Vulnerable Populations: Decisionally Impaired and Other Potentially Vulnerable Subjects.* Assessed November 13, 2006 at http://www.sjmercyhealth.org/documents/irb/sops/SJMHS% 20Policy%20-%20Vulnerable%20Populations%20Decisionally%20Impaire.pdf

Dubler, N.N., & Sidel, V.W. (1989). On research on HIV infection in correctional institutions. *Milbank Quarterly, 67*(2), 171-207.

Dubler, N.N. & Barnes, M. (2005). *Secretary's Advisory Committee on Human Research Protections: The Report of Subpart C Subcommittee.* Accessed November 16, 2006, http://www.os.dhhs.gov/ohrp/sachrp/mtgings/mtg01-05/present2/barnesdubler_files/frame.htm

Eckenwiler, L. (2001). Moral reasoning and the review of research involving human subjects. *Kennedy Institute of Ethics Journal, 1*(1), 37-69.

Goffman, E. (1957). Characteristics of total institutions. In *Symposium on Preventative and Social Psychiatry*, Sponsored by the Walter Reed Army Institute of Research, the Walter Reed Army Medical Centre, and the National Research Council, Washington (Government Printing Office), pp. 43-93 [revised version of Interpersonal Persuasion; revised in *Asylums*, pp. 1-124].

Goffman, E. (1961). *Asylums: Essays on the social situation of mental patients and other inmates*. New York: Doubleday Anchor; Harmondsworth: Penguin, 1968.

· Gostin, L.O., Cori, V., & Andrew, P. (Eds.) (2006). *Ethical considerations for research involving prisoners*. Washington DC: National Academy of Sciences.

Henry, S. (2005). The threat of incarceration does not deter criminal behavior. In J. Haley (Ed.), *Prisons*. Farmington Hills: Green Haven Press, pp. 41-48.

Lane, Eleish O'Neil (2005). Decision-making in the human subjects review system. Unpublished dissertation, School of Public Policy, Georgia Institute of Technology. Available at: http://hdl.handle.net/1853/6834.

OHRP (Office for Human Research Protections 2004). *OHRP guidance on the involvement of prisoners in research*. Washington DC: Department of Health and Human Services.

Stark, L. (2006). *Morality in science: How research is evaluated in the age of human subjects*. Unpublished doctoral dissertation. Princeton, NJ: Princeton University.

University of Washington (2006). *IRB member composition*. Seattle, WA: University of Washington, Human Subjects Division.

AUTHORS' NOTES

Alan Mobley, PhD, is Assistant Professor, School of Public Administration and Urban Studies, San Diego State University, 5500 Campanile Drive, San Diego, CA 92182-4505 (E-mail: alan.mobley@sdsu.edu).

Stuart Henry, PhD, is Professor and Director, School of Public Affairs, San Diego State University, 5500 Campanile Dr., San Diego, CA 92182-4305 (E-mail: stuart.henry@sdsu.edu).

Dena Plemmons, PhD, Division of Research Affairs, is Adjunct Assistant Professor, Graduate School of Public Health, San Diego State University, 5500 Campanile Drive, San Diego, CA 92182 (E-mail: plemmons@mail.sdsu.edu).

doi:10.1300/J076v45n01_03

Mental Health Issues in the Criminal Justice System. Pp. 47-54.
Available online at http://jor.haworthpress.com
© 2007 by The Haworth Press, Inc. All rights reserved.
doi:10.1300/J076v45n01_04

Justice Is in the Eye of the Beholder

MICHAEL WEAVER

ABSTRACT An individual tells his story of how mental health problems got him to prison and how prison mental health services were difficult to obtain and inappropriate at times. He had to demand that he receive adequate treatment. Mike Weaver currently advocates for mental health services and treating people rather than extending their prison sentences. doi:10.1300/J076v45n01_04 *[Article copies available for a fee from The Haworth Document Delivery Service: 1-800-HAWORTH. E-mail address: <docdelivery@haworthpress.com> Website: <http://www.HaworthPress.com> © 2007 by The Haworth Press, Inc. All rights reserved.]*

KEYWORDS Prison mental health services, prison, bi-polar

INTRODUCTION

The old saying goes that "beauty is in the eye of the beholder" and it is the same way with the courts and the resulting jail and prison sentences that follow. "Justice is in the eye of the beholder." It makes a big difference whether one is a defendant with a mental illness, a prosecutor, judge, psychologist or defense attorney. If one listens to the multitude of former prosecutors on news and semi-news shows on television, one might think that we have not gained much since the mid 20th century.

Mental illnesses were considered character weaknesses or flaws. Religious leaders thought mental illnesses could be "prayed away" or removed by laying on of hands. The same nonsense is propagated today and unfortunately, it is within the justice system that this is so prevalent. I am thankful for those enlightened souls who are beginning to utilize mental health and substance abuse courts.

I am a person who has had bipolar disorder for twenty years and at the age of thirty-six encountered the courts and incarceration for the first time. I will preface this with the statement that I tell groups of the mentally ill often: "mental illness is not an excuse for bad behavior, but it is an explanation." People who commit crimes while mentally incapacitated should not be excused for their actions. There is a difference between them and those who intentionally break the law. While operating a support group for people with bipolar disorder, I met a man who ultimately killed his very young twin daughters. Many people believe it was premeditated because he had homicidal urges before the murders. The very nature of his psychotic illness prohibited him from telling anyone because he feared what would happen. He had a lot of remorse afterward and later appeared to be very lucid. Nevertheless, it is my belief that he was driven by the illness and instead of grabbing for a life sentence to avoid the death penalty, his attorney should have gone with an insanity plea.

Despite the increasing knowledge about mental illness, there appears to be increasing confusion. The DSM-IV diagnostic manual is much thicker than the DSM-III and the next manual is purported to be much thicker. Treatment manuals abound but judges, defense attorneys and prosecutors lack the time to really understand mental illness. I constantly hear attorneys and news people using the wrong terms to describe mental illnesses.

MY STORY

When I arrived at the maximum security Soledad State Prison, I was still in shock. I was a white middle class male, son of a minister and one of fourteen children. I was in the middle of a successful career as a teacher and administrator. Accolades and honors such as Teacher of the Year had been bestowed upon me but the combination of heavy stress and not following a medication regimen brought me to the point of acute mania and delusion. Why does an intelligent person not follow medical advice? Well, I was a typical California health nut. I worked out six days a week, ate whole wheat, sugar free organic foods and did not like to take medicine. Until the time that I was diagnosed in 1987, I never even took aspirin.

Thus, during a stressful time, being department chair and chairing numerous other committees, I read a book, *Toxic Psychiatry*, by a psychiatrist, Dr. Peter Breggin. This book stated emphatically that all medications were "poisonous" or "toxic" to the human body. Psychotropic drugs such as lithium were extremely bad in his view. I already had enough side effects from the lithium (tremors, diarrhea, sweating and dry mouth) that I bought this hook, line and sinker. I did not stop taking the 40 mg of Prozac that had been prescribed. This launched me into the most severe mania of my life and to places I thought I would never visit.

The long, almost 400-mile ride in a Department of Corrections bus, with one guard with a shotgun in front and one behind me, caused me to think how I had arrived at this place in my life. Until recently, I had not known the difference between a misdemeanor and a felony. Looking down at the adobe roofs of Santa Barbara, I thought about the many vacations I had spent there. Cars below were scurrying around in their freedom, unaware of the misery in the bus next to them. I realized then, that I had to be in charge of my mental health. My thinking processes did need improvement but I don't know if I could have prevented what had happened without the knowledge I have now. I had needed a "ghost of Christmas past" to show me before I lost it all.

I did not expect to receive any better medical treatment in prison than I had in county jail. It took me many days and sleepless nights to start receiving medications and only after family members and friends had made several calls to the jail. On one occasion I had told a cellmate that I was suicidal after witnessing a severe beating of an inmate by another. The so-called hospital I was referred to have beds attached to each other by about six inches and were only eight inches from the floor. I spoke to a psychiatrist once through a 2-inch slit in the door. This was not a therapeutic environment. Extremely psychotic people were all around me and especially the one next to me. I left there plenty suicidal, but I faked it so I could get back out into the general population. The number one duty of the technicians there was to write down what we said and how much of our meals we ate.

Nevertheless, upon entering the Salinas Valley prison at Soledad, I met with a prison psychiatrist. He immediately informed me that I was not bipolar and he would not prescribe me medications. I urged him to reconsider, as it probably wouldn't be too good for me to complete my sentence if I did without medications. I told him that I had thirteen brothers and sisters and a mother who would be inquiring about me. This is one of the biggest problems with prisons. Families have given up on inmates and the system does whatever they want with them. Anyway,

I told this doctor that I had been diagnosed by five private psychiatrists in two states along with clinical psychologists and an eleven-person research team at the University of California at San Diego. I had nine hospitalizations. I reminded him that lithium was not expensive and certainly not a feel good drug. Cost is a major factor in what jails and prisons give to inmates. In jail, I had received an old tricyclic antidepressant, Elavil, which had nasty side effects but at least aided sleep. This psychiatrist finally prescribed me lithium, a mood stabilizer and Zoloft, an antidepressant. He specifically said they didn't give Zyprexa to people with bipolar because it was too expensive and I could forget about Klonopin.

During the duration of my stay there, I saw a psychiatrist twice. He wanted to know why my attorney had not brought up my mental illness as a mitigating circumstance. Despite the fact that I had paid $21,000 to an attorney, he adamantly refused to mention my mental illness to the judge. It was election time, he said, and the OJ case was affecting everything. California is considered to be a liberal, nutcase, fruit flake state but its law enforcement is much tougher than the southern state I reside in now. And most of the time a person is in court, it is not the deliberate pace one sees in murder trials on television. Everything happens so fast; one does not know what happened.

I know the US has a better system than most countries, but it is confusing for the average person.

My mental health treatment besides the meds I received in prison, was me exhaustively looking for books that could encourage me, reading the Bible, listening to my black market radio, seeking out the few people who I could have good conversations with, and the telephone. Good intelligent conversation was at a premium in jail and prison. The telephones were my lifeline with the real world. I would have to spend four hours out on the yard to use the only inmate telephones. There were twelve telephones on each end, some for northern or southern Mexicans, some for the Crips and Bloods, some for the Others, and three phones for the whites that evidently had lost the wars. I did my running everyday while out there but the wait for a ten-minute phone conversation could be two hours. Thankfully, I had people to call. While I waited in line, I could watch two guys doing heroin off a spoon, talk to a Neo-Nazi, get propositioned by a transsexual or wait for the next riot to kick off. That would result in hitting the dirt, having guards fire live ammunition overhead from the towers, watching the Mexicans beat up on each other and then losing a week to total lock down in the cell except for an occasional shower.

I attended the Protestant and Catholic chapels just to be in a better environment. The Protestants could really sing. It was the only place one could let tears flow and the old hymns never sounded better. The Catholic priest was a liberal theologian but extremely intelligent, compassionate and a breath of fresh air every week. I lived in a three-tier wing with about three hundred men. There were seven thousand men housed at this prison. What I did learn in prison was patience. Something that took minutes on the outside took hours in there. Showers, laundry, getting meds, going to medical were lengthy propositions. I had to pay an inmate ten dollars of canteen material to get in to see the dentist. It was a brutal cleaning and I never went back. Depression was abundant as was evil. The evil did not exist just within the inmates. Many guards and employees in the system let the inmates dictate their attitudes. They call mentally ill people "Crazies" to their face and basically dehumanize them so they can justify their treatment of them. Two guards worked me over quite well one day. The one guard came back and told me he had to do it. My attorney said it happened every day and to forget about it. I worked as a teacher's aide with the younger sixteen- and seventeen-year-old inmates with a teacher who seemingly hated all inmates and really made it rough on those who worked for her, especially when she found out I had bipolar disorder. Entering that prison school was weird after having been a teacher for many years. It was a scary place. I met one guard who was a retired minister and not long from state retirement. He would say something encouraging every time on the way to dinner. Would it be possible to change the hiring template for a guard from the current model to that of this retired minister? I think he probably had the best chance of a guard not getting hurt at that prison.

The never-ending threats of violence (by inmates and guards), the dreariness of the prison itself–concrete and steel, the heavy carbohydrate diet and the total lack of niceness provided me with a constant battle with depression. I was housed on the second tier because those with mental illness could not be housed on the third tier. Nevertheless, I would visit people on the third tier and look down at the concrete floor and think about jumping. But I hung on, reading many of the seventy books I had in my cell. I believe the limit was five. I wore earplugs to sleep, stayed away from trouble and managed not to get a shank stuck in me. I washed my clothes in my cell to avoid getting them ripped off in the laundry. I followed the inmate rules which were basically segregation although I did occasionally have conversations with blacks and used their phones at my risk occasionally.

CONCLUDING COMMENTS

There is nothing to be learned that is radically new here. We pay now or we pay later. If we invest in a "correctional" system that aims not just to warehouse inmates, then we will benefit with communities that are not at much as risk for violence and criminality. I had a good job before prison and many friends and family members who helped me when I got out. Yet, the five years after prison were much tougher than the years in prison. When I got out I never anticipated the difficulty I would have not only obtaining a good job but also finding housing for someone considered a felon. As far as programs go, there were almost none. I found a program in Boston but it was basically for manual labor individuals and the person leading the group seemed to resent that I had higher education. There were no groups available for my peer group that I could find. I proceeded to look for managerial jobs in industries that did not check my background carefully but since 9/11 that is increasingly difficult. When parole is complete the payment to society is not. I lost jobs that I knew I was qualified for after the check was made. In two of these I had answered the question truthfully but the question asked for a limited number of years. Despite my outstanding performance, I was let go when they finally looked at my record. I worked as a teacher and administrator at two schools despite the convictions but I had to bare my entire life in front of the school board. I was paid accordingly. It is apparent that organizations do not have the capability or the desire to distinguish between crimes that were committed long ago and the circumstances in which they were committed. I am in my position today because of a supervisor who looked beyond the conviction and saw my value. She said that my record did not frighten her, that it was an example of a person with bipolar disorder who had come to terms with it. She saw me from a strengths aspect, not a deficit stance. My years of retail work and developing five support groups on a volunteer basis served to put me into a position to succeed today. I had help from my family and friends, but governmental or community programs were not there for me.

Surprisingly, housing was also an issue when I left prison. Many places would not accept me based on the felony record. I rented from people, not always the best places, who I knew did not do background checks. It wasn't until recently at a fair housing seminar that I found out that I could ask for a reasonable accommodation based on the fact that I had been in the midst of a mental health crisis when the crime occurred. Since I had no problems for some time I would be eligible for this. There are reasons to exclude people from housing but it is the consumer's responsibility to know the law and ask for the accommodation. The landlord does not have to advertise the law.

Receiving mental health treatment after prison was a challenge and without insurance I ended up going to the county mental health system for many years. The psychiatrists were extremely good but therapy was another story. The main barrier to this system was learning not to take the system's attitude personally. Also, one had to be prepared to sit in the waiting room with some very seriously ill individuals.

Nevertheless, I have received the right to vote. I will apply for a pardon to have my conviction expunged in 2009 and hopefully by that time, I will be totally able to leave this nightmare behind me. Most of the individuals that end up incarcerated are going to wind up back on the streets with all of us someday. How they are treated there has to have an effect on their psyche. This is not a plea to be soft on crime. I realize how dangerous some of these guys are. Threats to my safety were a daily occurrence in prison.

Specifically, with regard to people who have mental illnesses and commit crimes, the mental health courts that are springing up across America and even in my community are a necessary part of the process to increase fairness. Judges and attorneys who are knowledgeable will conduct these courts. I meet with the Mental Health Court Group in my community and am happy to report that we have received $119,000 to start the court. We are anticipating additional community funding. We are advocating having a peer, one with mental illness, as part of the Mental Health Court Team. Groups for men and women in prison who have illnesses need to be funded. In the California system, I saw nothing. There were no AA, NA, Anger Management, or Mental Health related groups. Understandably, individual counseling could be costly but so are the forty four + prisons for men and women in California.

My informal interviews of inmates in prisons and jail probably reach close to one thousand. I met very few who had good starts in life. For the ones who were there due to substance abuse, it was difficult to determine whether their mental difficulties started the drug abuse or the opposite. Most have hair trigger tempers, a horrible attitude toward authority, misogynistic views of women and racist views. Most of these people grew up in a shame-based environment. Jail and prison are all about shame. Every aspect of one's life is open to all. Many of them believe they are just a part of what has become one of the two top industries in California. What is the answer? Encourage the legislatures to continue to lengthen penalties? Or is there a way within the jail and prison system to effect more humane treatment of those with mental illnesses who are incarcerated?

I support our nation's law enforcement system but I also support the fair and humane treatment of all incarcerated people in jails and prisons. Especially, there is an ongoing need to examine the way we sentence mentally ill people and the way we treat them in prisons and state hospitals. We must realize that every single person on this earth has value. There is still a need for our whole society to understand mental illness better.

As part of the Mental Health Association, it is my job to educate the public. My experience in jail and prison has also made it easier for me to communicate with those who are experiencing the painful realities of having mental illness. My life has been much more difficult as a result of what happened in a few minutes years ago. But I take the attitude that life could have been better and it also could have been worse. In spite of the treatment I received, I survive. I do think that I am an anomaly. It is my belief that those like myself in the system need much more help. My many conversations with those with severe mental illness in prison revealed that. The state prison systems are secretive, scary places that produce little hope. We are spending a great deal of money in this area. I do think the federal, state and local governments can be more intentional about how we are treating the mentally ill in jail and prison. I understand that violent crime is down statistically but we have a very large correctional system that mostly punishes.

People do not create the genes that cause them to get psychotic, manic or depressed. Yes, they can work on managing everything around that illness so that it does not get out of control. For most, like myself, we don't always learn it in time. It is the individual's job to work on managing his or her life, but it is our job to make sure that our fellow citizens with mental illnesses are afforded a recovery environment, one that provides hope, choice and empowerment so that we all are safe when people who have committed offenses reenter our society.

AUTHOR'S NOTE

Michael Weaver, MS, is Director of Supportive Services, The Mental Health Association in Greensboro, Inc., 330 S. Greene St., Suite B-12, Greensboro, NC 27401 (E-mail: mweaver@mhag.org).

doi:10.1300/J076v45n01_04

Mental Health Issues in the Criminal Justice System. Pp. 55-57.

Available online at http://jor.haworthpress.com

© 2007 by The Haworth Press, Inc. All rights reserved.

doi:10.1300/J076v45n01_05

An "Extended Care" Community Corrections Model for Seriously Mentally Ill Offenders

RAYMOND SABBATINE

ABSTRACT Our system fills every bed before it is built. Supply and demand have never had a better relationship. We need to refocus our public policy upon a correctional system that heals itself by helping those it serves to heal themselves through service to others even less fortunate. Let us term this new paradigm a "Correctional Cooperative," where mentally ill and substance abusers receive treatment while they work the floors of a detox unit, where the stabilized mentally ill become "buddy watchers" for those on suicide watch. Instead of warehousing offenders let us require their time to be productive, healing others while they heal themselves. doi:10.1300/J076v45n01_05 *[Article copies available for a fee from The Haworth Document Delivery Service: 1-800-HAWORTH. E-mail address: <docdelivery@haworthpress.com> Website: <http:// www.HaworthPress.com> © 2007 by The Haworth Press, Inc. All rights reserved.]*

KEYWORDS Jail, community corrections, extended care community corrections

INTRODUCTION

While diversion efforts, CIT programs and Mental Health Courts function to minimize the number of offenders with mental illness occupying our nation's jails, the most seriously mentally ill will always be our residents. Just as the promises of deinstitutionalization failed to come to fruition through the creation of our Community Mental Health System, jail will always be the institutions of last resort for the seriously mentally ill. The reason for these governmental failures is twofold. First and foremost, a jail is the only institution in government that does not have admission criteria. Jails must accept everyone legally presented for custody. Second, as long as forensic hospitalization averages $500 per day and a jail's housing cost is $50 per day, jails will always be the preferred choice.

Regardless of the rhetoric of the nation's mental health community, they continue to drive the seriously mentally ill into jail by creating hospital admission criteria prohibiting violent felons from entering their system and involuntary commitment criteria that does the same. The Mental Health System has excused its behavior by hiding behind the limited ability their hospitals have to provide the needed security to manage violent felons with mental illness. In reality, the violent mentally ill require huge outlays of institutional resources over extended periods of time and at $500 a day it would bankrupt their system. In addition to the resource drain, the seriously mentally ill are seldom a treatment success, therefore requiring a lifetime of difficult and expensive care.

If this is the reality and not likely to change, then what is the morally responsible approach to the humane care of our most seriously mentally ill offenders posing a long-term risk to themselves and to the community? The seriously mentally ill are not good candidates for community mental health placement because they victimize and are frequently victimized. Currently they are sentenced to 10 days at a time for the rest of their life, alternating with short stints on the street, homeless and hopeless, until they die or seriously victimize someone. This is morally reprehensible for those suffering from mental illness and equally disturbing for those victimized by their violence.

Maybe the solution is a true community corrections model, one that has a host of custodial housing and treatment options. If jails are the most economical solution to the humane treatment of our seriously mentally ill then let us develop a system of care that focuses upon public safety and adequate care. Jails have high security housing capacities needed by the more violent offenders. Jails seldom focus upon long-term, low security and transitional housing. Whether it is a stabilized mentally ill offender or a recovering substance abuser, the return to the community without employment and housing is a sure formula for failure. Transitional housing is most difficult to obtain in the community. Campusing transitional or "extended care" housing on a correctional complex could help solve this dilemma and provide a safe and secure environment in the process. The complex already provides medical care, mental health care, food service and law enforcement supervision. Employment opportunities in food service, facility maintenance and off-campus community work programs would allow residents to earn their care in the "extended care" community. Some residents could actually transition to the community and others may become long-time productive members of this unique community. Jails would have to enhance their mental health services through true alliances with the Community Mental Health Network. "Extended Care Communities" could be made eligible for reimbursable community mental health services that are traditionally revoked during periods of incarceration. A true collaboration between the correctional staff and the community mental health staff would be necessary for the success of this innovation.

To make such an "Extended Care Community" a reality, laws would have to be enacted to permit the co-housing of civil and criminal commitments. Mandatory reviews of the civil commitments would also be necessary to protect the civil rights of the residents. A basic paradigm shift would be necessary to support such an effort. We must come to the realization that some repeat offenders with violent histories and mental illness may never be capable of a successful return to the community. Now we return them to the street knowing they will fail and hoping that they will not seriously injure another or become a victim themselves. "Extended Care Community Corrections" may be the only time when thinking "inside the box" may be better than thinking "outside the box."

AUTHOR'S NOTE

Raymond Sabbatine, MA, is President, Sabbatine & Associates, 110 Royal Court, Georgetown, KY 40324.

doi:10.1300/J076v45n01_05

Mental Health Issues in the Criminal Justice System. Pp. 59-68.
Available online at http://jor.haworthpress.com
© 2007 by The Haworth Press, Inc. All rights reserved.
doi:10.1300/J076v45n01_06

A Story Telling of Tragedy:
Mental Illness, Molestation, Suicide,
and the Penalty of Death

CRAIG J. FORSYTH
OUIDA F. FORSYTH

ABSTRACT This paper describes the experience of mitigation experts in first degree murder cases in the penalty phase of the trial. The first author, who is a sociologist, has worked in capital murder cases since 1988, as a mitigation expert in over 200 such cases. The second author assists in the mitigation process by analyzing mental health and educational records. The focus of the paper is a discussion of a specific case in which the defendant committed suicide before the case went to trial. doi:10.1300/J076v45n01_06 *[Article copies available for a fee from The Haworth Document Delivery Service: 1-800-HAWORTH. E-mail address: <docdelivery@haworthpress.com> Website: <http://www.HaworthPress.com> © 2007 by The Haworth Press, Inc. All rights reserved.]*

KEYWORDS Death penalty, mitigation, mental illness

INTRODUCTION

Most defendants in cases of homicides received sentences as a result of plea bargains (Forsyth & Mire, 2006) while for a lesser number their sentence is a result of trial. In one such case the defendant committed suicide in a south Louisiana jail cell before any plea bargaining or trial took place. This paper describes the experiences/roles of the authors in mitigation generally in such cases and specifically in this case.[1] The paper will then address the methods used both to obtain and to validate data in these cases. Lastly, a study and discussion of this case is presented.

THE ROLE OF THE SOCIOLOGIST AS EXPERT IN CASES OF HOMICIDE[2]

The relevance for sociological knowledge in criminal defense has been aptly stated by several researchers (Charvat, 1996; Forsyth, 1995, 1996, 1997, 1998, 1999; Forsyth & Bankston, 1997; Najmi, 1992; Radelet, 1987; Thoresen, 1993; Wolfgang, 1974).

If justice . . . is based on impartial judgments of the facts of a case, then what gets introduced is itself a moral deliberation on the limits of fairness. Limiting the facts of a case to an act, to its physical and, perhaps, psychological representations, is likely to make it easier to reach a verdict. Introducing sociological knowledge in a court of law, however, is likely to increase the range of plausible explanations and perspectives, expanding the opportunity for . . . fairness while making it more difficult to reach a decision . . . To know a defendant was battered as a child and as an adult abused drugs after several failed attempts to find work is . . . of less importance than the fact that he murdered his wife, but knowing the defendant in this more complicated fashion may save his life . . . (Kroll-Smith & Jenkins, 1996, p.14).

Any matter the judge regards as relevant to sentencing may be offered as evidence in the penalty phase. Mitigating circumstances are the most important elements of the penalty phase of a trial for the defense. Mitigating circumstances are facts that do not justify or excuse an action but can lower the amount of moral blame, and thus lower the criminal penalty for the action.[3] Depending on the expertise of the sociologist, one or several mitigating circumstances will frame the testimony. The U.S. Supreme Court has held that courts must consider any and all relevant mitigating evidence that is available (Hall & Brace, 1994). The legal basis for mitigation has already been stated, but one could add that any aspects of the defendant's life which demonstrate that he/she is not deserving of the death penalty would also be considered as mitigating circumstances. The prosecution, on the other hand, presents aggravating circumstances. Generally, aggravation includes actions or occurrences that lead to an increase in the seriousness of a crime, yet which are not part of the legal definition of that crime (Oran, 1983).[4]

Debates about sentencing focus on two adversarial positions: the circumstances of the crime versus the social psychological qualities of the client (Brodsky, 1991; Dayan, 1991; Forsyth, 1995, 1996, 1997, 1998, 1999; Najmi, 1992; Thoresen, 1993). Sociology is relevant to the questions of sentencing in criminal cases because it expands and explains the boundaries of mitigating factors.[5] The expert/sociologist, in addressing the issue of sentencing, attempts the difficult job of explaining how sociological factors have, at least partially, shaped the circumstances of the crime. The job of the sociologist can be summed up as the telling of the defendant's story so that the audience (jury, judge, prosecution) sees him as a human being. Indeed, to humanize the defendant may be the most important thing the defense team does. In this capacity the authors gather a complete social history of the defendant.

METHODS USED

A complete mitigation investigation involves a social and familial history of the client. The goal is to provide a full social portrait of the client and relate that to his criminality. The researchers gather data about the defendant's family life, education, drug and alcohol use patterns, mental health and work history, etc. Everyone who plays a role in the life of the defendant is interviewed. The defendant is interviewed several times, as well as parents, siblings, grandparents, wives, children, other relatives, neighbors, friends, probation officer(s), teachers, employers, work supervisors, and fellow employees. Some of these persons are interviewed by phone, but personal face-to-face interviews are more productive. The home setting of the client is always visited. In addition, various records are reviewed: prison, education, mental health. The research can become further integrated by the diagnostic needs of the psychologist and/or psychiatrist, if indeed, one is part of the defense team.

The authors use grounded theory or analytic induction in developing a mitigation history in each case. Evidence presented to the court by experts must be based on techniques or theories that have acceptance in the expert's field (Jasanoff, 1989). This methodology compares each aspect of the defendant's biography generating a constantly refined theory of a case; either confirming, fine tuning, or questioning the theory of the case (Babbie, 2001; Berg, 1989; Glaser & Strauss, 1961).

A SOCIAL HISTORY WAITING FOR A TRAGEDY

Sam is a 21-year-old white male.[6] He has never been married. His parents are divorced. He was accused of beating to death one male with a baseball bat. In addition, he was accused of attempting to murder three others with the same bat. It is these three other beatings that contributed to this as a case of capital murder.[7]

Sam had a cataclysmic childhood. He was raped at the age of five so badly that his anus had to be repaired surgically. Sam experienced feelings of being homosexual because of this. He also received little support from his family to cope with this conflict. His father did not live with him and has remarried with children. Sam lived in a female-headed household with his mother who is mentally ill; she was in a brief, abusive second marriage and her sons were with her. He has a younger brother who joined the army "to escape the town and his family." Sam's mother was diagnosed with Paranoid Schizophrenia. At least eight other members of the mother's family had been diagnosed with either some form of Schizophrenia or Bi-Polar Disorder. His mother has a long history of mental illness; spent time in mental institutions; had several episodes of bizarre behavior in public; hears voices; had her child from her second marriage taken away because she was judged unfit; kidnapped a baby in a public place to replace the one taken away; and has been charged with destruction of public property.

Sam's childhood is laced with indicators of his emotional problems. He had an eminent fear of the man who molested him. He slept with knives. The man was not sentenced until Sam was eight years old, indeed, he was free in the community. Sam was very worried about what would happen if the man saw him. Sam gave his mother an iron bar to defend herself. He had painted the bar black and hid it under a chair so if the man came back they could protect themselves with this "hidden weapon." He was always in fear that others would find out he was molested. He once confided his ordeal to a female friend and then repeatedly threatened her with violence if she told anyone. Sam bought a baseball bat, which he kept in the corner of his room, to beat up his mother or anyone who would tell people about him being molested. Sam claimed he started hearing voices at age seventeen, but did not receive counseling and/or medication. Sam was afraid of his mother when she was off medication and he wondered who would take care of "my mother."

Sam's biography would have been "hard to endure" with support, but neglected it was devastating. He drank and used drugs to cope with this conflict. He dated a lot of women, also referred to himself as a "mackdaddy" to portray the image of a ladies man. He was also very rough on all occasions with both genders. Any perceived threat to his manhood was met with exaggerated violent reactions. Sam never let this guard down.

He kept seeking help for his drug use; but the underlying cause of his drug use was this conflict. During the Summer of 2001 he was working full time and in the National Guard. He was arrested for possession of marijuana. He subsequently remained drunk at home; goes AWOL from the National Guard; does not show up for his court date; and became a fugitive. He admitted himself to short-term rehabilitation to get help and also to get out of trouble. During rehabilitation he never admits the underlying cause of his problems. On one occasion he overdosed on drugs and alcohol. The hospital tells his father he has little chance of surviving. He is airlifted 150 miles away, where he stayed two weeks. In early October 2001 he is released from the hospital having escaped a deadly crisis; but, indeed, the cause had not been resolved. He felt better but "wanted to permanently fix himself," so he entered long-term rehabilitation for six months. He was discharged in April 2002.

After discharge from rehabilitation he came to Louisiana to escape the environment of his drug use and all the abusive history. The problem with this strategy is that unbeknownst to Sam the old friend he will stay with, James, is a drug user and a homosexual. During the next several months James will spend little time with Sam because he is working and in school. His friend gets him a job in a restaurant whose clientele is mostly gay males, all the other waiters are gay. The friends that come over to visit James are mostly gay males. In interviews Sam indicated he was naive to the fact that all these men were gay. In reality because he was "living" with James, these visitors thought he was gay. These are the only friends that Sam has. In an incident a month previous to this homicide case, Sam attacked a man who approached him. He is charged with assault. He called his mother and father because he wanted to return home. During this visit his friends said he got into several fights and appeared to be particularly homophobic and angry. His friends ask that he stay home. He agreed but must go back temporarily to face the assault charges; for which he has been told he will receive probation.

On the night of the crime he was visiting a friend of James. He thought he was being sexually approached by the man. He brutally beat the man to death. He then goes into another apartment in the same complex and attacks three other friends of James. All of these men are injured, one severely. After the murder and assaults Sam drives to his home state where he is arrested. He is charged with capital murder. He is faced with the probability that he will remain in prison for the rest of his life or be sentenced to death. Sam will never leave prison; he committed suicide alone in his cell early one morning.

THE STORY TO BE TOLD MUST BE A HUMAN ONE

If justice is more than retribution, then violent acts like homicide must be understood in their complex association with a defendant's social history (Haney, 1998; Leonard, 2003). The audience must be made aware of those instances and themes in his life that portended an act of murder. Capital punishment has been a conspicuous and endless source of debate. The idea of an eye for an eye does not account for the "why." A reconstructed life history with an emphasis on sociological factors can contribute to a reasonable voice, balanced with a sense of fairness, in the explanation of seemingly nonsensical violent acts–it facilitates the story that must be told. This specific life history alerts us to the fact that murder is never an isolated act. Life histories are arguably beyond a defendant's control but act to influence and control behavior in manners so horrendous they beg for understanding, consideration, and compassion. Stories of a defendant's life also subtly humanize the defendant, a critical factor in avoiding a death penalty (Dayan, 1991).

Scientific story telling (Becker, 1998) creates, if you will, images in the mind of this person's life. There can be no unanswered questions in testimony. The story shows the basic picture–simple, clean, and intuitively obvious.[8]

Years are spent by both the prosecution and the defense in preparing for a first degree murder case. The defense team studies evidence, examines reports, and prepares witnesses in an attempt to compose a story which best describes the actions of the defendant. Literally everything counts and is considered. Perhaps the most important aspect is the humanizing of the defendant. Defendants are seen as something less than human because their acts are so horrible. The most important aspect of the job of the defense team is to make the defendant human again.

The prosecution in capital cases employs several mechanisms of moral disengagement which allow capital jurors to distance themselves from, and therefore make it easier to carry out, the distasteful task of ordering another human being's death at the hands of the state. One mechanism is the dehumanization of the defendant. The prosecution hopes that, once unable to recognize the defendant's humanity, jurors will be insensitive (Brewer, 2005) to the fact that they are ordering the death of a human being.

Humanizing the defendant is an influential part of a mitigation strategy designed to obtain a life sentence. Such evidence is mitigation in its most pure construct. The task is to tell a sociological story of a human being whose good character, although not a justification for murder, reveals a human being who is nonetheless not deserving of the death penalty. Indeed, all of the efforts of the defense team for obtaining a result less than a death sentence are directed toward portraying the client as a person with a complex character like all human beings. In other words, the expert humanizes the defendant so the jury can understand what led to the defendant's actions. The humanization process might entail a discussion of his abuse or neglect by his parents or guardians, his mental illness which went neglected or untreated, his substance abuse problem, his wife's abandonment of him and her promiscuity, and any other similar circumstances relating to the defendant. There is, indeed, one fact that makes this so onerous a task; unlike most other humans this person took the life of another. Yet, when considering all that brought a person such as Sam to the place where he committed murder, one cannot ignore the significance of mitigation–the story of Sam's life. Had Sam eventually gone to trial? Could we (jurors, judges, attorneys, experts, families) really see "an eye for an eye"?

NOTES

1. The first author of this paper has worked in death penalty cases since 1988, having served as a mitigation expert in over 200 such cases. The second author, because of her different expertise, assists the first in the mitigation process by analyzing mental health and educational records. Singular reference in this paper to the "expert" or the "author" will be in reference to the first author. The first author is typically hired by defense attorneys as a mitigation expert for the penalty phase of capital murder trials, but has also worked in the same role in other criminal cases to develop mitigation testimony.

2. Expert witnesses assist judges or juries in finding facts that bear on criminal, civil, and tort matters. It is the expert's ability to identify and interpret circumstances that are beyond the understanding of nonexperts that make him an expert. Trial judges are the gatekeepers who decide whether or not expert testimony applies. For an explanation of the acceptance of expert testimony by the court see: Frye v. United States, 1923 (referred to as the rule of general acceptance); Federal Rules of Evidence for United States Courts and Magistrates (1989); and Daubert v. Merrell Dow Pharmaceutical (1993).

3. In Louisiana, the jury weighs aggravating and mitigating circumstances before imposing sentences of death or life in prison without parole. Jury sentencing during this "second trial" is not required in some states. In those states, the trial judge, after hearing the arguments, determines the sentence to be imposed.

Louisiana law, although recognizing any relevant evidence as plausible mitigating testimony, generally classifies the factors to be appraised as such: The offender has no significant prior history of criminal activity; The offense was committed while the offender was under the influence of extreme mental or emotional disturbance; The offense was committed while the offender was under the influence or under the domination of another person; The offense was committed under circumstances which the offender reasonably believed to provide a moral justification or extenuation for his conduct; At the time of the offense the capacity of the offender to appreciate the criminality of his conduct or to conform his conduct to the requirements of law was impaired as a result of mental disease or defect or intoxication; The youth of the offender at the time of the offense; The offender was a principal whose participation was relatively minor; or mental retardation, brain damage, physical, sexual, or emotional abuse as a child or any other relevant mitigating circumstance.

4. These are the intentionality of the act; the propensity of the murderer to kill again and the heinous, atrocious and cruel nature of the murder.

5. Sociology has extraordinary capacity for the attorney. As suggested above, the utility of sociology in a murder case may be clearest in the penalty phase of the trial, but the data obtained and delivered by the sociologist has uses other than in the penalty phase. It can be used to negotiate a plea so that a trial never takes place or at a sentencing hearing for a conviction of manslaughter which has a range of sentences rather than a determinant sentence. Sociological data can be used to help shorten the sentence of the client. The sociologist's report can be filed in the record to be used at later hearings to reduce the sentence of the client. Sociological data can be used on appeal to convince the reviewing court of the questionable moral appropriateness of the death sentence in the client's case, or that the death sentence of the client is disproportionate (Forsyth, 1997).

6. Names are pseudonyms.

7. First degree murder is the intentional killing of another person; and involves another dictated circumstance, in this case attempted murder.

8. The first author routinely talks to members of the jury after a trial. A juror once told the author she believed his testimony and he was a good story teller. On another occasion after giving a three hour talk on the death penalty, an anthropologist also credited him with good story telling. This later comment caused the author to examine the concept. The author concluded being a good story teller is an essential part of mitigation.

REFERENCES

Babbie, Earl. 2001. *The Practice of Social Research*. Belmont, CA: Wadsworth Publishing.

Becker, Howard S. 1998. *Tricks of the Trade: How to Think About Your Research While You're Doing It*. Chicago: The University of Chicago Press.

Berg, Bruce. 1989. *Qualitative Research Methods for the Social Sciences*. Boston: Allyn and Bacon.

Brewer, Thomas W. 2005. "The Attorney-Client Relationship in Capital Cases and Its Impact on Juror Receptivity to Mitigation Evidence." *Justice Quarterly* 22(3), 340-363.

Brodsky, Stanley L. 1991. *Testifying in Court: Guidelines and Maxims for the Expert Witness*. Washington, DC: American Psychological Association.

Charvat, Ann. 1996. "Mitigation Evaluation: Preparation for a Death Penalty Trial." *Clinical Sociology Review 14*, 119-135.

Daubert v. Merrell Dow Pharmaceutical, 113 S. Ct. 2786 (1993).

Dayan, Marshall. 1991. "The Penalty Phase of the Capital Case: Good Character Evidence." *The Champion*: 14-17.

Federal Rules of Evidence for United States Courts and Magistrates. 1989. St. Paul, MN: West.

Forsyth, Craig J. 1995. "The Sociologist as Mitigation Expert in First Degree Murder Cases." *Clinical Sociology Review 13*, 134-144.

Forsyth, Craig J. 1996. "Sociology and Capital Murder: A Question of Life or Death." Pp. 57-69 in *Witnessing for Sociology: Sociologists in the Courtroom*, edited by Pamela Jenkins and Steven Kroll-Smith. New York: Greenwood Press.

Forsyth, Craig J. 1997. "Using Sociology and Establishing Sociological Turf: The Sociologist as Expert in Capital Murder Cases." *Sociological Spectrum 17*(4), 375-388.

Forsyth, Craig J. 1998. "The Use of the Subculture of Violence as Mitigation in a Capital Murder Case." *Journal of Police and Criminal Psychology 13*(2), 67-75.

Forsyth, Craig J. 1999. "Too Terrible to Talk About: A Case Study of the Rape and Murder of a Child." *International Journal of Sociology of the Family 29*(1), 97-106.

Forsyth, Craig J. & Carl L. Bankston III. 1997. "Mitigation in a Capital Murder Case with a Vietnamese Defendant: The Interpretation of Social Context." *Journal of Applied Sociology 14*(1), 147-165.

Forsyth, Craig J. & Scott M. Mire. 2006. "Plea Bargaining: Notes and Observations of a More Indispensable but Less than Perfect System." *The International Journal of Crime, Criminal Justice and Law 1*(1), 79-91.

Frye v. United States, 293 F.1013 , 1014 (D.C. Circuit, 1923).

Glaser, Barney & Anselm Strauss, 1967. *The Discovery of Grounded Theory*. Chicago: Aldine.

Hall, Melinda Gann & Paul Brace, 1994. "The Vicissitudes of Death by Decree: Forces Influencing Capital Punishment Decision Making in State Supreme Courts." *Social Science Quarterly 75*,136-151.

Haney, Craig. 1998. "Mitigation and the Study of Lives: On the Roots of Violent Criminality and the Nature of Criminal Justice." Pp. 351-384 in *America's Experiment with Capital Punishment*, edited by James R. Acker, Robert M. Bohm, and Charles S. Lanier. Durham, NC: Carolina Academic Press.

Jasanoff, S. 1989. "Science on the Witness Stand." *Issues in Science and Technology 6*(1), 80-87.

Kroll-Smith, Steve & Pamela J. Jenkins, 1996. "Old Stories, New Audiences: Sociological Knowledge in Courts." Pp. 1-15 in *Witnessing for Sociology: Sociologists in the Courtroom*, edited by Pamela Jenkins and Steven Kroll-Smith. New York: Greenwood Press.

Leonard, Pamela Blume. 2003. "A New Profession for an Old Need: Why a Mitigation Specialist Must Be Included on the Capital Defense Team." *Hofstra Law Review 31* (Summer), 1143-1156.

Najmi, M.A. 1992. "Sociologist as Expert Witness." *The Useful Sociologist 13*: 4.

Oran, Daniel. 1983. *Oran's Dictionary of the Law*. New York: West Publishing Company.
Radelet, M.L. 1987. "Sociologists as Expert Witnesses in Capital Cases: A Case Study." Pp. 119-134 in *Expert Witnesses: Criminologists in the Courtroom*, edited by P.R. Anderson and L.T. Winfree. Albany: State University of New York Press.
Thoresen, Jean H. 1993. "The Sociologist as Expert Witness." *Clinical Sociological Review 11*, 109-122.
Wolfgang, Marvin. 1974. "The Social Scientist in Court." *Journal of Criminal Law & Criminology 65*, 239-247.

AUTHORS' NOTES

Craig J. Forsyth, PhD, and Ouida F. Forsyth, MS, are affiliated with the University of Louisiana, Lafayette.

Address correspondence to Craig J. Forsyth, PhD, Department of Criminal Justice, University of Louisiana, Lafayette, P.O. Box 41652, Lafayette, LA 70504-1652 (E-mail: cjf5714@louisiana.edu).

doi:10.1300/J076v45n01_06

Mental Health Issues in the Criminal Justice System. Pp. 69-80.
Available online at http://jor.haworthpress.com
© 2007 by The Haworth Press, Inc. All rights reserved.
doi:10.1300/J076v45n01_07

Gaols or De Facto Mental Institutions? Why Individuals with a Mental Illness Are Over-Represented in the Criminal Justice System in New South Wales, Australia

CORINNE HENDERSON

ABSTRACT The over-representation of people with mental illness in the criminal justice system highlights the need for legislative reform and the implementation of programs breaking the cycle of mental illness, poverty, unemployment and substance abuse across Australia. Whilst there is no inherent association between mental illness and crime, there is a strong causal link between mental illness and incarceration. The fragmentation of mental health services and the closure of many community-based services have led to the criminalisation of the mentally ill. As a consequence, unsurprisingly, gaols and juvenile detention centres have become "de facto" mental institutions. doi:10.1300/J076v45n01_07 *[Article copies available for a fee from The Haworth Document Delivery Service: 1-800-HAWORTH. E-mail address: <docdelivery@haworthpress.com> Website: <http://www.HaworthPress. com> © 2007 by The Haworth Press, Inc. All rights reserved.]*

KEYWORDS Mental illness, criminal justice system, violence

INTRODUCTION

It has long been acknowledged that there is an over-representation of people with mental illness in the criminal justice system. Despite numerous government inquiries over the past 15 years into mental health in Australia (both state and federally), evidence exists indicating that the situation has further deteriorated.

The problem is compounded by the fact that the (New South Wales) *NSW Mental Health Act 1990* and *Mental Health (Criminal Procedures) Act 1990* make no specific provision for people with intellectual disability who may frequently be classified as "forensic" patients. As a consequence, there is a 10% over-representation of people with intellectual disability in the criminal justice system as against representation in the general population. Whether intellectual disability is present as a result of developmental disability, brain damage, illness or genetic disorder, intellectual disability is not a mental illness which can be managed by medication or therapeutic practices from which there is "recovery."

The absence of a consistent definition of intellectual disability in the relevant Mental Health Acts has led to considerable confusion, particularly where co-morbidity of intellectual disability and mental illness occur. A revised *NSW Mental Health Act* has been tabled in the NSW Parliament in December, 2006, and the forensic provisions of the Act are under review. Nevertheless, reform as a result of further consultation and inquiry will no doubt take considerable time. In the interim, unless increased diversionary programs are provided, people with intellectual disability will continue to be over-represented in the criminal justice system whether they present with co-morbidity or not.

PREVALENCE OF MENTAL ILLNESS AND BURDEN OF COST TO THE AUSTRALIAN COMMUNITY

In order to understand the link between mental illness and the criminal justice system, it is important to be aware of the extent to which mental illness is present in the general population, together with the socioeconomic and environmental factors that frequently lead to interactions with the criminal justice system.

A number of studies have indicated that one in five Australians will be affected by mental illness at some time in their life. Recent estimates internationally suggest that this could be a gross underestimation of the prevalence of, and disability caused by, mental illness. Based on figures in the National Survey of Health and Wellbeing (ABS, 2002), approximately 2.4 million Australians are thought to experience a mental health problem during any 12-month period. Over 1 million are estimated to suffer from a mental disorder, with almost half of these affected long-term.

Mental disorders account for almost 30% of the non-fatal burden of disease in Australia (Mathers, Yos, & Stevenson, 1999). Depression is the most common mental disorder reported, both recent and long-term, and has been identified as one of the most pressing priorities for mental health care. In 2001-02, total spending on mental health services was $3.1 billion, a 65% increase in real terms since 1993.

Nevertheless, Australia lags behind other western nations in the proportion of national wealth spent on mental health care, and specialised mental health services accounted for only 6.4% of Australia's recurrent health expenditure. An analysis by the Australian Institute of Health and Welfare (AIHW, 2005) shows that the proportion of mental health expenditure will rise to 9.6% if substance abuse and dementia are included. Substance abuse accounts for 11.5% of mental health costs in Australia (AIHW, 2005).

According to estimates from the Australian Bureau of Statistics (ABS), the cost of mental health disorders is dominated by years lost due to disability, responsible in 1996 for 13.3% of total Disability Adjusted for Life Year (DALY) (Mathers et al., 1999). These figures emphasise mental illness not as a major direct cause of death, but as a major cause of chronic disability (ABS, 1998d).

Identifying the breakdown of burden in terms of mental illness and gender, the ABS stated the major cause of mental disorder for females to be affective disorder, accounting for 39% of women's mental health disability. This was represented almost entirely by depression (87%) and anxiety disorder (22%). Men are more than twice as likely as women to have substance use disorder (11%). Young adults of both sexes (18-24 years) have the highest prevalence (27%) of mental disorder (Mathers et al., 1999).

STIGMA AND A PREOCCUPATION WITH EXCESSIVE RISK MANAGEMENT

Despite the high incidence of mental illness in the general community, there remains widespread fear, misunderstanding and stigma. Community attitudes concerning mentally ill offenders and their treatment by the criminal justice system are no exception. Much of this misunderstanding comes from dramatic depictions of mentally ill persons in films, on television, and sensationalised reports in the media.

Mullen (2001) writes that current preoccupation with risk assessment "privileges policies of control and containment as against support and management." As a consequence, resources are diverted from the mentally disordered towards those believed to be of potential risk. This encourages stigmatising constructions of the mentally disordered, giving primacy to their supposed level of dangerousness and has resulted in the development of a "spurious technology of risk management" which has come to dominate a broad spectrum of clinical practice, obfuscating actual causes of crime in the community.

However, it has long been established that mentally ill persons are much more likely to be a danger to themselves than to others. The "Tracking Tragedy" report on suicide deaths of recent mental health inpatients (2003) highlighted the vulnerability of people with mental illness to suicide and self-harm, following acute episodes of mental ill health.

In NSW, a defence of mental illness is commonly viewed as a loophole used to escape punishment. Debate surrounds the offender's state of mind—whether they must be "mad" to commit a crime or simply "bad." The perception that a perpetrator feigning madness can avoid a sentence is not supported by evidence.

THE REAL FACTS

The NSW Bureau of Crime Statistics and Research (1996) has estimated that only 1% of charges are dismissed under the *NSW Mental Health (Criminal Procedure) Act (1990)*. This accounted for only 0.3% (555) of the total criminal charges finalised in NSW local courts in 1996. In view of the high incidence of people with a mental illness who do not have their charges dismissed, it is unsurprising that NSW gaols and juvenile detention centres have become "de facto" mental institutions.

Individuals whose charges are dismissed may be transferred through court diversionary programs, whilst those who become forensic patients may spend a longer period incarcerated than had they received a guilty verdict. Although NSW has undergone reform relating to persons found unfit to be tried, a person found not guilty of an offence due to mental illness still may face the prospect of indefinite detention. There is no limit placed on length of time for which a person may be detained after a special verdict is handed down, and since the individual ceases to be a forensic patient only if the Executive Council orders his or her un-conditional release, or on the expiry of any conditions of release, it is therefore possible, in practice, that a person may be detained for a pe-riod longer than the maximum penalty for the offence for which he or she has been acquitted.

Despite acquitees having been classed as NGMI (not guilty by virtue of mental illness), the very nature of the criminal justice system and interpretation of the Act supports an underlying concept of culpabil-ity–the need for a NGMI to serve some period of incarceration that represents a sentence at least similar to what they would have received under "normal" circumstances (opinion of the author).

In a study of 500 psychiatric patients in the United Kingdom, a lifetime prevalence of crime was rated at 4%, which is comparable to the popu-lation in general and applicable to Australia (Gunn, 1987). Whilst there is no inherent link between mental illness and crime, there is a strong causal link between mental illness and incarceration. Furthermore, there is extensive evidence that people with severe mental illness are more likely to be convicted of misdemeanours than their mentally healthy counterparts, and tend to be incarcerated for longer periods (Lamberti et al., 2001).

A study in 1983 observed no relationship between mental illness and general crime, when controlled for age, race, socioeconomic status and previous hospitalisation or imprisonment (Monahan, 1992). Such dem-onstrative statistics imply the existence of another variable or variables that may have an association with both mental illness and imprisonment.

Similar scrutiny must also be applied to the notion that people with a mental illness are more violent than the general population. The Australian Institute of Criminology (1990) stated that "violence and violent crime are commonly regarded by the public as the domain of the mentally ill." Public misconception about the true nature of mental illness, as distinct from personality disorder or behavioural disorder, frequently associates extreme violence with mental illness. The evidence base has long displayed greater scepticism.

Whilst a weak association between mental disorder and violent be-haviour has been demonstrated, it is limited to people with mental illness not receiving treatment or who have a history of violence and/or abuse of alcohol or drugs (Steadman et al., 1998; Swartz et al., 1998; Better Health Channel, 2005; Munetz et al., 2001). Research has noted this relationship may be mediated by a range of factors including: gender; socioeconomic status; age; and substance abuse.

Substance abuse in particular has been identified by many researchers as a powerful co-morbid factor. Monahan (1992) also noted that increased risk was evident only in the immediate presence of psychotic symptoms, thus eliminating the vast majority of people with mental disorder. For people with mental disorders, co-morbidity is common and individuals may have more than one disorder, exacerbated by a high prevalence of coexisting substance disorder which exists, depending on the population sample, in 30% to 80% of people with a mental illness in the community (NSW Health, 2000).

Socioeconomic status can clearly be seen as impacting on the prevalence of mental illness. People who live in the most socioeconomically disadvantaged circumstances (depending on age) are between 1½ and 3½ times more likely to have mental or behavioural problems as compared with people who live in the least socioeconomically disadvantaged circumstances (ABS, 2001). Hence the high percentage of Indigenous people with a mental illness in the criminal justice system.

The 2001 National Health Survey did not include information on Indigenous mental health, due to concerns about the cultural appropriateness of the mental health-related questions in that survey. However, hospitalisation and mortality rates from intentional injury or self-harm (over twice as prevalent in the Indigenous community) may be indicative of mental illness and distress (ABS, AIHW, National Hospital Morbidity Database, 2003c).

According to the Australian Census (2004), NSW correctional and forensic facilities contained 8,510 adults and 300 juveniles. This figure represented a snapshot of the annual throughput of approximately 18,000 adults and 6,000 juveniles.

Justice Health (NSW) reported in the same year that 78% of the male prison population and 90% of the female population presented at reception with a broad spectrum of mental disorders (Halpin et al., 2004). Whilst acknowledging that the figures are not directly comparable, it is noteworthy to mention that in state of Victoria (2003) the Department of Justice reported that 28% of inmates had a mental illness when they presented at reception.

This disparity, one might suggest, could be seen as a reflection of the more favourable access to appropriate community services in Victoria, and the establishment of a secure facility, the Thomas Embling Hospital in 2001. It is instructive also to consider the diversity of outcomes across Australia in association with state spending per capita and allocation of resources to the NGO sector, which average at 5.5% of the total national mental health expenditure. Over the last year, the NSW government has made a commitment to increase resources for non-government organisations which in 2005 were 2.4%, as compared to 9.6% in Victoria (AIHW, 2005).

OTHER INFLUENTIAL FACTORS

If there is no fundamental causality between mental illness and crime, and only a tenuous link between mental illness and violence, what other factors may explain the over-representation of people with a mental illness in the criminal justice system?

A study in the UK (Hodgins, 1993) was one of the first able to examine clinical associations between mental illness and crime. The research identified that people with a mental illness are at a higher-than-average risk of offending, not because of mental illness per se, but because of the higher-than-average prevalence of substance abuse in this population. In a 2001 study of people with a mental illness in prison, two thirds of their crimes were related to substance use, usually non-violent (Munetz et al., 2001).

Fragmentation of mental health services and the accompanying risk factors of mental illness–poverty, poor education, unemployment, poor social skills and family support–lead the mentally ill to situations of high exposure to psychoactive substances (Drake & Mueser, 2000). These are the people who are described as "falling through the gaps"–"the gaps are wide and the fall is hard" (NSW Health, 2000b). Such high exposure factors are reflected in the 2004 Census figures highlighting the level of socioeconomic disadvantage prior to incarceration (Justice Health, 2004).

On Census Night, 2001, approximately 100,000 people were homeless, 14% were "sleeping rough." More than half (54%) of the homeless population were adults over 24 years of age; of the 46% under 24 years of age, 26% were between 12-18 years old. Less than half (42%) of homeless people were female. Single homeless people represented 58% of the numbers, while 19% were couples and 23% were homeless families.

Statistics on juvenile offenders in the Young People in Correction Health Survey (YCPiCHS, 2003) clearly identified some of problems leading to incarceration in addition to the prevalence of coexisting mental illness and substance abuse. This included a close relationship between child sexual abuse and physical violence, and the continuation of young people remaining homeless. Speaking at a National Congress on Homelessness (2003), David Tully of Adelaide Central Mission in South Australia referred to abuse as the primary factor causing young people to seek safety by leaving home.

CRIMINALISATION OF THE MENTALLY ILL

In 2002, Justice Health NSW noted that within the prison population, "50% of males and 30% of females warrant mental health referral for major depression." Approximately 80% have been incarcerated for offences relating to drug and alcohol use. In an environment in which substance abuse so closely accompanies mental illness, a policy of zero tolerance with regards to drug crimes automatically leads to an increase in interactions with the criminal justice system.

The combination of inadequate community mental health services, heightened legal imperatives and shrinking facilities for people with mental illness requiring acute care have resulted in an increased reliance on the police for crisis management and referral, regardless of the mental state of the individual. Police have become "de facto" ambulances transferring people from one hospital to another. Frequently failing to secure a hospital admission, the police must "do something," and "arrest by default" (Davis, 1992).

Unfortunately, the most appropriate treatment is usually unavailable within the criminal justice system. Effective treatment is one that emphasises recovery and appropriate support to facilitate integration back into the community. This is no less applicable to mentally ill inmates as forensic patients for whom gaol is an unsuitable environment in which "management" and "medication" rather than "recovery" and "rehabilitation" are the main focus (NSW Mental Health Sentinel Events Review Committee, 2003).

In a review of the relationship between mental disorders and offending behaviours, and the management of mentally abnormal offenders in the health and criminal justice services, Mullen (2001) writes that "the correctional culture and physical realities of prisons are rarely conducive to therapy. Rigid routines, the pedantic enforcement of a plethora of minor rules, the denial of most of that which affirms our identity, add to the difficulties of managing vulnerable and disordered people" (p. 36).

Another probable cause of increased criminalisation of mentally ill persons may be as a result of closure of many "living skill" and "drop in centres," limited access to appropriate coordinated community-based services, absence of planning of discharge arrangements and the support crucial in avoiding lapse and relapse into crisis, and recidivism. Many, who would have benefited from treatment for their mental illness, received none prior to being imprisoned (Halpin et al., 2004).

Apart from high risk of interactions with the criminal justice system as a consequence of the relationship between mental illness and substance abuse, the additional likelihood of homelessness together with treatment non-adherence bring about the greatest challenges for intervention–due to the segmented nature of services, barriers to access, assessment and treatment and the implications of complex need on receptiveness to treatment.

The over-representation of people with a mental illness in the criminal justice system is demonstration of the extent to which the social environment gives rise to mental illness, highlighting the urgent need for legislative reform and implementation of collaborative practices that break the cycle of mental illness, substance abuse, poverty, unemployment, domestic violence, and interactions with the criminal justice system. The importance of the non-government sector in providing services for early intervention, pre- and post-release programs cannot be too strongly emphasised. Non-government organisations are often less constrained by institutional and political influences, are more flexible and able to react swiftly to changing social conditions.

In order to fulfil our responsibilities as a humane society, it is critical to protect and preserve the human rights of people with mental illness as stated in the principles of the Australian National Mental Health Strategy: National Mental Health Plan, 2003-2008, and the NSW guidelines and standards which support a collaborative approach emphasising a recovery model of mental health service provision within the criminal justice system; and that removes itself from notions of culpability and a need for detention and punishment in order to manage the perceived risk.

As identified in UN Resolution 46/119 to which Australia is a signatory, those rights are primarily embodied in Principle 1: Fundamental freedoms and basic rights. These principles are central to all our endeavours when addressing the needs of the mentally ill–a population group often the most vulnerable and marginalised in our society:

- *All persons have the right to the best available mental health care, which shall be part of the health and social care system.*
- *All persons with a mental illness shall be treated with humanity and respect for the inherent dignity of the human person.*

- *All persons with a mental illness have the right to protection from economic, sexual and other forms of exploitation, physical or other abuse and degrading treatment.*
- *There shall be no discrimination on the grounds of mental illness. "Discrimination" means any distinction, exclusion or preference that has the effect of nullifying or impairing equal enjoyment of rights.*

REFERENCES

ABS. (1999). Australian Bureau of Statistics. National Survey of Health and Wellbeing: *Mental Health of Australian Adults* (1998b).

ABS (2001). Australian Bureau of Statistics. *National Health Survey: Mental Health.*

AIHW. Australian Institute of Health and Welfare (2002). *Australia's Health, 2002.* Canberra: AIHW.

AIHW. Australian Institute of Health and Welfare (2003). *Australia's Welfare, 2003.* (The Sixth Biennial Welfare Report of the Australian Institute of Health and Welfare). Canberra: AIHW.

AIHW & ABS (2003). Australian Institute of Health & Welfare, Australian Bureau of Statistics. *National Hospital Morbidity Database,* 2002a, 2003c.

AIHW. Australian Institute of Health and Welfare (2005). *Mental Health Expenditure and Priorities. Section 6.* Available: http://www.aihw.gov.au/publications/health/bdia/bdia-c06.pdf

Australian Census Analytic Program: *Counting the Homeless,* 2050.0.

Australian Institute of Criminology (1990). *Violence: Directions for Australia, in Crime and Violence Prevention.* Canberra: Institute of Criminology, pp. 74-76.

Better Health Channel (2005). Available: http://www.betterhealth.vic.gov.au/bhcv2/bhcarticles.nsf/pages/Mental_illness_and_violence_explained

Blood, R.W., Putnis, P., Payne, T., Purkis, J., Francis, C., McCallum, K., & Andrew, D. (2001). *The Media Monitoring Project: A Baseline Description of How the Australian Media Report and Portray Suicide and Mental Health and Illness: Case Studies.* School of Professional Communication, University of Canberra, & the Centre for Health Program Evaluation, University of Melbourne.

Bureau of Crime Statistics & Research (1996).

Commonwealth of Australia (2006).The Senate Select Committee on Mental Health. (2006). *A National Approach to Mental Health–from Crisis to Community: First Report.*

Davis, S. (1992). *Assessing the 'criminalization' of the mentally ill in Canada.* Canadian Journal of Psychiatry, 37, October, 532-538.

Draine, J., Salzer, M., Culhane, D.P., & Hadley, T.R. (2002). *Role of social disadvantage in crime, joblessness, and homelessness among persons with a serious mental illness.* Psychiatric Services, 53, 5, 565-573.

Drake, R.E., & Mueser, K.T. (2000). *Psychosocial approaches to dual diagnosis.* Schizophrenia Bulletin, 26, 1, 105-118.

Gunn cited in Henderson, A.S. (1988). *An Introduction to Social Psychiatry.* New York: Oxford Press, p. 123.

Halpin, R., Barling, J., & Levy, M. (2004). *Capturing Perceptions: 2004 NSW Inmate Access Survey.* Justice Health, NSW: Australia.

Henderson, A.S. (1988). *An Introduction to Social Psychiatry.* New York: Oxford Press, p. 123.

Henderson, C.D. (2007). *Submission to the Consultation Paper: Forensic Provisions of the NSW Mental Health Act, 1990 and Mental Health (Criminal Procedures) Act 1990,* p. 9.

Henderson, S. (2003). *Mental Illness and the Criminal Justice System.* Mental Health Co-ordinating Council, p. 9.

Hodgins, S. (ed.) (1993). *Mental Disorder and Crime.* London, Sage.

Hodgins. S. (2002). *Research priorities in forensic mental health.* International Journal of Forensic Mental Health, 1, 1, 7-23.

Human Rights and Equal Opportunity Commission (1993). *Human Rights and Mental Illness: Report of the National Inquiry into the Human Rights of People with Mental Illness.* AGPS, Canberra, p. 757.

James, G. QC. (2007). *Consultation Paper: Review of the Forensic Provisions of the Mental Health Act, 1990 and the Mental Health (Criminal Procedure) Act 1990.* NSW Health, p. 38.

Lamberti, J.S., Weisman, R.L., Schwarzkopf, S.B., Price, N., Ashton, R.M., & Trompeter, J. (2001). *The mentally ill in jails and prisons: Towards an integrated model of prevention.* Psychiatric Quarterly, 72, 1, 63-77.

Mathers, C., Yos, T., & Stevenson, C. (1999). *The Burden of Disease and Injury in Australia.* Australian Institute of Health and Welfare (AIHW): Canberra.

Mental Health Council of Australia (2002). *Submission 262,* p. 24.

Mental Health Council of Australia (2005). *Not for Service: Experiences of Injustice and Despair in Mental Health Care in Australia.*

Monahan, J. (1983). *The prediction of violent behavior: Developments in psychology and law.* Chapter in James C. Scheirer, & Barbara L. Hammonds (Eds). Psychology and the law. Master Lecture Series, 2, 151-176.

Mullen, P. (2001). *A review of the relationship between mental disorders and offending behaviours and on the management of mentally abnormal offenders in the health and criminal justice services.* Criminology Research Council, p. 23.

Munetz, M.R., Grande, T.P., & Chambers, M.R. (2001). *The incarceration of individuals with severe mental disorders.* Community Mental Health Journal, 37, 4, 361-371.

Northern Beaches Mental Health Consumer Network (2002), Submission 60, p. 20.

NSW Health (2000). *The Management of People with Co-Existing Mental Health and Substance Use Disorder–Service Delivery Guidelines,* NSW Health Department: Australia, p. 2.

NSW Mental Health Sentinel Events Review Committee (2003). *Tracking Tragedy.* First Report of the Committee (December, 2003). NSW Health, Australia. Available: http://www.health.nsw.gov.au/pubs/t/serc contents.html.

Probation and Community Corrections Officers' Association Inc. (2002). *Submission 503.*

Steadman, H.J., Mulvey, E.P., Monahan, J., Robbins, P. C., Appelbaum, P.S., Grisso, T., Roth, L.H., & Silver, E. (1998). *Violence by people discharged from acute psychiatric inpatient facilities and by others in the same neighbourhoods.* Archives of General Psychiatry, 55, 393-401.

Swartz, M.S., Swanson, J.A.W., Hiday, V.A., Borum, R., Wagner, H.R., & Burns, B.J. (1998). *Violence and severe mental illness: The effects of substance abuse and non adherence to medication.* American Journal of Psychiatry, 155, 226-231.

Tully, D. (2003). *Childhood Sexual Assault and Homelessness.* Paper presented at the 3rd National Conference 'Beyond the Divide' convened by the Australian Federation of Homelessness Organisations, April, 2003.

Weatherburn, D., Matka, E., & Lind, B. (1996). *Crime perception and reality: Public perception of the risk of criminal victimisation in Australia.* Bureau of Crime Statistics & Research (1996).

Whiteford, H.A., & Buckingham, W.J. (2005). *Ten years of mental health service reform in Australia: are we getting it right?* MJA, 2005, 182, 8, 396-400.

AUTHOR'S NOTE

Corinne Henderson, MA, is Senior Policy Officer, Mental Health Coordinating Council, Rose Cottage, Collan Park, P.O. Box 668, Rozelle, Sydney, NSW 2039, Australia (E-mail: corinne@mhcc.org.au).

doi:10.1300/J076v45n01_07

Mental Health Issues in the Criminal Justice System. Pp. 81-104.
Available online at http://jor.haworthpress.com
© 2007 by The Haworth Press, Inc. All rights reserved.
doi:10.1300/J076v45n01_08

Offenders with Mental Illness in the Correctional System

MAUREEN L. O'KEEFE
MARISSA J. SCHNELL

ABSTRACT The escalating mentally ill population in prisons has created unique challenges for correctional systems, Colorado being no exception with 25% of its incarcerated population having mental health needs. This study examined correctional offenders with mental illness (OMIs) and found a growing number of OMIs in Colorado's prison system. Not only is this population expanding, OMIs have higher rates of recidivism, oftentimes a result of failing under parole supervision. OMIs present with characteristics that differentiate them from the general offender population, exhibiting greater rehabilitation needs and prison adjustment difficulties, which has a direct impact on the resources required to house them. doi:10.1300/J076v45n01_08 *[Article copies available for a fee from The Haworth Document Delivery Service: 1-800-HAWORTH. E-mail address: <docdelivery@ haworthpress.com> Website: <http://www.HaworthPress.com> © 2007 by The Haworth Press, Inc. All rights reserved.]*

KEYWORDS Offenders, mental illness, recidivism, prevalence rates, prison adjustment

INTRODUCTION

The criminalization of persons suffering from mental illness is a critical component of the escalating prison population. Largely initiated by the deinstitutionalization period of the 1960s, many persons with serious mental illness, who at one time would have been treated in mental hospitals, are displaced into correctional facilities. According to the Bureau of Justice Statistics (James & Glaze, 2006), prevalence estimates reveal approximately 24% of U.S. inmates incarcerated in state facilities are mentally ill–a number that is continually growing. Furthermore, it is possible this estimate might minimize reality, as research suggests many offenders with mental illness (OMIs) go undetected during entrance screening (Birmingham, Gray, Mason, & Grubin, 2000). Data illustrating that approximately 2.6% of persons in the populace are mentally ill (Beck & Marushak, 2001) makes it evident that they are disproportionately represented in the criminal justice system. Repercussions from the lack of community resources can be traced back to deinstitutionalization and persist in the present.

Historical Antecedents

The migration of OMIs from mental hospitals to prisons was precipitated by the period of time subsequent to World War II known as deinstitutionalization, an era marked by changes in state mental health-care systems. Changes were catalyzed by media sources publicizing negative depictions of state mental hospitals (e.g., abuse, neglect, unsanitary living conditions) and were intended to improve treatment of patients. During this time new psychotropic medications were developed. It was thought that these drugs, when accompanied with increased community mental health-care placements, would facilitate a more humanitarian way of treating people with severe mental illness and eliminate the need for lengthy and costly inpatient hospital stays (Thomas, 1998).

Correspondingly, policymakers initiated reforms and advocated mental health legislation resulting in the closing of many state mental hospitals. The effects of this were seen in the dramatic decrease of in-patients from 560,000 in 1955 to 77,000 in 1994 and the closing of many state mental hospitals (U.S. Department of Health and Human Services, 1994).

Reforms accompanied deinstitutionalization with the implementation of the Community Mental Health Centers Act of 1963. This act was an attempt by the National Institute of Mental Health to create a community-based outpatient system so patients could be closer to their families and live more normal lives. Other mental health law reforms made it more difficult to involuntarily commit individuals to mental health institutions without lengthy judicial procedures, unless mental deterioration became extreme or a crisis ensued (Torrey, 1997).

Mental health law reforms seemed a positive change as they limited the number of people being unjustly institutionalized; however, these laws ended up being over-compensatory in nature, taking institutionalization to the opposite end of the spectrum. Now many people who are not necessarily classified as dangerous, but in serious need of mental health services, are not placed in hospitals where they can receive help.

The mental health law reforms would have been less detrimental had the community treatment centers been established as envisioned. Unfortunately, the upsurge of persons with mental illness back into the community coincided with financial strains imposed on society from the Vietnam War and economic crisis of the 1970s. As a result community-based substitutes could not be funded.

Limited community care resources are problematic chiefly because individuals with mental illness who do not have access to treatment and social services often have poor medication compliance, and experience survival difficulties that can elicit criminal activity. Studies have shown that 42% of crimes committed by the mentally ill are related to symptomatic expression and 30% are related to survival (Lurigio & Lewis, 1987; Lewis et al., 1994; as cited in Lurigio & Swartz, 2000). This finding is not unexpected when considering that persons with mental illness report high rates of homelessness, unemployment, and substance use prior to incarceration (Ditton, 1999; James & Glaze, 2006).

Decreased numbers of mental health placement beds make hospitalization an impractical alternative for people with mental illness when they commit crimes (Teplin, 1983). Thus, police officers who deal with mentally ill persons who are disruptive or engage in criminal activity have limited courses of action. In addition, stringent legal criteria for involuntary commitment, complicated admission procedures, and long emergency waiting room periods often make incarceration seem the most efficient alternative. Abram and Teplin (1991) observed police officers for a 14-month period and found they were most likely to arrest mentally ill persons in two types of circumstances: when a mentally ill person's behavior exceeded the public's limited tolerance for deviance (e.g., behavioral disruptions that disturbed the peace) or when the officer at the scene felt there was a strong likelihood that disruptions would continually necessitate law enforcement if the person was not arrested.

Challenges to the Criminal Justice System

Expanding incarceration rates of persons with mental illness pose many challenges for the criminal justice system and, in turn, confinement in correctional facilities can exacerbate preexisting mental health conditions. Meeting the rehabilitative needs of this special subgroup is complicated, costly, and often comes secondary to maintaining security and control. Criminal justice system challenges are largely related to screening difficulties and limited resources.

Screening challenges. The purpose of mental health screening upon intake is to determine which offenders need psychological treatment and placement in specialized accommodations. OMIs have differing treatment, medication, and social support needs than nonmentally ill offenders to enable them to cope with prison life and, therefore, need to be identified as such.

One of the most prominent assessment challenges correctional systems face is detection of mental illness. Teplin (1990) studied jail detainees and identified several factors that impact identification of mental disorders in offender populations. Perhaps the strongest contributing factor was having a charted history of mental illness. When offenders had a recorded treatment history, 91.7% of them were accurately detected as mentally ill, whereas only 32.5% were detected when treatment histories were unknown.

Detection is also influenced by the type of diagnosis. Teplin (1990) found a 7.1% detection rate for depression in comparison with a 45% detection rate for schizophrenia. One likely explanation is that mental disorders comprised of overt symptoms (e.g., hallucinations) are easier to recognize than those with less conspicuous symptoms, particularly if depressive symptoms including isolation and withdrawal do little to create prison disruption. These findings suggest that improved screening instruments and procedures are needed to ensure accurate identification of mental illness because depressed individuals in forensic populations are at a higher risk for suicide than those in the general public (Liebling, 1993; as cited in Jeglic, Vanderhoff, & Donovick, 2005).

In addition to disorders that easily go undetected, recognized psychological disorders may not be categorized as such, given various definitions of mental illness used across systems. The most common definition of serious mental illness encompasses Axis I disorders, specifically psychotic and mood disorders, and frequently does not include Axis II disorders (Lurigio & Swartz, 2000). When serious mental illness is limited in scope to only this definition, other disorders needing clinical attention may be neglected. Overlooking some of these disorders could create dangerous situations for inmates in the general prison population, correctional staff, and the individual OMI, in that certain psychiatric symptoms can include aggressive, self-harming, or suicidal behaviors.

Limited resources and treatment programs. Even when screening procedures identify OMIs, correctional budgetary constraints leave minimal funding available for mental health treatment and rehabilitative measures (Rice & Harris, 1997). Constricted resources for mental health care results in limited staff and restricted program variability (Dvoskin & Spiers, 2004). Seemingly, evidence suggests that the amount of time clinical personnel are available to assist OMIs is inversely correlated with their education and training (Human Rights Watch, 2003). Consequently, prison psychiatrists and psychologists have extremely large caseloads, which drastically limit the effectiveness of treatment per individual. Decreases in qualified mental health workers are largely a result of the low salaries offered and the high stressors produced in prison environments (Human Rights Watch). Limited staffing also restricts the availability of treatment groups and the number of participants. Hence, not all prisoners in need of treatment are placed into mental health groups.

Notwithstanding the limitations on group enrollment, most therapy programs do not address comorbid substance abuse disorders, which have been estimated to exist in three quarters of the OMI population (Abram & Teplin, 1991; Chandler, Peters, Field, & Juliano-Bult, 2004; James & Glaze, 2006). Many treatment groups focus on these areas individually or exclude offenders with dual diagnoses. This limits the treatment efficacy of OMIs, as mental illness and substance abuse interchangeably affect each other negatively (Hartwell, 2004; Van Stelle, Blumer, & Moberg, 2004; White, Goldkamp, & Campbell, 2006). Accordingly, it would be most logical to address these issues simultaneously.

Resource shortages not only affect staffing and treatment group availability, but also drive housing decisions. There are limited beds in mental health units as they are very costly for the correctional system; therefore, not every OMI can be placed in specialized accommodations (Human Rights Watch, 2003). Inevitably, large quantities of OMIs must be placed in the general prison population where they get less individual treatment and support. Sometimes OMIs are placed in or voluntarily opt for segregated living accommodations as a protective measure. The verdict remains undetermined as to whether or not segregating OMIs from the general population is a beneficial practice. It is suggested that while OMIs may be better protected in specialized living accommodations, they might not always have access to the same programs, privileges, and services offered within the general population (Wormith, Tellier, & Gendreau, 1988).

Adjustment to Prison Life

Screening difficulties and limited resources are best conceptualized as problems inherent to the criminal justice system as opposed to adjustment difficulties that can be characterized as innate to the individual. OMI behavioral responses to environmental stimuli are largely influenced by mental illness symptoms and accordingly cannot be controlled by correction officials. While in prison, OMIs' psychological health, behavior, and coping abilities are greatly affected by their medication compliance and the prison environment. Security and control in correctional settings are in part contingent on how OMIs are affected by these two variables.

Psychotropic medications relieve many of the manifestations of mental illness that precipitate behavioral infractions; therefore, disruptive behaviors are most likely to occur when OMIs are not taking their medication. Many mentally ill inmates refuse to take medications, and when this occurs, prison staff typically cannot forcibly administer them without a court order (Jacoby & Kozie-Peak, 1997). It is probable noncompliance occurs because OMIs want to avoid unpleasant side effects or benefit from selling or bargaining medications for desired amenities.

Detrimental effects of medication noncompliance are further agitated by environmental variables. The prison environment is comprised of many adverse conditions that negatively affect all prisoners, such as overcrowding, excessive noise and uncomfortable temperatures (Human Rights Watch, 2003). Additionally, lack of autonomy, uncomfortable physical limitation, and humiliation evoke fear and stress (Dvoskin & Spiers, 2004). The abrasive atmosphere in correctional facilities, when compounded by mental illness, can easily trigger behavioral infractions (e.g., yelling, aggression) which lead to punitive consequences.

Further evidence of prison adjustment issues was found in a 2006 study (James & Glaze) where 58% of OMIs were charged with rule violations in comparison to only 43% of nonmentally ill offenders. Additionally, OMIs' behavioral disturbances can sometimes agitate other inmates and result in aggression towards the individual causing the annoyance. Correspondingly, it was found that OMIs were twice as likely to sustain a fighting injury as their nonmentally ill counterparts (James & Glaze).

Limited behavioral control makes OMIs appear mentally weak and vulnerable, which greatly increases their chances of becoming victimized by other inmates for abuse and manipulation. OMIs are often targets of predacious inmates in part because of their compromised mental functioning and also because their allegations may be taken less seriously by prison staff.

Challenges to Reentry

Challenges persist for OMIs upon release from incarceration when they must attempt to reintegrate back into society. As a result of their illnesses, OMIs require more aid than nonmentally ill offenders, but discouragingly often receive very little by way of parole or halfway house accommodations (Petersilia, 2003).

Dually-diagnosed OMIs have decreased chances for community-based programs. Similar to correctional facilities, a large majority of treatment services in the community focus on specific disorders and do not address comorbid issues (Messina, Burdon, Hagopian, & Prendergast, 2004). Mental health programs often decline treating persons with substance abuse problems in apprehension that addicts may try to bring drugs into the program or will be disruptive. Substance abuse programs will often not accept clients with severe mental illness because they are not adequately equipped to deal with individuals with these disorders (Hartwell, 2004).

Discharge planning is one of the least frequently provided services for OMIs (Osher, Steadman, & Barr, 2003) who are often released with little or no mental health aftercare planning (Lamb, Weinberger, & Gross, 1999). Discharge planning could establish and maintain links to various social services (e.g., employment, housing assistance) and treatment resources.

Many challenges result from insufficient aftercare planning. One primary challenge is difficulty finding and maintaining employment. Studies show that all offenders have reduced chances of being hired for a job as a result of having a criminal record (Petersilia, 2003). If offenders are able to find employment, they commonly earn considerably lower wages and receive fewer benefits (Petersilia). OMIs' employment obstacles are exacerbated beyond those faced by offenders who are not mentally ill. Ditton (1999) showed approximately 38% of OMIs in state and federal prisons were unemployed in the month before they were arrested.

Lack of employment or social assistance is a major determinant of homelessness in mentally ill populations. Statistical analyses reflect that approximately 20% of OMIs were homeless at some point during the year before they were arrested (Ditton, 1999). Other possible antecedents of homelessness include substance abuse, weak social support systems, and limited access to medication.

Compliance with psychotropic medication regimens is often substantial in an OMI's adjustment when reentering society. Federal court rulings in *Wakefield v. Thompson* (1999) ordered that the state must provide newly released OMIs with enough medication to last until they are able to consult a doctor and obtain a new supply. The objective behind this ruling was to ascertain that OMIs would not be left without the medications upon which their daily functioning was contingent. Nevertheless, problems still exist due to OMIs' inability to pay the high costs of prescription medications (Weisman, Lamberti, & Price, 2004). Accordingly, many OMIs use alcohol or drugs as a way to self-medicate symptoms of mental illness as they are less costly and easier to obtain.

Even when prescriptions can be obtained, problems still arise. Side effects of medication and mental illness symptoms can cause cognitive impairments that hinder OMIs' abilities to adhere to parole requirements and attend appointments (Lurigio, 2001). This often results in technical violations and can eventually lead to rearrest.

OMIs in Colorado

The number of persons with mental illness being incarcerated has been escalating for the past 40 years (Thomas, 1998), negatively impacting the criminal justice system and adversely affecting the individual offender. As is the case across the nation, Colorado has struggled with its flourishing OMI population and the challenges they pose. Although the Colorado Department of Corrections (CDOC) has had a screening and assessment process in place for decades, scant resources limit the quantity and type of services for identified OMIs.

A 250-bed specialized mental health prison was opened in 1995 on the state hospital grounds, the mentally ill once again occupying the very facilities from which they were displaced, now the ward of a different custodian. This facility was intended to treat offenders whose psychiatric symptom acuteness was so serious that they could not be safely managed within the general population. Although the primary purpose of the facility is to stabilize offenders, programs and classes offered at this facility include basic education, substance abuse treatment,

work skills, mental health education, symptom and medication management, and institutional coping skills.

Even though Colorado has a dedicated mental health facility, CDOC
endorses a model whereby OMIs are integrated into the general population.
However, maintaining this population in a desegregated environment is
difficult. A recent study showed that not only were OMIs placed in
administrative segregation–long-term solitary confinement–more often
than their nonmentally ill counterparts, they represented the OMIs with
the most severe psychiatric problems (O'Keefe, this volume).

The ever present challenge of reducing rising rates of mentally ill
persons in the criminal justice system suggests the necessity to learn
more about this subgroup of offenders. The present study is an exploratory
one, designed to examine characteristics of OMIs in the Colorado
correctional system. Prevalence, release and recidivism data were investigated to understand the rates of OMIs entering, releasing, and returning
to prison. This study profiles mentally ill offenders across demographic,
criminal history, psychological, and needs areas as well as some prison
adjustment factors to determine how OMIs differ from the general
prison population, particularly in relation to findings in the literature.

METHOD

Participants

The present study has five sections with different cohorts for each,
although participants in all were offenders under the supervision of
CDOC. CDOC's jurisdiction includes adult inmates in state-run facilities,
privately operated prisons, transitional halfway houses and other community settings as well as parolees. Cohorts varied as function of the
type of information being examined and accordingly are explained in
greater detail in subsequent sections.

Offenders were grouped into three categories (qualifying, nonqualifying,
and none) according to their mental health diagnosis as determined
during the prison intake process or later by a mental health clinician. A
number of measures factor into an initial psychological code including
psychological assessments, previous inpatient and outpatient treatment,
prescription for psychotropic medications, medical examinations, and
prior successful not guilty by reason of insanity pleas. All inmates are
given a rating of 1 to 5 to denote severity of psychological needs, and
qualifier codes are assigned by clinicians to differentiate among offenders

who have a rating of 3 or higher. There are four qualifier codes: "C" for chronic disorders, "O" for organic disorders, "N" for nonqualifying diagnoses, and "T" for temporary or rule-out disorders.

Offenders classified as "qualifying" met the CDOC definition of OMI, which requires a C or O qualifier in addition to a psychological code of 3, 4, or 5. Individuals in the qualifying group had a diagnosis consistent with certain Diagnostic and Statistical Manual of Mental Disorders-text revision (DSM-IV-TR; American Psychological Association, 2000) Axis I and Axis II disorders, specifically those which encompass the most disruptive ones within a prison environment. These include bipolar disorder, major depressive disorder, depressive disorder not otherwise specified, dysthymia, paranoid and delusional disorders, schizophrenic disorders, schizophreniform disorder, schizoaffective disorder, psychotic disorder not otherwise specified, induced psychotic disorder, brief reactive psychosis, dissociative identity disorder, post-traumatic stress disorder, and cluster A personality disorders (schizoid, schizotypal, and paranoid).

Offenders in the "nonqualifying" group had a psychological code in the 3 to 5 range, but differentially were assigned an N, T, or no qualifier. Accordingly, offenders in the nonqualifying group presented with significant mental health needs, although either their diagnoses did not meet CDOC's stringent definition for OMI or they needed a diagnostic interview to rule out a qualifying disorder.

Offenders placed into the category labeled "none" were those with no diagnosis and only minimal mental health needs. These offenders had psychological codes of 1 or 2.

Materials

The Level of Supervision Inventory-Revised (LSI-R; Andrews & Bonta, 1995) is a 54-item assessment conducted in a semi-structured interview format. It measures offender recidivism risk and can be utilized to determine the amount of supervision necessary for offenders in the community. The LSI-R is administered to all people entering prison as part of the diagnostic assessment and, using norms set for Colorado parolees, scores between 0 and 12 designate offenders as low risk, 13 to 25 as medium risk, and 26 to 54 as high risk.

The Millon Clinical Multiaxial Inventory-III (MCMI-III; Millon, Davis, & Millon, 1997) is a 175-item assessment which uses a true/false response format to obtain information about clinical syndromes and personality pathology. Base rate scores above 75 indicate the presence of a personality trait or clinical syndrome, and scores above 85 indicate the presence of a personality disorder or the prominence of a clinical syndrome. The MCMI-III contains one 3-item validity scale and three modifying indices that measure disclosure, desirability, and debasement to determine if test scores are interpretable. The MCMI-III was administered to all Colorado offenders upon intake between 1996 and 2004; although it has since been replaced by the Coolidge Correctional Inventory (2004), more cases had data from the MCMI-III than the newer measure.

Procedure

Offender data for this study was downloaded from the CDOC administrative database. Electronic offender records are received from the judicial system with mittimus data, and CDOC adds assessment, classification, and behavioral data to offenders' official record.

Demographic data, criminal history, and offender needs information are gathered at intake through a variety of sources including official records, interviews, pencil and paper tests, and file reviews. Screening for mental health needs, including the administration of psychological assessments, is conducted during admission and again as warranted during an offender's incarceration. Subsequent interviews and test administrations are conducted as needed for individuals identified with serious mental health needs.

RESULTS

Prevalence Rates

Participants. Groups were accumulated for prison admissions and for prison populations for fiscal years (FY) 2001 through, 2005. Prison admissions encompass not only commitments sentenced by the court, but also parole or probation technical violations, interstate compact transfers, and failures in the youthful offender system. The admission cohorts included 6,959 in FY01, 7,735 in FY02, 7,728 in FY03, 8,063 in FY04, and 9,301 in FY05. There were five population cohorts, representing a snapshot of incarcerated offenders on the last day of each year. To provide a better comparison against prison admissions, only offenders incarcerated in a prison facility were included. There were 14,913 inmates in FY01, 15,435 in FY02, 16,171 in FY03, 17,003 in FY04, and 17,536 in FY05. Cases with missing psychological codes in the admission ($n = 363$) and population cohorts ($n = 377$) were excluded.

Findings. Inmates with a qualifying disorder declined among admissions yet increased within the population (see Table 1). Conversely, nonqualifying mental disorders increased among admissions, and the population stayed relatively stable until the final year. Taken together, there was a slight increase of OMIs (qualifying and nonqualifying) among admissions over the 5-year span, while OMIs among the prison population increased steadily.

An examination of psychological qualifier codes revealed that the T qualifier was used nearly four times as often for admissions in FY05 ($n = 711$) than in FY01 ($n = 187$). Similarly, use of this temporary code increased in the population from 174 cases in FY01 to 659 in FY05. Although this may be partly due to the introduction of a new qualifier code, the implications are that a growing number of prison intakes are assigned a temporary code rather than one derived from a diagnostic interview.

The rate of technical returns was examined by group across years. Of the offenders being returned for technical violations in FY01, 16% were qualifying OMIs, 8% nonqualifying OMIs, and 76% had no diagnosis. Compared to those figures are the FY05 statistics where 17% were qualifying OMIs, 13% were nonqualifying OMIs, and 70% had no diagnosis. Over time, the nonqualifying group was increasingly returned to prison for technical violations.

□ *Table 1: OMI Prevalence Rates for Prison Intakes and Population*						
	Qualifying		Nonqualifying		None	
	Admits	Population	Admits	Population	Admits	Population
FY01	15%	13%	9%	7%	76%	80%
FY02	14%	15%	9%	7%	77%	78%
FY03	13%	15%	11%	7%	76%	78%
FY04	13%	16%	12%	7%	75%	77%
FY05	13%	16%	12%	9%	75%	75%

Profile Analysis

Participants. Participant data for the CDOC offender population ($N = 26{,}442$) at the end of FY05, including inmates in prison and under community supervision and parolees, were used to profile OMIs. Some cases could not be grouped ($n = 281$) due to missing psychological codes. Of the available data, the qualifying group was comprised of 3,844 offenders (15%), the nonqualifying group included 1,996 offenders (8%), and the none group consisted of 20,321 offenders (77%).

Findings. The prevalence rates of OMIs were analyzed across supervision settings. State facilities had the highest concentration of both qualifying and nonqualifying OMIs at 26% while community-based inmates had the lowest at 15%. OMIs comprised 17% of private facilities and 20% of parolees.

Table 2 shows differences across all three groups for gender and ethnicity. The female population presented with greater mental health needs than males, as did Caucasian offenders relative to African Americans

☐ Table 2: Demographic Data of Inmates and Parolees

	Qualifying ($n = 3{,}844$)	Nonqualifying ($n = 1{,}996$)	None ($n = 20{,}321$)
Gender			
Male	76%	85%	92%
Female	24%	15%	8%
Ethnicity			
Caucasian	60%	60%	44%
African American	16%	14%	21%
Hispanic	21%	23%	32%
Other	3%	3%	3%
Highest grade completed			
0-8	11%	11%	10%
9-11	61%	62%	62%
12	16%	16%	17%
Post secondary	12%	11%	11%
Mean Age (*SD*)	36.4 (9.9)	34.3 (9.8)	35.1 (10.3)

and Hispanics. The average age for offenders varied slightly with the qualifying group being the eldest and the nonqualifying group the youngest.

Number of prior incarcerations did not differ between groups, although
all other crime variables did (see Table 3). Participants' most serious
offense was coded by type and felony class, where first is the most serious
and sixth degree the least serious. The qualifying group had higher rates
of violent crimes and lower rates of drug crimes than the other groups.
The nonqualifying group had higher rates of other crimes and committed
less serious crimes as noted by their felony class. Findings showed that
the nonqualifying group received shorter maximum sentences on average
than the others, which coincides with this group having less serious
offenses. Average sentence length data did not include offenders serving
life sentences; life sentences were more common among the qualifying

☐ *Table 3: Criminal History Data of Inmates and Parolees*			
	Qualifying (*n* = 3,844)	Nonqualifying (*n* = 1,996)	None (*n* = 20,321)
Prior incarcerations			
None	72%	73%	73%
One	20%	19%	19%
Two or more	8%	8%	8%
Crime type			
Violent	49%	42%	43%
Property	21%	22%	22%
Drug	18%	21%	23%
Other	12%	15%	12%
Felony class			
1	3%	2%	3%
2	6%	5%	6%
3	25%	21%	29%
4	44%	46%	41%
5	19%	20%	17%
6	3%	6%	4%
Mean max. sentence (*SD*)	9.4 (18.7)	8.0 (17.6)	9.2 (17.4)
% serving life sentence	8%	6%	6%
Mean LSI-R score (*SD*)	32.7 (7.9)	32.1 (7.7)	28.6 (7.7)

group than the other two groups, likely a function of this group committing a higher rate of violent offenses. Finally, higher LSI-R scores were found for OMIs than non-OMIs.

An examination of eight needs categories is presented in Figure 1. Similar to the psychological codes, offenders are scored on 5-point needs scales based upon a variety of data sources; scores of 3 and above represent moderate to severe needs. Vocational and substance abuse were the two areas where offenders in all groups showed the greatest needs.

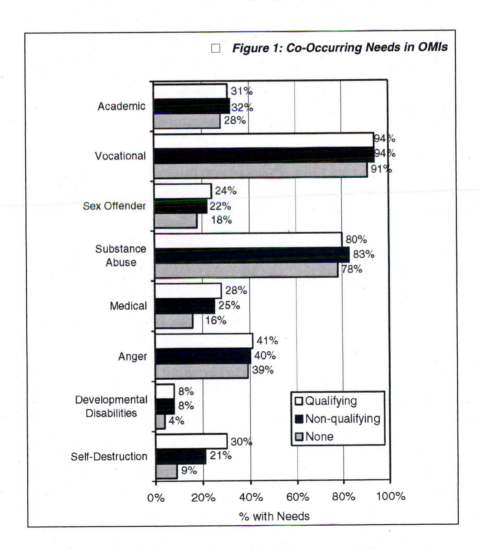

Figure 1: Co-Occurring Needs in OMIs

Needs were greater across all categories for both OMI groups than those with no diagnosis. Differences were more dramatic in self-destruction and medical than in other areas, two domains that are likely to affect monetary and staffing resources necessary to care for OMIs.

Valid MCMI-III profiles showed that passive-aggressive, avoidant, and antisocial personality disorders were the three most prominent *personality patterns* (see Table 4). Depressive, avoidant, and passive-aggressive

☐ **Table 4: MCMI-III Scores by OMI Group**			
% of Groups with Base Rate Score > 85	Qualifying (n = 2,083)	Nonqualifying (n = 949)	None (n = 9,483)	Total (N = 12,515)
Personality Patterns				
1- Schizoid	12%	9%	4%	6%
2a- Avoidant	22%	17%	9%	12%
2b- Depressive	25%	15%	7%	10%
3- Dependent	12%	7%	4%	5%
4- Histrionic	4%	4%	5%	5%
5- Narcissistic	8%	10%	11%	10%
6a- Antisocial	13%	14%	10%	11%
6b- Aggressive	13%	14%	8%	9%
7- Compulsive	1%	0%	1%	1%
8a- Passive-aggressive	21%	18%	12%	14%
8b- Self-defeating	10%	5%	2%	3%
s- Schizotypal	7%	4%	1%	2%
c- Borderline	8%	4%	2%	3%
p- Paranoid	7%	4%	2%	3%
Clinical Syndromes				
a- Anxiety	37%	29%	17%	21%
h- Somatoform	3%	2%	0%	1%
n- Bi-polar: manic disorder	4%	2%	1%	2%
d- Dysthymic disorder	10%	6%	2%	3%
b- Alcohol dependence	15%	14%	10%	11%
t- Drug dependence	20%	15%	10%	12%
r- Post traumatic stress	10%	5%	2%	3%
ss- Thought disorder	4%	2%	1%	1%
cc- Major depression	10%	5%	1%	3%
pp- Delusional disorder	5%	3%	1%	2%

personality disorders were the most common among OMIs. Offenders with no clinical diagnosis showed passive-aggressive, narcissistic, and antisocial as their most prominent personality disorders. Anxiety, alcohol dependence and drug dependence were the most commonly elevated *clinical syndromes* regardless of group.

Prison Adjustment

Participants. Two measures of how OMIs adjust to the prison environment were available from the official records: mental health crises and disciplinary violations. These measures can be thought of as behavioral reactions to the correctional environment, and accordingly provide some indication as to an offender's adjustment to this setting. Sampling for mental health crises and disciplinary violations was based on the numbers of events that occurred over the course of a year.

Findings. There were 1,195 recorded crisis incidents requiring mental health intervention during FY05, for which 686 inmates were involved. Approximately 65% of inmates were involved in a single crisis event, 31% in two to four events, and 4% in five or more incidents. As expected, the qualifying group had the highest rate of mental health crises (65%); however considerable frequencies also occurred in the nonqualifying (23%) and none groups (12%). In general, most crises were resolved with counseling and the return of offenders to their cells (48%). The next most common courses of action, mainly for self-harm and suicide attempts, involved the placement of offenders in observation cells (33%) or the prison infirmary (10%). Ambulatory (6%) and 4-point (2%) restraints were the least frequent responses to these situations. Infrequently did the outcomes result in a hospital admission (1%).

Disciplinary violations occurred at a greater rate than mental health crises as illustrated by 23,852 disciplinary violations during FY05. Qualifying OMIs were responsible for 22% of these events and nonqualifying for 12%, a disproportionately high rate as only 25% of the population was identified as qualifying or nonqualifying OMIs. Disobeying a lawful order was the most frequent violation, regardless of group. For the OMI groups, advocating facility disruption, unauthorized possession of contraband, and verbal abuse were the next most common violations. On the other hand, unauthorized possession, possession or use of dangerous drugs, and tattooing were the most common violations for the non-OMI group.

Release Rates

Participants. Data was obtained for offenders releasing from inmate status during FY05 to examine how groups varied across community transition factors. Releases occur when offenders are granted discretionary parole, begin a mandatory parole sentence, or discharge their sentence without further supervision. Infrequently, inmates release in other ways: probation, court ordered discharges, appeal bonds, inactivated cases, and death. Of the initial sample ($N = 8,251$), 11 cases could not be categorized due to missing psychological codes.

Findings. Release findings (see Table 5) yielded that offenders in the qualifying and nonqualifying groups were more likely to release from high custody levels–administrative segregation and close custody– and less likely to release from minimum security facilities than offenders with no diagnosis. Offenders with significant mental health needs were also less likely to receive a transitional halfway house placement or discretionary parole than offenders with no diagnosis. Qualifying OMIs had higher rates of discharge without community supervision than the other groups, while nonqualifying OMIs had the highest rates of mandatory parole releases. Contrary to literature that suggests OMIs

	Qualifying ($n = 1,294$)	Nonqualifying ($n = 589$)	None ($n = 6,357$)
☐ Table 5: Prison Release and Transitional Data			
Custody level at release			
Admin. segregation	7%	7%	3%
Close	16%	17%	8%
Medium	21%	23%	20%
Minimum-restrictive	24%	26%	26%
Minimum	28%	22%	39%
New/Unclassified	4%	5%	4%
Release Type			
Discharges	24%	19%	18%
Mandatory parole	57%	64%	56%
Discretionary parole	16%	14%	21%
Other	3%	3%	5%
Transitional placement	28%	28%	36%
Mean time served (*SD*)	3.0 (3.2)	2.6 (2.7)	2.9 (3.2)

serve significantly longer sentences than their nonmentally ill counterparts (Ditton, 1999), average time served did not appear to be influenced by mental health status, which may be skewed due to mandatory parole sentences.

Recidivism

Participants. Adult offender release cohorts for FY01 ($N = 6,122$), FY03 ($N = 6,972$), and FY05 ($N = 8,240$) were gathered to examine recidivism rates, excluding cases where psychological codes were unavailable. Recidivism was defined as returning to CDOC for new criminal charges, or technical violations of parole or probation requirements. Outcomes at 1-year post-release were examined using the FY05 cohort, 3 years using FY03 releases, and 5 years using FY01 releases.

Findings. Recidivism findings (see Figure 2) showed that offenders with mental health needs (qualifying and nonqualifying) were more likely to return to prison than offenders with no diagnoses at each follow-up period. Offenders in the nonqualifying group showed the highest recidivism rates. This finding is surprising given that the nonqualifying group had the least serious offenses and the shortest sentence lengths; however, it is congruent with the prevalence analyses that showed increased rates of nonqualifying OMIs among prison admissions for technical returns.

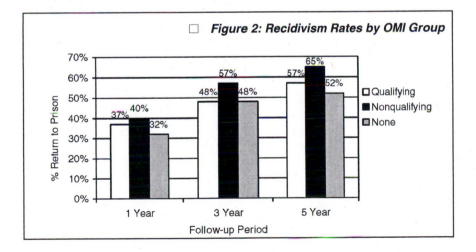

Figure 2: Recidivism Rates by OMI Group

DISCUSSION

The incidence of mental illness among Colorado's prison population models nationwide trends. In fact, study findings closely mirror national estimates that show 16% of inmates manifest serious and pervasive mental illness (Ditton, 1999) and 24% of state prisoners had a recent history of a mental health problem (James & Glaze, 2006). As of June 30, 2005, 16% of CDOC offenders were identified with a serious and pervasive psychiatric disorder. An additional 9% were classified as having mental health needs, although their diagnoses may be considered less serious within a prison environment than those meeting criteria for a qualifying diagnosis. Altogether, 25% of Colorado inmates presented with mental health issues.

Screening and Identification

The literature speaks to challenges in the detection of mental illness among inmates. Colorado has in place a well-established screening process which classifies offenders using various means including treatment history, psychological assessments and diagnostic interviews. This system is dynamic, allowing for status changes to be made anytime during an offender's incarceration as deemed appropriate by a mental health clinician.

The finding that Colorado's detection rate is the same as national averages suggests that CDOC is not impeded by screening problems. However, an increase in offenders carrying the "T" qualifier, a temporary code, may indicate resource limitations surrounding screening and assessment. Although there was a steady increase of T qualifiers over the entire 5-year period studied, that rate accelerated sharply beginning in FY03 when serious budget reductions struck.

Reentry Issues

Although there was only a modest 1% increase in the rate of OMIs among prison *intakes*, the sheer number grew 39% over a 5-year span as a result of prison growth. OMI prevalence rates within the prison *population* rose 5% over the same period. This phenomenon–the number of incarcerated OMIs increasing at a faster rate than among prison intakes–might be attributable to the higher rate of life sentences among qualifying OMIs. However, it must further be considered that mental health staff are identifying inmates with mental illness who were not detected during the screening process or experienced an onset of psychiatric symptoms following admission.

An important finding from this study was that technical returns are increasingly responsible for many of the OMI prison intakes. This supports the literature that indicates that mentally ill offenders are cycling in and out of the prison system. Indeed, recidivism rates showed that OMIs were more likely than non-OMIs to return to prison, even at 5 years post-release. Surprisingly, mentally ill inmates with a nonqualifying diagnosis had the highest recidivism rates. Even though there was nothing in their profile to suggest they were higher risk, they had the highest rate of mandatory parole releases, which is consistently associated with high recidivism rates (Rosten, 2007). Notably, individuals in the nonqualifying group were a mixed group, consisting of offenders diagnosed with less serious Axis I disorders (e.g., phobias, somatization), diagnosed with Axis II disorders which are generally considered untreatable, or needing a diagnostic interview where a qualifying disorder is possible (i.e., T qualifier). The present research did not explore how these subgroups within the nonqualifying group differed from each other.

While this study did not specifically explore reentry issues, several of the findings indicated that OMIs face greater barriers than non-OMIs, which is consistent with the literature. First of all, OMIs were more likely to release from administrative segregation or close custody than were their counterparts. This means that OMIs who already have difficulties assimilating into society are releasing from settings where they are more isolated than the average inmate. Secondly, they were less likely to have a transitional halfway house placement following their release from prison. Halfway house programs often provide reentry planning and assist in areas of housing, income, and treatment. Finally, it was found that OMIs, compared to the general population, were less likely to be granted discretionary parole and more likely to discharge their sentence. While it makes inherent sense that they would not be granted parole given their custody levels, those who discharge their sentence receive no post-release services.

The Person Behind the Mental Illness

Among the incarcerated, mental illness was more common among females than males. There was also a higher incidence of mental illness among Caucasians than other races. However, age and education were not discriminating factors. OMIs who had a qualifying disorder were more likely to be incarcerated on a violent crime and, consequently, were more likely to serve a life sentence. On the other hand, OMIs with a nonqualifying disorder appeared to have less serious offenses than other inmates and served slightly shorter sentences.

All in all, mental illness corresponded to greater needs across a host of areas–academic, vocational, sex offender, substance abuse, medical, anger, developmental disabilities, and self-destruction. These elevated needs translate into greater risk factors, as confirmed by elevated LSI-R scores. This means that many of the same individuals need services from a variety of treatment or program areas, and coordination of those services is essential.

Within a 1-year timeframe, 686 inmates were involved in crisis incidents. While it is impossible to make judgments about what is an acceptable rate, 4% of the prison population is far lower than the OMI prevalence rate, which suggests that most of them are being managed without crisis intervention if underreporting is not a problem. Additionally, when a crisis ensues, mental health staff were found to use a system of graduated responses such that low level responses were the most frequently used.

Unfortunately, the disproportionately high rate of disciplinary violations suggests that OMIs have a harder time adapting to their environment than non-OMIs. While their infractions were no more serious than others', their higher accumulation of infractions resulted in higher custody placements. Research conducted elsewhere (O'Keefe, this volume) has shown that OMIs are overrepresented in administrative segregation, a costly and highly restrictive environment.

In conclusion, this study provided a broad exploratory review of correctional OMIs in Colorado, corroborating many of the findings in the literature and representing what is likely occurring in other state systems. Although the seriously mentally ill offenders receive the most attention, this study suggests that those who have mental health needs but do not meet strict diagnostic criteria should not be neglected. Effective management and treatment of OMIs may be costly, but without these, the price paid by prisons and society may be even more costly.

REFERENCES

Abram, K. M., & Teplin, L. A. (1991). Co-occurring disorders among mentally ill jail detainees. *American Psychologist, 46,* 1036-1045.

American Psychiatric Association (2000). *Diagnostic and statistical manual of mental disorders* (4th ed. tr.). Washington, DC: Author.

Andrews, D. A., & Bonta, J. L. (1995). *LSI-R: The level of service inventory–revised.* Toronto: Multi-Health Systems.

Beck, A. J., & Marushak, L. M. (June, 2001). Mental health treatment in state prisons, 2000. *Bureau of Justice Statistics,* NCJ Publication No. 188215.

Birmingham, L., Gray, J., Mason, D., & Grubin, D. (2000). Mental illness at reception into prison. *Criminal Behavior and Mental Health, 10,* 78-87.

Burger, G. K., Calsyn, R. J., Morse, G. A., Klinkenberg, W. D., & Trusty, M. L. (1997). Factor structure of the expanded brief psychiatric rating scale. *Journal of Clinical Psychology, 53,* 451-454.

Chandler, R. K., Peters, R. H., Field, G., & Juliano-Bult, D. (2004). Challenges in implementing evidence-based treatment practices for co-occurring disorders in the criminal justice system. *Behavioral Science and the Law, 22,* 431-448.

Coolidge, F. L. (2004). *Coolidge Correctional Inventory.* Colorado Springs, CO: Author.

Ditton, P. M. (1999, July). *Mental health and treatment of inmates and probationers.* Washington, DC: U.S. Department of Justice, Bureau of Justice Statistics.

Dvoskin, J. A., & Spiers, E. M. (2004). On the role of correctional officers in prison mental health. *Psychiatric Quarterly, 75,* 41-59.

Hartwell, S. W. (2004). Comparison of offenders with mental illness only and offenders with dual diagnoses. *Psychiatric Services, 55,* 145-150.

Human Rights Watch (2003). *Ill-Equipped: U.S. prisons and offenders with mental illness.* New York: Human Rights Watch.

Jacoby, J. E., & Kozie-Peak, B. (1997). The benefits of social support for mentally ill offenders: Prison-to-community transitions. *Behavioral Sciences and the Law, 15,* 483-501.

James, D. J., & Glaze, L. E. (2006, September). *Mental health problems of prison and jail inmates.* Washington, DC: U.S. Department of Justice, Bureau of Justice Statistics.

Jeglic, E., Vanderhoff, H. A., & Donovick, P. J. (2005). The function of self-harm behavior in a forensic population. *International Journal of Offender Therapy and Comparative Criminology, 49,* 131-142.

Lamb, R. H., Weinberger, L. E., & Gross, B. H. (1999). Community treatment of severely mentally ill offenders under the jurisdiction of the criminal justice system: A review. *Psychiatric Services, 50,* 907-913.

Lurigio, A. J. (2001). Effective services for parolees with mental illness. *Crime and Delinquency, 47,* 446-461.

Lurigio, A. J., & Lewis, D. A. (1987). The criminal mental patient: A descriptive analysis and suggestions for future research. *Criminal Justice and Behavior, 14,* 268-287.

Lurigio, A. J., & Swartz, J. A. (2000). Changing the contours of the criminal justice system to meet the needs of persons with serious mental illness. *Policies, Process and Decisions of the Criminal Justice System, 3,* 45-100.

Millon, T., Davis, R. D., & Millon, C. (1997). *Manual for the Millon Clinical Multiaxial Inventory-III (MCMI-III)* (2nd ed.). Minneapolis: National Computer Systems.

O'Keefe, M. L. (this volume). Administrative segregation for mentally ill inmates. *Journal of Offender Rehabilitation.*

Osher, F., Steadman, H. J., & Barr, H. (2003). A best practice approach to community reentry from jails for inmates with co-occurring disorders: The APIC model. *Crime and Delinquency, 49,* 79-96.

Overall, J. E., & Gorham, D. R. (1962). The brief psychiatric rating scale. *Psychological Reports, 10,* 799-812.

Petersilia, J. (2003). *When prisoners come home: Parole and prisoner reentry.* New York: Oxford University Press.

Rice, M. E., & Harris, G. T. (1997). The treatment of mentally disordered offenders. *Psychology, Public Policy, and Law, 3,* 126-183.

Rosten, K. L. (2007). *Statistical report: Fiscal year, 2006* [Technical Report]. Colorado Springs, CO: Department of Corrections.

Teplin, L. A. (1983). The criminalization of the mentally ill: Speculation in search of data. *Psychological Bulletin, 94,* 54-67.

Teplin, L. A. (1990). Detecting disorder: The treatment of mental illness among jail detainees. *Journal of Consulting and Clinical Psychology, 2,* 233-236.

Thomas, A. (1998). Ronald Reagan and the commitment of the mentally ill: Capital interest groups, and the eclipse of social policy. *Electronic Journal of Sociology.* Retrieved July 11, 2006, from http://www.sociology.org/content/vol003.004/thomas.html.

Thomas, A., Donnell, A. J., & Young, T. R. (2004). Factor structure and differential validity of the expanded brief psychiatric rating scale. *Assessment, 11,* 177-187.

Torrey, E. F. (1997). *Out of the shadows: Confronting America's mental illness crisis.* New York: John Wiley & Sons.

U.S. Department of Health and Human Services (1994). *Resident patients in state and county mental hospitals.* Rockville, MD: Author.

Van Stelle, K. R., Blumer, C., & Moberg, D. P. (2004). Treatment retention of dually diagnosed offenders in an institutional therapeutic community. *Behavioral Sciences and the Law, 22,* 585-597.

Wakefield v. Thompson, 177 F. 3d. 1160 (9th Cir. 1999).

Weisman, R. L., Lamberti, J. S., & Price, N. (2004). Integrating criminal justice, community mental healthcare, and support services for adults with severe mental disorders, *Psychiatric Quarterly, 75,* 71-85.

White, M. D., Goldkamp, J. S., & Campbell, S. P. (2006). Co-occurring mental illness and substance abuse in the criminal justice system. *The Prison Journal, 86,* 301-326.

Wormith, J. S., Tellier, M. C., & Gendreau, P. (1988). Characteristics of protective custody offenders in a provincial correctional centre. *Canadian Journal of Criminology, 30,* 39-58.

AUTHORS' NOTES

Maureen L. O'Keefe, MA, is QA Officer, Rehabilitation Programs, Colorado Department of Corrections, 2862 South Circle Drive, Colorado Springs, CO 80906 (E-mail: Maureen.Okeefe@doc.state.co.us).

Marissa J. Schnell, BA, is affiliated with Arrowhead Correctional Center, P.O. Box 300, Canon City, CO 81215.

doi:10.1300/J076v45n01_08

Mental Health Issues in the Criminal Justice System. Pp. 105-122.
Available online at http://jor.haworthpress.com
© 2007 by The Haworth Press, Inc. All rights reserved.
doi:10.1300/J076v45n01_09

The Helping Alliance in Juvenile Probation:
The Missing Element
in the "What Works" Literature

BETSY MATTHEWS
DANA HUBBARD

ABSTRACT Over the past 20 years, much has been learned about the elements of effective correctional interventions through a body of literature known as "what works." The primary foci within this literature are assessment, treatment models, and treatment setting. Relatively little is said about the specific knowledge, attitudes and skill sets that correctional staff should possess to be effective change agents, or about the importance of the relationships that form between correctional staff and the offenders they serve. This stands in contrast to the counseling profession, where the therapeutic, or helping, alliance has long been viewed as an intermediate criterion of counseling effectiveness. The purpose of this article is to examine the role of the helping alliance in juvenile probation settings. Strategies for facilitating the development of the helping alliance and suggestions for future research are discussed. doi:10.1300/J076v45n01_09 *[Article copies available for a fee from The Haworth Document Delivery Service: 1-800-HAWORTH. E-mail address: <docdelivery@haworthpress.com> Website: <http://www.HaworthPress.com> © 2007 by The Haworth Press, Inc. All rights reserved.]*

KEYWORDS Juvenile probation, probation officer, therapeutic alliance, protective factor, interpersonal skills, counseling, "what works"

INTRODUCTION

Although recent research has identified specific treatment models that are effective in changing youth behavior (e.g., cognitive-behavioral therapy), very little research has examined how the relationship between a probation officer and youth impact behavioral change within a community setting (Florsheim, Shotorbani et al., 2000). Aside from a few recent articles (see Clark, 2000; Taxman, 2002), the probation literature is relatively silent about the specific knowledge, attitudes and skill sets that probation officers should possess to be effective change agents. In fact, it is questionable as to whether or not probation officers even see their role as change agents given the more punitive nature of juvenile justice in recent years. This silence and role ambiguity may undermine the power of the helping relationship and impede a probation agency's ability to achieve important treatment goals with the youths they serve.

The purpose of this article is to examine the potential role that the relationships between youth and probation officers could play in enhancing the effectiveness of juvenile probation services. We begin by reviewing the major tenets of the "what works" literature, and discussing a potential shortcoming within the literature and associated initiatives. Next we describe the therapeutic alliance, a concept drawn from the counseling literature, which has been associated with improved therapeutic outcomes. We then begin to build a case for applying this concept to the juvenile probation setting by discussing its significance to gender-responsive programming and by emphasizing the value of youth-adult relationships within the risk-protection framework that is popular among juvenile justice settings. Next, we identify factors within juvenile probation settings that may threaten the viability of developing this type of relationship with youths, and suggest agency strategies for creating an organizational culture that is more conducive to the development of trusting and respectful relationships between youth and probation officers. We close the article with suggestions for future research.

"WHAT WORKS": AN OVERVIEW

Ever since Martinson's (1974) infamous proclamation about the failures of rehabilitation, researchers have been grappling with the question of "what works" to reduce offender recidivism. Using various research methodologies, these researchers have arrived at remarkably similar conclusions. Programs that reduce recidivism share several common characteristics: They were conducted in the community (Izzo and Ross, 1990; Lipsey and Wilson, 1998; Palmer, 1974; Whitehead and Lab, 1989); included multimodal programming (Clements, 1988; Lipsey, 1992; Lipsey and Wilson, 1998; Palmer, 1992, 1996); involved the family in the offender's treatment (Clements, 1988; Gendreau and Ross, 1987; Palmer, 1996); and were cognitive-behavioral in nature (Andrews, Zinger et al., 1990; Gendreau and Ross, 1987; Pearson, Lipton et al., 2002).

From this body of research, more specific characteristics have been identified and referred to as "the principles of effective intervention." These principles have appeared in many articles, in many forms (see Andrews, Bonta, and Hoge, 1990; Gendreau, 1996; Gendreau and Andrews, 1990), but their essence remains the same. An abbreviated version of the principles as discussed by Smith, Gendreau, and Goggin (2004, pp. 287-288) appears below:

1. The treatment is based on behavioral strategies (e.g., radical behavioral, social learning, or cognitive-behavioral).
2. The program has a manual that describes the theory and data justifying the program, as well as a curriculum that details the discrete steps to be followed in presenting the material.
3. The treatment is located, preferably, in the offender's natural environment.
4. The treatment is multimodal, offering a variety of interventions that address a range of offender needs, particularly criminogenic needs.
5. The intensity of treatment should be approximately 100 hours of direct service over a three-to four-month period.
6. The treatment emphasizes positive reinforcement contingencies for prosocial behaviors, and is individualized as much as possible.
7. According to the risk principle, the behaviors targeted are those that are predictive of future criminal behavior and are dynamic in nature (e.g., antisocial attitudes and associates), and it is the medium-to higher-risk offenders who will benefit the most from treatment.
8. According to the responsivity principle, the treatment should be designed to match key offenders' characteristics and learning styles with relevant therapist characteristics and program features in order to facilitate the learning of prosocial values.

9. Once the formal phase of treatment has ended, continuity through aftercare on an as-needed basis is required.
10. Several system factors must be in place for effective service delivery including the quality of program implementation, the training and credentials of program directors and staff, the degree to which the organization engages in advocacy brokerage, the participation of staff in program decision-making, effective case management, and the quality of the therapeutic practices of the staff.

The body of research attesting to the validity of these principles continues to grow. National organizations, both private-nonprofit (e.g., the American Probation and Parole Association, International Community Corrections Association) and federal (National Institute of Corrections, Office of Juvenile Justice and Delinquency Prevention), have facilitated their implementation through the provision of training and technical assistance. By all accounts, it appears that the "what works" research and its associated iniatives have provided corrections and juvenile justice agencies and professionals a new sense of direction and a positive outlook for the future.

Where "What Works" Falls Short

Despite its many contributions to correctional practice, we have identified what we perceive to be a major shortcoming of the "what works" agenda. Our reading of the literature, and ongoing consultation with corrections and juvenile justice agencies, suggest that little attention is given to the crucial role that probation officers and other corrections professionals can play in promoting positive behavioral change.

Throughout the many versions of these "principles of effective intervention" references are made to staff qualifications (e.g., interpersonal sensitivity, firmness, consistency, professional training), staff attitudes (e.g., beliefs supportive of rehabilitation) and effective therapeutic practices (e.g., anti-criminal modeling, reinforcement and disapproval, relationship practices, and motivational interviewing). Beyond that, there is little discussion or research devoted to the role that the relationship between the probation officer and the client plays in promoting positive behavioral change. The bulk of the research and training on effective correctional interventions seems to be devoted to the implementation and evaluation of specific assessment tools and various cognitive-behavioral programs, with the softer technologies of interpersonal skills and relationship building taking a back seat.

Supporting this perception, are studies suggesting that little emphasis is placed on helping correctional staff develop and practice the interpersonal skills needed to establish trusting and respectful relationships. For example, a 2002 survey of training administrators in 35 state juvenile justice agencies revealed that only 11 (37.9%) offered interpersonal skills training as part of their basic skills curriculum (Reddington and Wright Kreisel, 2003). Moreover, an analysis of skills among 720 adult probation officers revealed that officers infrequently used the communication skills set known to contribute to rapport with offenders (e.g., open ended questions, affirmation, reflective responses) (Taxman, 2002). Braswell (2004) claims that helping agents within adult and juvenile corrections are often instructed to avoid getting too close to the client. He argues that these mandates undermine the human spirit and the power of the helping relationship.

This tendency to downplay the offender-officer relationship may be an unintended consequence of the emphasis that the "what works" agenda places on the importance of directive therapeutic approaches, such as cognitive skills training, during which the helping agent is active and solution-focused. This focus on directive therapeutic approaches is in response to studies suggesting that client-centered, or non-directive therapy, is not an effective therapeutic approach for antisocial or delinquent youths who lack verbal skills and insight (Latessa, Cullen, and Gendreau, 2002).[1] In an effort to disassociate themselves from this client-centered type of therapy, correctional agencies seem to have discarded the important skills and characteristics that, although associated with Rogers' (1951) client-centered therapy, have also been associated with positive therapeutic outcomes.

In contrast to corrections, the relationship between the client and the helping agent takes center stage in research and training within the counseling profession. According to Bordin (1980, p. 2), this relationship is considered the element that "makes it possible for the patient to accept and follow treatment faithfully."

THE THERAPEUTIC ALLIANCE

The therapeutic alliance has been defined as the collaborative relationship that develops within a helping relationship. In the counseling profession, the therapeutic alliance has long been viewed as an intermediate criterion of counseling effectiveness–that is, stronger alliances contribute to better outcomes (Frieswyk, Allen et al., 1986; Horvath and Symonds, 1991; Stiles, Agnew-Davies et al., 1998). The positive association found between the alliance and outcomes is believed to be generic, or transtheoretical (Clark, 2001; Florsheim et al., 2001). That is, the importance of the therapeutic relationship to outcome is evident across both residential and outpatient settings (Florsheim et al., 2000), and across different types of treatment including behavioral, cognitive, and psychodynamic therapies (Horvath, 2005; Horvath and Symonds, 1991).

The three primary components of a high quality alliance include: (1) agreement between the change agent and the client on the goals of intervention; (2) collaboration on the development and completion of tasks devised to achieve the goals; and (3) a trusting and respectful relationship that provides a safe context for self-examination and personal growth (Florsheim et al., 2000). Staff characteristics that have been found to be associated with strong therapeutic alliances and positive behavioral change include genuineness, acceptance, and empathy (Rogers, 1951, 1992; Traux and Carkhuff, 1967; Miller and Rollnick, 1991). According to Rogers (1992), genuineness requires personal introspection and congruence between what you are feeling, what you believe, what you say, and what you do; acceptance is demonstrated through positive expression of feelings and respect for the client; and empathy speaks to the helping agent's ability to identify the client's core feelings and accurately communicate them back to the client.

Some things about being an effective helping agent are innate; you either have it or you don't. There are, however, some key communication skills that can be learned, and these skills go a long way toward promoting the genuineness, acceptance, and empathy necessary for developing strong helping relationships with youth. Attending is the most fundamental of all communication skills. It includes listening carefully to verbal exchanges, observing nonverbal cues, and communicating to the client that you are paying attention. Asking open-ended questions encourages clients to explore their feelings or situations in more depth. Paraphrasing, reflection of feeling, and summarizing are all skills that demonstrate to youths that you are interested in what they have to say, and that you understand how they are feeling. Lastly, self-disclosure by the helping agent has been shown to help build trust and rapport, increase the likelihood that the youth will perceive the helping agent as genuine, and foster feelings of empathy (Gaines, 2003; Rabinor, 2003).

As suggested earlier in this article, these skills are not always emphasized in training or practice within adult and juvenile probation agencies.

Clark (2000) draws on findings regarding the importance of the therapeutic alliance to encourage a more therapeutic approach for juvenile courts. He contends that probation staff, while not clinically trained, can become effective change agents through the development of mutually trusting and respectful relationships with youth. The remainder of this article expands on Clark's contention by suggesting strategies for promoting the development of these types of relationships within the juvenile justice context.

ENHANCING THE APPEAL OF THE HELPING ALLIANCE

In order for agencies and staff to embrace the concept, the therapeutic alliance must be made more relevant to probation officers who are quick to make distinctions between their role and that of counselors. Based on lessons learned from training juvenile justice practitioners, we have found that simple terminology can make a difference in how receptive probation officers are to the concept and to building skills associated with a strong therapeutic alliance. We have replaced the term "therapeutic alliance" with "helping alliance," to reflect the nonclinical setting in which probation services are delivered, and to reflect the notion that any professional within a youth-serving agency is a change agent with the capacity to promote positive change among the youths they serve. Another way to increase receptiveness is to demonstrate how the helping alliance supports other current initiatives or philosophies within the context of juvenile probation. Two such initiatives include gender-responsive services for girls and a risk-protection framework for offender intervention.

The Helping Alliance as an Essential Element for Gender-Responsive Services

Although also relevant for boys, the helping alliance is particularly relevant when working with girls. Girls are socialized to listen to others and value the emotional exchange that takes place within intimate relationships with others (Amaro, Blake et al., 2001; Belknap, Holsinger, and Dunn, 1997; Maccoby, 1990). Boys, on the other hand, are socialized to be achievement oriented and to prefer relationships that are characterized by well-defined roles and a directive style of interaction (Belknap et al., 1997; Maccoby, 1990). According to the responsivity principle, then, change agents should modify their approach to accommodate these differences in interpersonal styles and preferences.

Advocates for gender-responsive interventions support programs rooted in the "relational model" (Covington, 2000; Gilligan, 1982; Miller, 1986). According to the relational model, many of the problems that girls experience can "be traced to disconnections or violations within relationships" (Covington, 2000, p. 197). Thus, Covington (2000) argues, positive change for girls is dependent on developing mutually trusting and empathetic relationships that do not cause them to repeat their experiences with loss, neglect, and abuse.

It should be noted that neither the "what works" literature nor the "gender-responsive" literature provides much instruction on how to build trusting relationships or address girls' interpersonal preferences. A recent survey of probation officer perceptions of girls suggests that this is something that should not be left to chance. The officers surveyed characterized girls as "criers, liars, and manipulators" (Gaarder, Rodriguez, and Zatz, 2004). Although these findings are not reflective of all probation officers, they certainly make a sad statement about some of the persons we have working with our girls. By neglecting to equip staff with the basic communication skills needed to formulate strong helping alliances, and failing to match girls with staff who respect and empathize with the challenges girls encounter, youth-serving agencies may be recreating the type of relationships that have played destructive roles in the lives of girls.

Using the Helping Alliance to Promote Resiliency Among Juvenile Offenders

The helping alliance also fits well into the risk-protection framework, a popular model for intervention in juvenile justice agencies. Hawkins, Catalano, and Miller (1992) assert that programs with the best chance of preventing delinquency are those that try to reduce known risk factors and, simultaneously, implement strategies designed to enhance identified protective factors.

Risk factors are those factors that increase a youth's likelihood of engaging in delinquency and other antisocial behaviors. Studies on the predictors of delinquency reveal significant correlations between delinquency and many family and neighborhood factors. Children who come from a single-parent home, have inadequate supervision, experience inappropriate discipline, suffer from emotionally strained familial relationships, are economically deprived, and live in high crime neighborhoods have an increased likelihood of delinquency (Farrington, 1995; Howell, 2003; Yoshikawa, 1994). There are many children, however, who are able to beat the odds, and despite exposure to multiple risk factors, grow into productive, law-abiding citizens (Brewer, Hawkins et al., 1995; Katz, 1997). The difference for these children typically lies in some factor in their lives, either internal or external, that makes them resilient and enables them to overcome adversity.

Resiliency refers to the capacity for successful adaptation to disruptive, stressful, or challenging circumstances (Richardson, Neiger et al., 1990; Cicchetti and Garmezy, 1993). Protective factors are what moderate the effects of adversity and promote resilient responses to risk (Hawkins et al., 1992). Three categories of protective factors have been identified in the literature: (1) positive personality and social orientation; (2) warm and supportive relationships with family members or other adults; and (3) prosocial family and community norms (Garmezy, 1985; Howell, 2003).

A supportive relationship with a caring adult has consistently emerged in research as an important protective factor (Garmezy, 1985; Hawkins et al., 1992; Rutter, 1987; Werner and Smith, 1992). By fulfilling this need for a relationship with a caring adult, probation officers can potentially give youths a chance to overcome the adversity they experience in their family and neighborhood context.

Researchers have found that supportive relationships with adults mitigate the effects of high-risk environments in three key ways. First, they alter youths' self-perceptions. A longitudinal study of youths exposed to multiple risk factors found that supportive relationships with adults contributed to improvements in self-esteem and self-efficacy (Werner, 1993). Another study of economically disadvantaged youth found significantly higher levels of educational and occupational aspirations among youths involved in mentoring relationships for more than one year as compared to a group of youths on the waiting list for the same mentoring program (Lee, 1999). Rutter (1990) suggested that intimate relationships bolstered how youths viewed themselves by giving them an increased sense of mastery. Others have suggested that as the result of positive and consistent interactions with caring adult mentors, youths begin to believe that they are loved and valued (Morrow and Styles, 1995) and gain a sense of "felt-security" (Bretherton, 1985; McCartney, Styles and Morrow, 1994.) Given the impact that self-perceptions have on human performance (Bandura, 1977; Harter, 1998), improvements in how youths view themselves are particularly salient in programs aiming to prevent delinquency

The second way in which the presence of a caring adult may serve a protective capacity is by modifying youths' perceptions of other relationships in their lives. Positive interactions experienced in mentoring relationships can demonstrate to youth that positive relationships with adults are possible (Olds, Kitzman et al., 1997) and, thus, reduce the resentment that youth often feel toward adults, and more specifically, toward parental authority. Mentoring relationships have been found to improve parent-child interactions by modelling effective conflict resolution (Flaxman, Ascher, and Harrington, 1988). Werner and Smith (1992) found that children subjected to the chronic psychiatric problems of their parents were better able to detach themselves from the discord at home when they had a caring adult to whom they could turn. In these ways, relationships with caring adults may buffer the effects of family risk factors.

Third, a relationship with a caring adult has been identified as the most important protective factor for children who have experienced major trauma or stress in their lives (Anderson, 1994). According to Unger and Wandersman (1985), it is the feelings of love and belonging that youth gain from these relationships that counteract both psychological and physical consequences of stress. van der Kolk (1994) suggested that the benefits of current social supports outweigh the effects of past terror and encourage healthy ways of coping.

Clearly, providing youth with a trusting and safe relationship with a caring adult is a viable strategy for promoting resiliency. The question here is, can probation officers play that role by developing a more nurturing, trusting, and open relationship with youth?

BUILDING AN ORGANIZATIONAL CULTURE CONDUCIVE TO THE DEVELOPMENT OF HELPING ALLIANCES

There are several organizational factors that may impede probation officers' capacity for developing alliances with youth. First, as addressed previously, is the lack of organizational focus on the offender-officer relationship and the interpersonal skills necessary for developing such relationships. Second, during the 1990s, many states enacted laws and other policy changes making their juvenile justice systems more punitive (Griffin, 2000). Also during this time, the missions of juvenile courts shifted from a sole focus on "serving the best interest of the youth" to a more balanced approach designed to provide more rights to victims of juvenile crime and interject more offender accountability (Maloney and Umbreit, 1995). Although these philosophical shifts have not precluded the development of helping relationships with youth, they have contributed to a stronger focus on control and enforcement among juvenile probation officers than previously existed.

Third, human resources are stretched thin within many juvenile probation agencies. The number of cases placed on probation from 1985-2002 increased by 44 percent (Livsey, 2006), making it difficult to maintain reasonable caseload sizes. Average caseload sizes range from a low of 20 in Kentucky to a high of 80 in West Virginia (www.ncjj.org, retrieved April 10, 2007). Moreover, in addition to supervising offenders, many juvenile probation officers also are responsible for conducting intake screening and preparing predispositional reports for the court (Torbet, 1996). Clearly, these high caseloads and multiple duties restrict the amount of time an officer can devote to building trusting relationships with youth.

Given the demand for offender accountablity and the current budget situation, these barriers are unlikely to dissipate in the near future. Strong leadership is needed to build an organizational culture that supports the development of strong helping alliances between officers and youth in spite of these constraints. The following strategies are recommended:

1. **Hire people with the right values and skills:** It is difficult to fully assess applicants' values and skills during the interview process. At the very least, we should inquire about their philosophies regarding changing youth behavior, and attempt to assess their interpersonal skills through the use of some standardized assessments that measure the key characteristics and skills of effective helping agents.

2. **Train staff on the interpersonal skills needed to develop strong therapeutic relationships:** At a minimum, basic training should include an opportunity to learn about, and practice, the aforementioned interpersonal skills. It is also recommended that follow-up training be provided to reinforce these skills. "Motivational Interviewing," a training developed by Miller and Rollnick (1991), is an example of a training curriculum that covers these basic skills

and more advanced skills designed to enhance a client's readiness for change.

3. **Match staff and youth based on personality characteristics, interests, and skills (i.e., apply the responsivity principle):** Not everyone can work effectively with all types of youth. When making case assignments or referrals, consideration should be given to the interests and personal characteristics of staff.

4. **Assess staff's capacity to develop strong therapeutic relationships**. This capacity can be assessed through supervisor observation and skill rating or the completion of client perception scales. Examples of client perception scales include the Treatment Satisfaction Index (Dennis, Titus et al., 2002), and the Working Alliance Inventory (WAI; Horvath and Greenburg, 1989).

5. **Support staff in their work**: If we truly believe in social learning theory, then we ought to apply its tenets to our staff. Management should treat staff with the respect that they are expected to give to their clients, model the type of communication skills expected from staff, and reward staff's ability to develop strong therapeutic relationships with youth.

FUTURE RESEARCH

Although the research on counseling is instructive, research must be conducted within the probation context to make it more relevant to officers. Research on the helping alliance within the juvenile probation context should be designed to answer two basic research questions: (1) How does the strength of the helping alliance impact probation outcomes (e.g., reduction in risk, compliance with rules and regulations of probation, participation in treatment, completion of treatment goals, cognitive skills, antisocial attitudes, recidivism)? (2) What factors are associated with strong helping alliances between youth and probation officers? Figure 1 reflects an evaluation logic model that could be used to guide this research.

The policy implications of such research are twofold. First, the research may reveal information that can be used to guide staff hiring, training, and performance evaluation. Second, consistent with the "responsivity principle" of effective correctional intervention (Andrews, Bonta, and Hoge, 1990), the research may highlight factors that

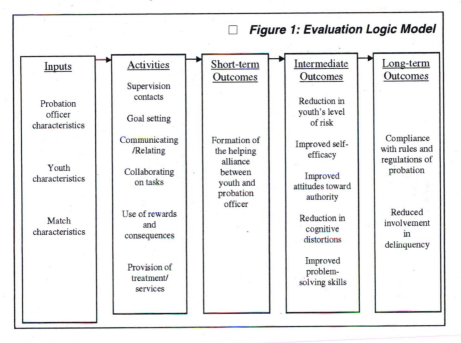

☐ **Figure 1: Evaluation Logic Model**

Inputs	Activities	Short-term Outcomes	Intermediate Outcomes	Long-term Outcomes
Probation officer characteristics	Supervision contacts		Reduction in youth's level of risk	
	Goal setting			Compliance with rules and regulations of probation
	Communicating /Relating	Formation of the helping alliance between youth and probation officer	Improved self-efficacy	
Youth characteristics	Collaborating on tasks		Improved attitudes toward authority	
Match characteristics	Use of rewards and consequences		Reduction in cognitive distortions	Reduced involvement in delinquency
	Provision of treatment/ services		Improved problem-solving skills	

should be considered when pairing youth with probation officers in an effort to increase a youth's amenability to supervision and treatment.

CONCLUSION

There is sufficient evidence to suggest that building a helping alliance with youth is a viable strategy for addressing treatment needs and reducing delinquency. Thus, the issue requires further exploration as we continue the movement toward the implementation of "what works" and evidence-based practices within juvenile probation. The more knowledge we can gain about the importance of building strong relationships with youth, the more likely we are to challenge the current culture of many modern day probation agencies–a culture that appears to impede the development of helping alliances. There is, of course, the possibility that research may reveal that it is too difficult to build helping alliances with youth, or that these alliances are insignificant in the lives of delinquent youth. Either way, research on this issue is likely to uncover information that will enhance our understanding and capacity for delivering effective probation services.

NOTE

1. In client-centered therapy, most associated with Carl Rogers (1951), the focus is on relationship building and developing client insight about past events; little attention is given to goals or skill building. Throughout his work with client-centered therapy, Rogers identified several characteristics of effective change agents that were found to contribute to the development of robust therapeutic relationships.

REFERENCES

Amaro, H., Blake, S., Schwartz, P., and Flinchbaugh, L. (2001). Developing theory-based substance abuse prevention programs for young adolescent girls. *Journal of Early Adolescence, 31*(3), 256-93.

Anderson, M. L. C. (1994). High juvenile crime rate: A look at mentoring as a preventive strategy. *Criminal Law Bulletin, 30*(1), 54-75.

Andrews, D. A., Bonta, J. D., and Hoge, R. D. (1990). Classification for effective rehabilitation: Rediscovering psychology. *Criminal Justice and Behavior, 17*, 19-52.

Andrews, D. A., Zinger, I., Bonta, J. D., Gendreau, P., and Cullen, F. T. (1990). Does correctional treatment work? A psychologically informed meta-analysis. *Criminology, 28*, 369-404.

Bandura, A. (1977). *Social Learning Theory, 1st Edition.* Upper Saddle River, NJ: Pearson Professional.

Belknap, J., Holsinger, K., and Dunn, M. (1997). *Moving Toward Juvenile Justice and Youth-Serving Systems that Address the Distinct Experiences of the Adolescent Female: A Report to the Governor.* Office of Criminal Justice Services, Columbus, OH.

Bordin, E. S. (1980). *Of Human Bonds that Bind or Free.* Pacific Grove, CA: Society for Psychotherapy Research.

Braswell, M. (2004). The function of correctional counseling and treatment. In P. Van Voorhis, M. Braswell, and D. Lester (Eds.), *Correctional Counseling and Rehabilitation, 5th Edition* (pp. 3-19). Cincinnati, OH: Anderson Publishing.

Bretherton, I. (1985). Attachment theory: Retrospect and prospect. In I. Bretherton and E. Waters (Eds.), *Growing Points of Attachment Theory and Research.* Chicago: University of Chicago Press.

Brewer, D. D., Hawkins, J. D., Catalano, R. F., and Neckerman, H. J. (1995). Preventing serious, violent and chronic juvenile offending: A review of evaluations of selected strategies in childhood, adolescence, and the community. In J. C. Howell, B. Krisberg, J. D. Hawkins, and J. J. Wilson (Eds.), *Sourcebook on Serious, Violent and Chronic Juvenile Offenders* (pp. 61-141). Thousand Oaks, CA: Sage.

Cicchetti, D., and Garmezy, N. (1993). Prospects and promises in the study of resilience. *Development and Psychopathology, 5*, 497-502.

Clark, M. D. (2000). Influencing positive behavior change: Increasing the therapeutic approach of juvenile courts. *Federal Probation, 65*(1), 18-27.

Clements, C. (1988). Delinquency prevention and treatment: A community-centered perspective. *Criminal Justice and Behavior, 15*, 286-305.

Covington, S. (2000). Helping women recover: Gender-specific treatment for substance abuse in community corrections. In M. McMahon (Ed.), *Assessment to Assistance: Programs for Women in Community Corrections* (pp. 139-170). Lanham, MD: American Correctional Association.

Dennis, M. L., Titus, J. C., White, M. K., Unsicker, J. I., and Hodgkins, D. V. (2002). Global Appraisal of Individual Needs (GAIN): Administration guide for the GAIN and related measures. Bloomington, IL: Chestnut Health Systems. [Online] Available at: www.chestnut.org/li/gain.

Farrington, D. P. (1995). The development of offending and antisocial behaviour from childhood: Key findings from the Cambridge Study in Delinquent Development. *Journal of Child Psychology and Psychiatry, 360*, 929-964.

Flaxman, F., Ascher, C., and Harrington, C. (1988). *Youth Mentoring: Programs and Practices.* New York: Columbia University, Teachers College. (Available from the ERIC Clearinghouse on Urban Education, Institute for Urban Minority Education, Box 40, Teachers College, Columbia University, New York, NY 10027).

Florsheim, P., Shotorbani, S., and Guest-Warnick, G. (2000). Role of the working alliance in the treament of delinquent boys in community based programs. *Journal of Clinical Child Psychology, 29*(1), 94-107.

Frieswyk, S., Allen, J., Colson, D., and Coyne, L. (1986). Therapeutic alliance: Its place as a process and outcome variable in dynamic psychotherapy research. *Journal of Consulting and Clinical Psychology, 5*, 483-489.

Gaarder, E., Rodriguez, N., and Zatz, M. (2004). Criers, liars, and manipulators: Probation officers' views of girls. *Justice Quarterly, 21*(3), 547-578.

Gaines, R. (2003). Therapist self-disclosure with children, adolescents and their parents. *Journal of Clinical Psychology, 59*(5), 569-580.

Garmezy, N. (1985). Stress resistant children: The search for protective factors. In J. E. Stevenson (Ed.), *Recent Research in Developmental Psychopathology. Journal of Child Psychology and Psychiatry, Book Supplement No. 4.* Oxford: Pergamon.

Gendreau, P. (1996). The principles of effective intervention with offenders. In A. T. Harland (Ed.), *Choosing Correctional Options that Work* (pp. 117-130). Thousand Oaks, CA: Sage.

Gendreau, P., and Andrews, D. A. (1990). Tertiary prevention: What the meta-analyses of the offender treatment literature tell us about what works. *Canadian Journal of Criminology, 32*, 173-184.

Gendreau, P., and Ross, R. (1987). Revivification of rehabilitation: Evidence from the 1980s. *Justice Quarterly, 4*, 349-407.

Gilligan, C. (1982). *In a Different Voice.* Cambridge, MA: Harvard University Press.

Griffin, P. (2000). Rethinking juvenile probation: The desktop guide to good juvenile probation practice revisited. *NCJJ in FOCUS, 2*(1), 1-8.

Harter, S. (1998). Effects of child abuse on the self-system. *Journal of Aggression, Maltreatment and Trauma, 2*(1), 147-169.

Hawkins, D. J., Catalano, R. F., and Miller, J. M. (1992). Risk and protective factors for alcohol and other drug problems in adolescence and early childhood: Implications for substance abuse prevention. *Psychological Bulletin, 112*, 64-105.

Horvath, A. O. (2005). The therapeutic relationship: Research and theory. *Psychotherapy Research, 15*(1/2), 3-7.

Horvath, A. O., and Symonds, D. B. (1991). Relationship between working alliance and outcome in psychotherapy: A meta-analysis. *Journal of Counseling Psychology, 38,* 139-149.

Horvath, A. O., and Greenberg, L. S. (1989). Development and validation of the Working Alliance Inventory. *Journal of Counseling Psychology, 36,* 223–233.

Howell, J. C. (2003). *Preventing and Reducing Juvenile Delinquency: A Comprehensive Framework.* Thousand Oaks, CA: Sage Publications.

Izzo, R., and Ross, R. (1990). Meta-analysis of rehabilitation programs for juvenile delinquents: A brief report. *Criminal Justice and Behavior, 17,* 134-142.

Katz, M. (1997). Overcoming childhood adversities: Lessons learned from those who have "beat the odds." *Intervention in School and Clinic, 32*(4), 205-211.

Latessa, E. J., Cullen, F. T., and Gendreau, P. (2002). Beyond correctional quackery-professionalism and the possibility of effective treatment. *Federal Probation, 66*(2), 43-49.

Lee, J. (1999). The positive effects of mentoring economically disadvantaged students. *Professional School Counseling, 2*(3), 172-179.

Lipsey, M. W. (1992). Juvenile delinquency treatment: A meta-analytic inquiry into the variability of effects. In T. D. Cook, H. Cooper, and T. Cordray (Eds.), *Meta-Analysis for Explanation: A Casebook* (pp. 83-127). Thousand Oaks, CA: Sage.

Lipsey, M. W., and Wilson, D. B. (1998). Effective intervention for serious juvenile offenders: A synthesis of research. In R. Loeber and D. P. Farrington (Eds), *Serious and Violent Juvenile Offenders: Risk Factors and Successful Interventions* (pp. 313-345). Thousand Oaks, CA: Sage Publications.

Livsey, S. (2006). Juvenile delinquency probation caseloads, 1985-2002. *OJJDP Fact Sheet.* Washington, DC: Office of Juvenile Justice and Delinquency Prevention.

Maccoby, E. (1990). Gender and relationships: A developmental account. *American Psychologist. 454,* 513-520.

Maloney, D. M., and Umbreit, M. S. (1995). Managing change: Toward a balanced and restorative justice model. *Perspectives, 19*(2), 43-46.

Martinson, R. (1974). What works? Questions and answers about prison reform. *The Public Interest, 35,* 22-54.

McCartney, C. A., Styles M. B., and Morrow, K. V. (1994). *Mentoring in the Juvenile Justice System: Findings from Two Pilot Programs.* Philadelphia, PA: Public/Private Ventures.

Morrow, K.V., and Styles, M. B. (1995). *Building Relationships with Youth in Program Settings: A Study of Big Brothers/Big Sisters.* Philadelphia, PA: Public/Private Ventures.

Miller, B. J. (1986). *Toward a New Psychology of Women.* Boston: Beacon Press.

Miller, W. R., and Rollnick, S. (1991). *Motivational Interviewing: Preparing People to Change Addictive Behavior.* New York: The Guilford Press.

National Center for Juvenile Justice. http://www.ncjrs.org. Retrieved April 10, 2007.

Olds, D., Kitzman, H., Cole, R., and Robinson, J. (1997). Theoretical formulations of a program of home visitation for pregnant women and parents of young children. *Journal of Community Psychology, 25,* 9-26.

Palmer, T. (1974). The Youth Authority's Community Treatment Project. *Federal Probation, 381,* 3-13.

Palmer, T. (1992). *The Reemergence of Correctional Intervention*. Newbury Park, CA: Sage.

Palmer, T. (1996). Programmatic and nonprogrammatic aspects of successful intervention. In A. T. Harland (Ed.), *Choosing Correctional Options that Work* (pp. 131-182). Thousand Oaks, CA: Sage.

Pearson, F. S., Lipton, D. S., Cleland, C. M., and Yee, D. S. (2002). Effects of behavioral/cognitive-behavioral programs on recidivism. *Crime and Delinquency, 48*(3), 476-496.

Rabinor, J. R. (2003). The therapist's voice: Healing through connection–Self disclosure in psychotherapy. In S. Nye (Ed.), *Eating Disorders: The Journal of Treatment & Prevention, 11*(3), 235-240.

Reddington , F., and Wright-Kreisel, B. (2003). Basic fundamental skills training for juvenile probation officers–Results of a nationwide survey of curriculum content. *Federal Probation, 67*(1), 41-45.

Richardson, G. E., Neiger, B. L., Jensen, S., & Kumpfer, K. L. (1990). The resiliency model. *Health Education, 216*, 33-39.

Rogers, C. (1951). *Client-Centered Therapy: Its Current Practice, Implications, and Theory*. Boston, MA: Houghton Miflin.

Rogers, C. (1992). The necessary and sufficient conditions of therapeutic personality change. *Journal of Consulting & Clinical Psychology, 60*(6), 827-833.

Rutter, M. (1987). Resilience in the face of adversity: Protective factors and resistance to psychiatric disorder. *British Journal of Psychiatry, 147*, 598-611.

Rutter, M. (1990). Psychological resilience and protective mechanisms. In J. Rolf, A. S. Maste, D. Cicchetti, K. H. Nuechterlien, and S. Weintraub (Eds.), *Risk and Protective Factors in the Development of Psychopathology*. New York, NY: Cambridge University Press.

Smith, P., Gendreau, P., and Goggin, C. (2004). Correctional treatment: Accomplishments and realities. In P. Van Voorhis, M. Braswell, and D. Lester (Eds.), *Correctional Counseling and Rehabilitation, 5th Edition* (pp. 285-294). Cincinnati, OH: Anderson Publishing.

Stiles, W. B., Agnew-Davies, R., Hardy, G. E., Barkham, M., and Shapiro, D. A. (1998). Relations of the alliance with psychotherapy outcome: Findings in the second Sheffield Psychotherapy Project. *Journal of Consulting and Clinical Psychology, 66*, 791-802.

Taxman, F. (2002). Supervision–Exploring the dimensions of effectiveness. *Federal Probation, 66*(2), 14-27.

Torbet, P. M. (March, 1996). Juvenile probation: The workhorse of the juvenile justice system. *Juvenile Justice Bulletin*. Washington, DC: Office of Juvenile Justice and Delinquency Prevention.

Truax, C. B., and Carkhuff, R. R. (1967). *Toward Effective Counseling and Psychotherapy*. Chicago: Aldine.

Unger, D. G., and Wandersman. A. (1985). The importance of neighbors: The social, cognitive, and affective components of neighboring. *American Journal of Community Psychology, 13*, 139-169.

Van der Kolk, B. A. (1994). *Trauma and Development in Children*. Albany: State-Wide Grand Rounds, Sponsored by the Bureau of Psychiatric Services, New York State Department of Mental Health.

Werner, E. E. (1993). Risk, resilience, and recovery: Perspectives from the Kauai Longitudinal Study. *Development and Psychopathology, 5*, 503-515.

Werner, E. E., and Smith, R. S. (1992). *Overcoming the Odds: High Risk Children from Birth to Adulthood.* New York: Cornell University.

Whitehead, J., and Lab, S. (1989). A meta-analysis of juvenile correctional treatment. *Journal of Research in Crime and Delinquency, 26*, 276-295.

Yoshikawa, H. (1994). Prevention as cumulative protection: Effects of early family support and education on chronic juvenile delinquency and its risks. *Psychological Bulletin, 115*(1), 28-55.

AUTHORS' NOTES

Betsy Matthews earned her PhD in Criminal Justice from the University of Cincinnati and is now an Associate Professor, Departmental of Correctional and Juvenile Justice Studies at Eastern Kentucky University, 521 Lancaster Ave., Richmond, KY 40475.

Dana Hubbard earned her PhD in Criminal Justice from the University of Cincinnati and is now an Assistant Professor, Department of Sociology at Cleveland State University, 2121 Euclid Ave., Cleveland, OH.

doi:10.1300/J076v45n01_09

Mental Health Issues in the Criminal Justice System. Pp. 123-148.
Available online at http://jor.haworthpress.com
© *2007 by The Haworth Press, Inc. All rights reserved.*
doi:10.1300/J076v45n01_10

The Mental Health of Young Offenders Serving Orders in the Community: Implications for Rehabilitation

DIANNA T. KENNY
CHRISTOPHER J. LENNINGS
PAUL K. NELSON

ABSTRACT Young offenders internationally have a higher incidence of mental health problems compared with adolescents in the general population. Mental health issues, particularly comorbid presentations, affect the response to and outcome of rehabilitation and hence recidivism of offending. Most information on the mental health of young offenders has derived from studies of incarcerated young offenders, potentially a more disturbed sample of young people than the majority of young offenders who are placed on community orders. Our study investigated young offenders serving community-based orders (n = 800); the sample comprised almost 29% of the available population. Approximately 40% had at least one score in the severe range for psychopathology as assessed by the Adolescent Psychopathology Scale-Short Form (APS-SF) and 17% reported at least one comorbid condition. Twenty-six percent (26%) and 19% of young offenders scored in the severe range on the Substance Abuse and Conduct Disorder scales respectively and 8% scored in the severe range on both scales. Eighteen percent (18.5%; n = 145) had scores in the severe range for Substance Abuse and at least one other subscale (excluding Conduct Disorder); 10.8% (n = 85) had scores in the severe range for Conduct Disorder and at least one other subscale (excluding Substance Abuse); and 2.7% (n = 21) had scores in the severe range for at least two scales excluding Substance Abuse and Conduct Disorder. Young women reported between two and four times greater internalizing pathology and self-harm behavior than young men; however, young women were more characterized by externalizing disorders and anger than they were by depression or anxiety. Notwithstanding, high/very high levels of psychological distress were reported (25%) on the Kessler-10. This sample also reported high rates of child abuse and neglect on the Childhood Trauma Questionnaire and these experiences were associated with more severe externalizing pathology. In the year prior to the study, 8% of the sample had considered suicide, 5% had attempted suicide and 16% had considered or attempted other forms of self-harm. Although as a group the sample revealed high levels of behavioral disturbance and high needs for treatment, a low number reported engagement in any treatment. Recommendations for early intervention as well as tertiary treatment programs are considered. doi:10.1300/J076v45n01_10

KEYWORDS Juvenile offenders, mental health, child abuse, conduct disorders and substance misuse, rehabilitation

INTRODUCTION

There is a strong association between mental health, substance abuse and criminal offending in young offenders (The National Centre on Addiction and Substance Abuse at Columbia University (CASA), 2004; Gordon, Kinlock, & Battjes, 2004; Hammersley, Marsland, & Reid, 2003; Prichard & Payne, 2005) and longitudinal studies of delinquency (Dembo et al., 1991; Loeber & Farrington, 2001; Moffitt, 1997) highlight the important roles that mental health and substance abuse play in delaying the trajectory out of offending.

It is difficult to identify the absolute risk of mental health concerns in young offenders compared with the general adolescent population. A number of methodological issues including sampling practices, setting (e.g., custodial, treatment and community) and methods for determining mental health status affect outcomes. For example, mental health status has been assessed by psychiatric interview (Dixon, Howie, &

Starling, 2004), and psychometric examination [e.g., Adolescent Psychopathology Scale (APS) (Allerton et al., 2003; Bickel & Campbell, 2002); APS-Short Form (APS-SF) (Kenny et al., 2006); Child Behaviour Checklist (CBCL) and the MACI-111 (reported in Bickel & Campbell, 2002); and SCL-90R (Lennings & Prichard, 1999)]. While such sample and setting differences produce different estimates of risk, all studies report significantly elevated risks over general adolescent community samples. Grisso (1999) reported on three large studies from the United States that indicated juvenile offenders had a prevalence rate of mental health concerns (however defined) of 40% to 50%, with girls reporting higher rates than boys. Compared to the general population of adolescents, juvenile delinquents were four times more likely to be diagnosed with Conduct Disorder, 10 times more likely to be diagnosed with a Substance Abuse Disorder, and three times more likely to have an affective disorder. However, they had anxiety disorders at the same rate as the general population of adolescents.

Mental illness is a less clearly defined term for adolescents than adults except for that very small proportion who have been diagnosed with schizophrenia (Grisso, 1999). Adolescence represents a time of rapid physical, cognitive and emotional development, in which symptoms may appear and mutate, and in which the course of a problem is dynamic and may not achieve the stability usually assumed with adult manifestations of disorder (see Cicchetti & Rogosh, 2002). Conduct Disorder is one of the most frequently diagnosed conditions in adolescents, particularly in young offenders. There is a debate, however, as to whether Conduct Disorder is a psychopathological condition or a description of anti-social behaviour. For this report, we adopted an operational definition of mental health that was assessed by a series of norm-referenced psychological tests. Because we used the Adolescent Psychopathology Scale–Short Form (APS-SF), which includes Conduct Disorder as a subscale, Conduct Disorder is reported as one of the psychopathologies in young offenders. Insofar as Conduct Disorder is related to dysfunctional parenting and child abuse and neglect, the presence of this diagnosis may reflect contextual elements that explain offending behaviour (Van Zeijl et al., 2006).

The issue of comorbidity is also problematic for the categorical diagnostic system in current use. Kruger and Piasecki (2002) quote findings from a large epidemiological survey in the United States that revealed that 79% of all respondents with at least one lifetime diagnosis of a mental illness reported an additional diagnosis. Further, 59% of the sample had comorbidity for three or more disorders within the last 12 months.

Kruger and Piasecki (2002) argued for a dimensional approach, based on the observation that even in adult populations diagnoses are not stable, that comorbidity is the norm, not the exception, and that studies using path analytic and confirmatory factor analytic approaches to diagnosis have revealed that the super-ordinate dimensions of Internalising and Externalising Disorders may be more useful. Whitmore et al. (1997) noted the high co-occurrence between Conduct Disorder, Attention Deficit Hyperactivity Disorder and Substance Abuse in an incarcerated adolescent population. They also noted a high correspondence between these disorders and depression in young substance-dependent persons. Dixon, Howie and Starling (2004) assessed 100 female offenders and found that while Conduct Disorder and Substance Abuse diagnoses were most prevalent, 55% met criteria for a diagnosis of Depression, 37% for a diagnosis of Post Traumatic Stress Disorder and 9% for Psychosis. Seventy-eight percent of the sample had three or more diagnoses, an indicator of complex cases with poor prognostic outcomes.

An assessment of self-harm and suicide should form part of any mental health assessment, particularly in adolescence. Expectations of lethality vary among different samples of suicidal youth (Howard et al., 2003) and the boundary between deliberate self-harm and suicide can be difficult to discern. Self-harm may occur on a continuum of maladaptive behaviors and similar factors may predict criminality, substance abuse and violence (Lennings, 1994). Lifetime suicidal ideation in the general adolescent population has been estimated at 29.9% (Evans et al., 2005). Rates of self-harm in the general adolescent population vary from 6.2% to 12.4% (DeLeo & Heller, 2004). In Australian young offenders, suicide has been identified as the leading cause of mortality after drug-related deaths (Coffey et al., 2003). The assessment of incidence and prevalence of self-harm can vary based on the means of assessment (self-report, clinical interview or psychometric instruments (see Goldston, 2003).

Help Seeking. Although juvenile justice systems were established with the expectation that they would provide appropriate rehabilitative strategies, there appears to be a somewhat pessimistic perception regarding the effectiveness of treatment amongst young people (Gorske, Srebalus, & Walls, 2003) especially those who exhibit antisocial features. In an authoritative meta-analysis of 69 studies of programs investigating the impact of treatments within the criminal justice system to reduce drug related crime, Holloway, Bennett and Farrington (2005) concluded that offenders assigned to treatment were 41% more likely to show a reduction in criminal behavior than non-treated groups. Forty-four of 52 studies analyzed were effective in reducing crime on at least one measure.

Treatment was more effective for juvenile than for adult offenders. However, young offenders do not actively seek out treatment and are hard to maintain in treatment. Young offenders are also highly mobile, have low psychosocial stability, and relatively low levels of social support, all additional factors that affect the maintenance in and outcomes of treatment.

The aim of this paper was to report the outcomes of screening for mental health concerns in young offenders serving community orders and to (i) assess the relationship between Conduct Disorder, substance use and child abuse and neglect history, (ii) the degree of comorbidity; (iii) self-harm and suicidal ideation and behaviour; and (iv) help seeking and treatment.

METHOD

Ethics

Ethics approval was independently granted by the University of Sydney Human Research Ethics Committee, the Research Applications Subcommittee of the Department of Juvenile Justice Collaborative Research Unit, Justice Health Human Research & Ethics Committee (formerly Corrections Health), and the Aboriginal Health and Medical Research Council. Written consent was required as a condition of participation. Parental consent was required for participants under the age of 14 years.

Participants and Procedures

The sample was comprised of young offenders serving community orders with the New South Wales (NSW) Department of Juvenile Justice (DJJ) between October 2003 and December 2005. Eligibility was limited to those on supervised, community-based orders during the study period. Supervised orders issued by the courts are either custodial or community-based. Custodial orders confine a young person to detention for a specified period of time. The large majority of supervised orders, however, are served in the community, and the Department supervises young offenders who receive supervised good behaviour bonds and probation orders, community service work orders, parole orders and suspended sentences. The Department also supervises young offenders on conditional bail and those remanded in custody pending finalization of their court matters. Clients on custody and/or bail orders only or dealt with under Section 32 or 33 of the *Mental Health (Criminal Procedure) Act 1990* (amended via the *Crimes Legislation Amendment Act 2002*) were excluded. These latter exclusions may have resulted in an underestimation of mental health indicators and substance abuse.

Approximately 4,036 young offenders were serving a community-based supervision order with DJJ during the study period. They were supervised in one of the JJCS (Juvenile Justice Community Service Centres) offices located throughout the state of New South Wales, Australia. Participants were interviewed in locations across NSW that were stratified into three main areas: Sydney, Other Metropolitan and Regional. Sydney is the major metropolitan centre of NSW. Other metropolitan includes the other major cities in NSW (Wollongong, Newcastle and Gosford, each with populations of more than 100,000). Regional includes smaller cities and towns (e.g., Albury, Dubbo, and Lismore). Young offenders were classified according to the DJJ office responsible for supervision of their community order; hence, some of those interviewed in regional DJJ offices may have been from remote areas supervised by that office. This method applied adapted classification rules from the RRMA (Rural, Remote and Metropolitan Areas), and ASGC (Australian Standard Geographical Classification) systems (ASGC, 2005; Aylward & Bamford, 2000). Remoteness, according to these classifications, describes areas in terms of relative distance from, and population size of, Australia's major cities and regional areas.

Clients from 22 of the 38 Juvenile Justice offices were seen at 39 sites during the study period. Some were visited on multiple occasions, some on only one occasion due to geographical distance and cost. Approximately 50% (469) of the clients in sites visited once only were either not eligible to participate because they were not on orders at the time of testing or were not available on the day the testing team arrived. There were 745 young offenders in sites not visited. The sample frame therefore comprised 2,822 young offenders, of whom 800 were included as participants in the study. Of the 2,022 who did not participate, approximately 1,000 either did not respond to several attempts to contact them or failed to attend after several bookings were made; approximately 500 were approached but refused to participate; approximately 400 had no current contact details; 100 (90 males and 10 females) were excluded because of serious mental health problems, substance withdrawal or excessively disruptive behavior on the day of testing.

The final sample comprised 800 young offenders: 682 (85%) males and 118 (15%) females. This gender distribution matched the population gender distribution during the study period, but regional and ethnic distributions were somewhat different (see Table 1). Our sample included 155 (19%) Indigenous young people (i.e., those of Aboriginal and Torres Strait Islander origin) who were underrepresented in our sample compared to DJJ population proportions (33%). Mean age of the total sample was 17 years. The sample was segmented into five subgroups to compare mental health indicators by gender; ethnicity [English Speaking Background (ESB); Indigenous; Culturally and Linguistically Diverse (CALD)]; region [Urban (i.e., Sydney), Outer Metropolitan and Regional)]; IQ (<70; 70-84; 85+); and age (<16; >16 years). Table 1

	Table 1: Sample and Comparative Population Characteristics					
	YPoCOHS		CO population[i]		NSW	
	N	%	N	%	N	%
Male	682	85.3	3429	85	430K	51[ii]
Female	118	14.8	607	15	414K	49[ii]
ESB	527	65.9	2154*	55.8		18[iii]
Indigenous	155	19.4	1275**	33	n/a	2[iii]
CALD	118	14.8	253*	6.5		20[iii]
Sydney	603	75.4	1809	44.8	–	68[iv]
Other metro	95	11.9	572	14.2	–	32[iv]
Regional	102	12.8	1413	41.0^	–	
IQ <70	119	15.2				2[v]
IQ 70-84	307	39.3	n/a		n/a	13[v]
IQ 85+	355	45.5				85[v]
<16 years	176	22	606	15	–	–
16+ years	624	78	3430	85	–	–

i Data extracted from NSW Department of Juvenile Justice Client Information Management System
ii & iii Australian Bureau of Statistics Cdata01. ii: young offenders aged 15-24; iii: all ages
iv Australian Bureau of Statistics: Australian Social Trends 2006 Table 2.1: NSW
v Wechsler Abbreviated Scale of Intelligence Full Scale IQ tables
* 181 (4.5%) non-Indigenous young offenders had no recorded ethnicity data
** 173 (4.3%) young offenders had no recorded Indigenous status or ethnicity data
^ Includes 242 (6%) from rural and remote areas not visited by YPoCOHS

shows the sample (YPoCOHS: Young People on Community Orders Health Survey), the DJJ population on community orders during the study period from which it was drawn (CO), and young offenders aged 12-21 in NSW by gender, ethnicity, region, IQ and age.

Measures

Adolescent Psychopathology Scale–Short Form (APS-SF)

The Adolescent Psychopathology Scale–Short Form (APS-SF) is a multidimensional measure that generates 12 clinical scales to assess a range of psychological and psychiatric symptoms and two validity scales to assess the consistency of responding and the degree of defensiveness in responding to the items on the test (Reynolds, 2000). It is derived from the Adolescent Psychopathology Scale (APS), has been extensively standardised on a USA population, and demonstrates significant correlations with scales from the MMPI and other psychosocial measures (Reynolds, 2000). Six clinical scales focus on DSM-IV (APA 1994) symptomatology associated with Conduct Disorder, Oppositional Defiant Disorder, Post-Traumatic Stress Disorder, Generalised Anxiety Disorder, Major Depressive Disorder and Substance Abuse Disorder (Reynolds, 2000). Conduct Disorder and Oppositional Defiant Disorder are the most commonly reported externalizing disorders in conjunction with adolescent substance abuse in the literature; depression and anxiety are the most commonly reported Internalizing disorders. The other six clinical scales assess domains of adolescent psychosocial problems and competencies (Reynolds, 2000).

Cronbach's alpha demonstrated high internal consistency of the APS-SF clinical scales (range: α = .80 to .91; CND = .80, SUB = .85). High test-retest reliability is not typically expected of measures of adolescent psychopathology over extended time frames due (for example) to routine fluctuations in mood-based symptoms (Reynolds, 2000). Reasonable short-term reliability is desirable, however, to demonstrate that scores are not purely related to external factors. R_{tt} for the APS-SF was moderately high to high, ranging from .76 to .91 (CND = .76; SUB = .86). Test-retest reliability measures were conducted on 64 adolescents, at a two-week interval.

The APS-SF mean T score is 50 [Standard Deviation (SD) = 10]; T scores from 65 to 69 are coded in the mild clinical symptom range; T scores from 70 to 79 in the moderate clinical symptom range; T scores of 80 and above are coded in the severe clinical symptom range. Elevated scores (T = 65 and above) are not diagnostic of DSM-IV disorders but provide an indication of possible disorders that may require direct and expeditious referral or intervention (Reynolds, 2000).

Prior to interpretation of the scores on the APS-SF, an assessment of consistency and defensiveness of responding was conducted for the key subgroups of the sample (gender, region, ethnicity, IQ, age). Ninety-six percent (96%) of APS-SF protocols were responded to consistently according to the APS-SF consistency scale. Inconsistency was not related to any of the grouping variables. Inconsistent protocols were removed prior to analysis of the APS-SF results. An analysis of the defensiveness scale of the APS-SF by key subgroups indicated that CALD were more likely to score in the moderate or severe range for Defensiveness on the APS-SF than either of the other ethnic subgroups. No other subgroup differences in defensiveness were found. Given the higher CALD defensiveness pattern, CALD results on the APS-SF may represent an underreporting of psychopathology for this group.

Kessler Psychological Distress Scale (K-10 LM)

The Kessler Psychological Distress Scale (K-10 LM) (Kessler et al., 2002) is a 10-item questionnaire yielding a global measure of psychosocial distress. The questions examine the level of anxiety and depressive symptoms experienced in the previous four weeks. Scores range from 10 (no distress) to 50 (severe distress) and are categorized into four groups: low (10 to 15), moderate (16 to 21), high (22-29) and very high (over 30). Scores in the very high range are associated with a high probability of having an anxiety or depressive disorder (Andrews & Slade 2001). Population norms suggest that between 11% and 12% of the general population have high to very high scores on the K-10 (Andrews & Slade, 2001). Because this is the first time that the K-10 has been used in an adolescent sample, reliability was assessed using Cronbach's alpha = .835.

Childhood Trauma Questionnaire (CTQ)

The Childhood Trauma Questionnaire (CTQ) (Bernstein & Fink, 1998) examines experiences of physical, emotional and sexual abuse and assesses the degree to which people minimize or deny experiences of abuse or trauma. Scores are classified as low, moderate, or severe depending on the level of abuse.

Prior to interpretation of scores on the CTQ, an assessment of minimization and denial was conducted for the key subgroups of the sample (gender, regions, ethnicity, IQ, age). Thirty-eight percent (38.2%) of profiles indicated responses in the moderate to severe range for minimization and denial. Forty percent (40%; n = 270) males and (29%; n = 35) females endorsed items on the Minimization/Denial Scale of the CTQ, suggesting substantial underreporting of abuse, neglect or trauma. ESB (n = 177; 33.7%) were significantly less likely to minimize or deny abuse than either Indigenous (n = 67; 43.5%) or CALD (n = 60; 52%). Young offenders with an intellectual disability (n = 61; 51.7%) and young offenders with IQ70-84 (n = 137; 44.6%) were more likely to have scores in the moderate/severe range on the CTQ than young offenders with IQ > 85 (28.4%). No other subgroup differences in minimization or denial were found. Given the overall high level of minimization and denial in this sample, results on the CTQ may represent an underreporting of abuse and neglect, in particular for the CALD group and for young offenders with an intellectual disability.

Assessment of Suicide and Self-Harm Ideation and Behavior

The physical health questionnaire was modeled on a number of adolescent health surveys addressing health care needs, risk behaviours and service utilization. These included the Youth Risk Behaviour Questionnaire (YRBQ) (Brener et al., 1995), Youth Risk Behavior Survey (CDC 2001), Western Australian Child Health Survey (Zubrick et al., 1994), National Longitudinal Survey of Children and Youth (Sprott Jenkins & Doob, 2000), Young Offender Risk and Protective Factor Survey (Carroll, 2002), NSW Corrections Health's Inmate Health Surveys (Brown & Butler, 1997; Butler & Milner, 2003), National Household Drug Use Survey (AIHW, 2002), Adolescent Health and Wellbeing Survey (Bond et al., 1998), and The National Longitudinal Study of Adolescent Health (Udry, 1998). Some items were adapted for this sample.

Statistical Analyses

Subgroup differences assessed by categorical variables were assessed using Pearson's Chi Square, and analysis of variance (ANOVA) was used to assess group differences for continuous variables. Because of the large number of analyses conducted, we avoided the risk of spuriously significant findings by setting the p value for the Chi square tests at <.001. We also assessed the standardized residuals for cell proportions and report only those values >2.14 (1.5 SD units). Except where otherwise indicated, trends were identified for p values <0.01.

RESULTS

Adolescent Psychopathology Scale–Short Form

Forty percent (40%; 311) (40% males, 38% females) reported symptoms in the severe range on at least one subscale. Twenty-six percent (26%; 207) reported symptoms of Substance Abuse Disorder in the severe range; (19%; 147) reported symptoms of Conduct Disorder in the severe range, the most prevalent disorders occurring in the severe range (Table 2); and four percent (4%; 27) reported symptoms for Academic Problems in the severe range. As predicted by defensiveness patterns, CALD (74.3%) were significantly less likely than ESB (60.6%) or Indigenous (56.7%) to have scores in the severe clinical range. Table 2 presents percentages of young offenders with scores in the mild, moderate and severe ranges of the APS-SF. On the Conduct Disorder and Substance Abuse Disorder scales, 52% males and 54% females scored in the normal range for Substance Abuse Disorder; 49% males and 57% females scored in the normal range for Conduct Disorder.

Proportions of young offenders with Substance Abuse Disorder scores in the severe range were as follows: ESB (n = 151; 29.9%); Indigenous (n = 35; 23.2%); CALD (n = 21; 19.3%). ESB were significantly more likely than CALD to have a Substance Abuse Disorder. Proportions of young offenders with Conduct Disorder scores in the severe range were as follows: ESB (n = 90; 17.8%); Indigenous (n = 32; 21.3%); CALD (n = 15; 13.8%). Indigenous were significantly more · likely to have a Conduct Disorder than either ESB or CALD. Younger offenders (<16 years) were more likely to have scores in the severe range on the Conduct Disorder scale (n = 48; 28.7%) than older offenders (n = 99; 16.6%) but were less likely to have scores in the severe range on Substance Abuse Disorder (n = 33; 19.8%) than older offenders (n = 174; 29.2%). Males (n = 74; 11.4%) were less likely (trend) to have two or more scores in the severe range on the APS-SF than females (n = 22; 19.3%).

☐ Table 2: APS-SF Scale Scores in the Mild, Moderate and Severe Range (%)						
	Mild		Moderate		Severe	
APS-SF scales	Male	Female	Male	Female	Male	Female
Substance Abuse Disorder	9	8	13	9	26	29
Conduct Disorder	9	8	23	17	19	18
Academic Problems	11	10	13	12	3	6
Anger/Violence Problems	12	14	14	23	3	5
Posttraumatic Stress Disorder	7	13	7	14	2	4
Suicide	3	2	4	10	1	4
Oppositional Defiant Disorder	9	12	7	9	1	5
Interpersonal Problems	7	15	4	11	1	1
Major Depression	5	9	3	12	1	3
Self-Concept Problems	6	8	3	3	<1	3
Eating Disorders	3	11	3	9	<1	3
Generalized Anxiety Disorder	1	9	2	7	<1	3

Male: Community = 666-668; Female: Community = 117

The APS-SF subscale profiles of the sample were examined to identify comorbid psychopathology, defined as scores in the severe range on two or more subscales. Thirty percent (30%) had scores in the severe range on two APS subscales and 13% (n = 101) reported symptoms (in the severe range) on more than two clinical disorders. Of particular interest were profiles that had comorbid Substance Abuse Disorder and Conduct Disorder, and either of these disorders in conjunction with any other disorder assessed by the APS-SF. For the sample as a whole: 10% (n = 80) had scores in the severe range for Substance Abuse and at least one other subscale (excluding Conduct Disorder); 10.8% (n = 85) had scores in the severe range for Conduct Disorder and at least one other subscale (excluding Substance Abuse); 8.0% (n = 62) had scores in the severe range for both Substance Abuse and Conduct Disorder; and 2.7% (n = 21) had scores in the severe range for at least two scales excluding Substance Abuse and Conduct Disorder. Of those young people scoring in the severe range for Conduct Disorder, significantly more (57%) reported that at least one of their close relatives abused drugs or alcohol.

K-10 Psychological Distress Scores

Figure 1 summarizes the distribution of scores on the K-10 by gender.

Twenty-five percent (25%; 193) community sample had high or very high psychological distress, consistent with a greater than 50% chance of having an anxiety or depressive disorder; 7% (56) had an 80% chance of having an anxiety or depressive disorder [6%; 42 males; 12%; (7) females)]. More females (n = 40; 35.7%) tended to score in the high/very high range on K-10 than males (n = 153; 23.0%). There were no other significant differences with respect to distribution of K-10 scores across the other key subgroupings. The correlation between the K-10 and the anxiety and depression scales on the APS-SF were r = .59 and r = .67 respectively, both significant at p < .001. Correlations with Conduct Disorder and Substance Abuse Disorder with K-10 were also significant (p = .05) (CD = .21, SUB = .25).

The relationship between concurrent self-reported substance use and psychological distress was also assessed. Table 3 shows the association between the proportion of young offenders who reported high/very high psychological distress and no, single and poly substance use in the past four weeks.

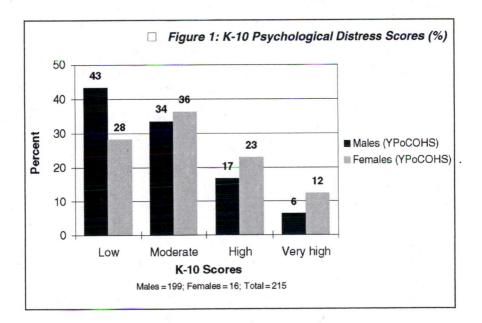

☐ **Table 3: Numbers and (Percentages) of Young People Abusing Substances in Past Four Weeks and Score Range on K-10**

Drug use in past 4 weeks	K-10		Total
	low/moderate	high/very high	
No drug use in last 4 weeks	244	54	298
	(81.9)	(18.1)	
Single drug use in last 4 weeks	239	80	319
	(74.9)	(25.1)	
Poly drug use in last 4 weeks	96	58	154
	(62.3%)	(37.7%)	
Total	579	192	771

Poly drug users were significantly more likely to score in the high/very high range on the K-10 than those who had not used drugs in the past four weeks. Similarly, those young offenders with scores in the severe range on the Substance Abuse Disorder Scale of the APS-SF were significantly more likely to score in the high/very high range on K-10 compared to those with scores in the lower ranges (35.7% vs. 21.2%).

The Childhood Trauma Questionnaire (CTQ)

Seventy-two percent (72%) of young people had experienced some form of abuse or neglect in their childhood (low, moderate, or severe abuse or neglect). Table 4 presents the percentages of young offenders who reported abuse and/or neglect on the CTQ in the low, moderate and severe ranges.

Females reported significantly more abuse and neglect in the severe range than males on all categories of abuse and neglect on the CTQ.

Figure 2 presents the results for the young offender sample by gender with comparative normative scores for males and females taken from the manual of the CTQ using the population (adolescent psychiatric inpatients) on which the test was normed. The figure shows that young offenders reported similar levels and patterns of abuse and neglect as those young people receiving inpatient psychiatric treatment.

Females (n = 14; 12.3%) were four times more likely than males (n = 19; 3%) to report three or more severe forms of abuse and significantly less likely than males to report no abuse (females: n = 71; 62%; males: n = 508; 78.3%). Males and females did not differ with respect to

Table 4: Percentages of Young Offenders in Each of the Childhood Trauma Questionnaire Scale Score Classifications

CTQ scales	Low		Moderate		Severe	
	Males	Females	Males	Females	Males	Females
Emotional Abuse	24	30	10	14	9	20
Physical Abuse	17	16	5	11	8	14
Sexual Abuse	3	8	4	19	2	11
Emotional Neglect	29	28	11	6	9	23
Physical Neglect	17	11	11	18	8	16
Any abuse (above)	59	58	32	45	23	38

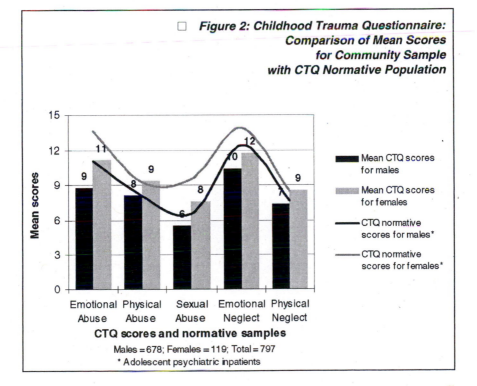

Figure 2: Childhood Trauma Questionnaire: Comparison of Mean Scores for Community Sample with CTQ Normative Population

Males = 678; Females = 119; Total = 797
* Adolescent psychiatric inpatients

their reporting of one or two severe forms of abuse. Table 5 shows that young people with scores in the severe range for Conduct Disorder scored significantly higher on the emotional and physical abuse scales of the CTQ than those not scoring in the severe range for Conduct Disorder. There were no differences for sexual abuse or emotional or physical neglect between the two groups.

Table 6 shows that for all scales on the CTQ, those young people with scores in the severe range for Substance Abuse scored significantly higher than those not scoring in the severe range for substance abuse.

Suicide and Self-Harm

Seventeen percent (17%) of the sample reported suicidal ideation; 9% reported a suicide attempt in their lifetime. Eight percent (8%) reported recent (in the last year) suicidal ideation and 5% reported a recent (in the last year) suicide attempt. Self-harm ideation and gesture rates were almost double the suicide rates. Young women were more than twice as likely to report self-harm and suicide ideation and to report

☐ Table 5: Analysis of Variance for CTQ Scales (Raw Scores) by Conduct Disorder Categories						
	N	Category	Mean	SD	F	Sig.
Emotional Abuse	636	Not severe	8.94	4.31	8.24	0.004
	146	Severe	10.10	4.82		
	782	Total	9.16	4.43		
Physical Abuse	636	Not severe	8.10	4.18	7.77	0.005
	146	Severe	9.22	5.20		
	782	Total	8.31	4.40		
Sexual Abuse	636	Not severe	5.80	2.74	0.53	0.467
	146	Severe	5.99	2.99		
	782	Total	5.84	2.78		
Emotional Neglect	636	Not severe	10.44	4.75	2.17	0.141
	146	Severe	11.08	4.87		
	782	Total	10.56	4.77		
Physical Neglect	636	Not severe	7.47	3.17	1.10	0.294
	146	Severe	7.77	2.98		
	782	Total	7.53	3.14		

CTQ scale	N	Category	Mean	SD	F	Sig.

☐ **Table 6: Analysis of Variance for CTQ Scales (Raw Scores) by Substance Abuse Categories**

CTQ scale	N	Category	Mean	SD	F	Sig.
Emotional Abuse	573	Not severe	8.81	4.13	13.27	0.000
	207	Severe	10.10	5.00		
	780	Total	9.15	4.41		
Physical Abuse	573	Not severe	7.97	4.01	12.65	0.000
	207	Severe	9.23	5.28		
	780	Total	8.30	4.41		
Sexual Abuse	573	Not severe	5.71	2.55	4.62	0.032
	207	Severe	6.19	3.33		
	780	Total	5.84	2.79		
Emotional Neglect	573	Not severe	10.31	4.69	6.70	0.010
	207	Severe	11.30	4.94		
	780	Total	10.57	4.78		
Physical Neglect	573	Not severe	7.31	3.03	10.75	0.001
	207	Severe	8.14	3.37		
	780	Total	7.53	3.14		

self-harm and suicide attempts. Table 7 summarizes the suicide and self-harm information for males and females. The sample overall reported a decrease in active self-harm ideation over the last year, but a small group reported an increase in ideation.

Seventy-one (71) young offenders (50 males and 21 females) reported self-harming. Multiple responses were permitted for self-harm methods. Methods in order of frequency were attempted hanging (37%: 42% males, 24% females); cutting/slashing of wrists (32%: 18% males; 67% females); and overdoses (30%: 26% boys, 39% females).

Recent self-harm attempters were more likely to report high K-10 · scores (21.6 vs 24.22 t = −2.37, d.f. 126, p < .05); higher APS-SF Depression scores (55.8 vs 60.30, t = −2.26, d.f. 126, p < .05); higher Conduct Disorder scores (63.47 vs 69.82, t = −2.26, d.f. 125, p < .01); and higher substance abuse scores (67.66 vs 77.51, t = −3.05, d.f. 126, p < .01). Those who reported a recent self-harm attempt were more likely to report any high score on the CTQ (n = 23; 12.2%) compared to low CTQ scores (n = 44; 7.5%). Whilst the trends were in the same direction for suicide attempts, the results did not reach statistical significance.

□ **Table 7: Percentages and Frequencies (n) of Suicidal and Self-Harm Ideation and Behaviour in Young Offenders Ever and in Past 12 Months**

	Males	Females	Total
Suicidal Ideation			
Considered suicide (ever)	14 (92)	32 (37)	17 (129)
Considered suicide (past 12m)	7 (47)	14 (16)	8 (63)
Made suicide plan (ever)	9 (59)	13 (15)	9 (74)
Made suicide plan (past 12m)	5 (32)	8 (9)	5 (41)
Self-harm Ideation			
Considered self-harm (ever)	19 (125)	40 (46)	22 (171)
Considered self-harm (past 12m)	10 (66)	27 (31)	12 (97)
Made plan to self-harm (past 12m)	4 (26)	13 (15)	5 (41)
Self-harm ideation decreased*	7 (43)	18 (21)	(64)
Self-harm ideation increased*	1 (9)	3 (3)	(12)
Suicide Attempts			
Attempted suicide (ever)	8 (52)	18 (21)	9 (73)
Attempted suicide (past 12m)	4 (27)	9 (10)	5 (37)
One suicide attempt (past 12m)	2 (13)	2 (2)	2 (15)
2-3 suicide attempts (past 12m)	2 (12)	4 (4)	2 (16)
>3 suicide attempts (past 12m)	<1 (2)	4 (4)	<1 (6)
Self-Harm Attempts			
Self-harm (ever)	15 (98)	28 (32)	17 (140)
Self-harm (past 12m)	7 (49)	16 (18)	9 (67)
1 self-harm incident (past 12m)	2 (16)	2 (2)	2 (18)
2-3 self-harm incidents (past 12m)	3 (20)	7 (8)	4 (28)
>3 self-harm incidents (past 12m)	2 (12)	4 (5)	2 (17)

Males = 665-667; Females = 114-116; Total = 779-783

Treatment

Thirty-three percent (33%) of young offenders reported that they had been diagnosed by a health professional with at least one mental health or behavioural problem. Of those who could recall receiving a diagnosis, most reported that they had received some treatment. Table 8 shows mental health disorders with which young offenders reported to have been diagnosed and the proportion of those diagnosed who had received treatment for the disorder. The most common self-reported disorders were ADHD/ADD/hyperactivity (19%) and depression (6%). The majority of those diagnosed report they received at least one session of treatment (Table 8).

	% diagnosed/
Table 8: Reported Mental Health Diagnoses and Treatment (n) (%)	
Mental health problem	treated (n)
Anxiety Disorders	2/1 (15)
ADHD, ADD, Hyperactivity	19/17 (144)
Conduct Disorder, Oppositional Defiant Disorder	2/2 (16)
Depression	6/5 (48)
Other mood disorder (non-depressive, elevated mood)	2/1 (10)
Intellectual Disability, Learning Difficulties	1/<1 (9)
Schizophrenia, psychotic disorder	3/2 (24)
Acute Stress Disorder, Post-Traumatic Stress Disorder	1/<1 (8)
Anger Management problems	4/3 (29)
Other	1/1 (9)

Males = 665-669; Females = 117; Total = 783-786

Help Seeking Behaviour

Psychiatrists (n = 243, 30.9%) and psychologists (n = 198, 25.2%) were most frequently seen, with a median number of four visits to a psychiatrist and five to a psychologist. Of those seen, 21.8% (n = 53) reported seeing a psychiatrist more than 10 times; 33% (n = 66) reported seeing a psychologist more than 10 times. Whilst Table 8 reveals relatively high rates of treatment for those formally identified with a mental health problem, we suspect that, other than those receiving stimulant medication for ADHD, there appear to be low rates of formal treatment provision. Despite relatively high levels of substance abuse (40%) and high involvement of substance abuse in crime, only 18% reported any substance abuse treatment, and of this group, only 7% reported engaging in formal drug abuse treatment.

DISCUSSION

This sample provides the first estimate of general psychological morbidity in young offenders serving community orders within the State of New South Wales, Australia. Relatively high rates of mental health problems were identified in our sample; 40% had scores in the severe range for the externalizing disorders–Conduct Disorder or Substance

Abuse Disorder. There were few gender differences. Although the APS-SF is only a screening instrument and hence false positives (and negatives) may occur, the use of only the severe category as a diagnostic marker of diagnosis minimizes the possibility that non-clinically impaired participants were identified as cases inappropriately. Further, since the APS assesses symptoms over a two-week to six-month period, and hence is not a prevalence measure, the data may have provided more conservative estimates of the prevalence of mental health concerns in our sample of young offenders compared with overseas data, which mostly provide prevalence rates for incarcerated young offenders (Chitsabesan & Bailey, 2006).

Comorbidity was identified in 18% of the sample, a figure lower than commonly reported, perhaps reflecting the strict definition of comorbidity used in the study (scores in the severe range on at least two scales of the APS-SF). Compared with other samples, primarily incarcerated young people, our study reveals that there are reasonably consistent levels of overall psychological vulnerability in young offender populations (Balenko & Dembo, 2003; Grisso, 1999). The degree of psychopathology revealed in our sample of young women is less than that generally reported in the literature (largely based on incarcerated young women: Dixon et al., 2004; Richards, 1996). Our sample revealed a group of young women characterized more by externalizing than internalizing disorders, a finding consistent with a recent comparison of male and female detained youth which showed higher than expected psychopathy indicators in females (Gavazzi, Yarcheck, & Chesney-Lind, 2006).

Our study is the first to our knowledge to use the K-10 with adolescents. The measure was reliable for this sample and the pattern of correlations with the APS-SF scale revealed primary associations with internalizing rather than externalizing disorders, as expected given the item content. Possible diagnoses of anxiety and depression were reflected in the relatively high levels of psychological distress reported by the sample, with 25% scoring in the high/very high range. Young women were more likely to report high distress than young men. Significantly greater numbers of participants scored higher on the K-10, as a measure of psychological distress, than in the severe range of scales assessing the internalizing disorders on the APS-SF. The K-10 assesses psychological distress over a four-week period whilst the items assessing anxiety and depression are assessed over a two-week period on the APS-SF. It is possible that the different time periods captured a greater range of distress on the K-10. It is also the case that the K-10 is a more general screening measure than the APS and by its nature more likely to identify false positives. Research is needed to assess the sensitivity and specificity of this measure for adolescent populations in general and young offender populations in particular.

Self-harm and suicide attempts were reported by the sample at similar rates to a sample of incarcerated young offenders (Allerton et al., 2003). Self-harm and suicidal behavior were strongly related to both internalizing and externalizing disorders, indicating that it is the psychological distress associated with the lifestyle of young offenders that constitutes the risk for these young people (Rohde, Seeley, & Mace, 1997). Baumeister (1990) identified self-harming behaviours as occurring on a continuum of maladaptive problem solving and avoidance behaviours of young people unable to envisage adaptive solutions to the crises occurring in adolescence.

Our community-based sample of young offenders had lower levels of psychopathology compared with a similar sample of incarcerated young offenders in the same juvenile justice jurisdiction (Allerton et al., 2003). Our data provide reason for caution against extrapolating findings from incarcerated young offenders or those attending mental health assessment clinics to those serving community-based orders. The risk of over-pathologizing community-based young offender populations may have significant implications for service planning and delivery. Community-based offenders appear to fit between incarcerated young offenders and the general adolescent population, since they showed lower rates of mental health issues compared with incarcerated youth and higher rates compared with the general adolescent population (Davies, Martin, Kosky, & O'Hanlon, 2000).

Both Conduct Disorder and substance abuse were strongly associated with childhood histories of severe abuse. Our findings support the contention that Conduct Disorder is related to dysfunctional parenting as represented by the higher rates of emotional and physical abuse experienced by young people who scored in the severe range on Conduct Disorder compared to those who did not, and that this diagnosis is indeed reflective of contextual elements rather than intrapersonal characteristics (Van Zeijl et al., 2006). Other research (Lennings, Kenny, Howard, Arcuri, & Mackdacy, in press) shows a clear relationship between youth offending, dysfunctional family background and mental health concerns. The more negative the family background the greater the involvement in substance abuse. A positive family background was protective against incarceration. In the current study, a strong association on all CTQ scales was observed for participants who scored in the severe range for Substance Abuse Disorder on the APS-SF. Substance abuse appears to be a (mal) adaptive response to the emotional distress that accrues to experiences of abuse during childhood. Current treatment programs for substance abusing young offenders need to maintain a strong focus on the management of issues related to abuse and abandonment in their programming. Referring, engaging and maintaining substance abusing young offenders is a major challenge confronting those in the field.

Our study, consistent with other reports (Balenko & Dembo, 2003; Newman, 1998; Wei, Makkai, & McGregor, 2003), indicated both low rates of referral to appropriate treatment and low uptake of treatment once offered. This finding concurred with another recent Australian study (Wei et al., 2003) that found that only 13% of 493 drug-abusing young offenders in a detained police sample had accessed treatment for substance abuse. The British Home Office study (Hammersley et al., 2003) found that 25% of the 293 young offenders in that sample had accessed treatment. Comparatively speaking, our sample appears to have accessed treatment at lower rates than those studies, although it should be noted that most studies did not identify the nature of treatment young people accessed or their compliance with it. Where a young person was identified as suffering from a psychiatric diagnosis, treatment followed. However, the most prevalent problem for our sample was substance abuse followed by Conduct Disorder. There was very little uptake of formal treatments of substance abuse, and the percentage of young offenders formerly diagnosed and treated for Conduct Disorder was well below the rate for the disorder as identified by the APS-SF. Whilst much emphasis deservedly should be placed on early intervention and primary prevention, analyses of gains made by treatment exposure show that tertiary treatment strategies, if properly constituted and of appropriate sensitivity, are well worthwhile (Holloway et al., 2005).

Appropriate, standardized mental health assessment protocols and policies within juvenile justice authorities that mandate such assessments once young people enter the juvenile justice system are needed to improve appropriate and timely referral for treatment for young offenders. Some progress toward achieving this goal has been made (Bailey et al., 2006; Grisso et al., 2005).

In summary, our study has revealed that community offenders tend towards similar overall rates of psychopathology as incarcerated offenders, but have lower rates of comorbidity. It is likely that incarcerated offenders represent a particularly problematic subgroup of young offenders, and data presented on incarcerated offenders may not be representative of the majority of young offenders who do not receive a custodial sentence. Notwithstanding, young offenders in the community showed high rates of externalizing disorders, substance abuse and child abuse/ neglect. They remain a highly psychologically vulnerable population with high rates of psychological distress. Compared with the general adolescent population they also showed high rates of self-harm and suicidal intent. Young women on community disorders appear to have significantly lower levels of psychopathology than their incarcerated counterparts, and despite the higher rates of internalizing disorders revealed in young women, they remain as a group more likely to exhibit higher rates of externalizing disorders.

Lower levels of pathology (such as in depression and comorbid presentations) in our sample may be due to our conservative inclusion criteria as well as the unavoidable exclusions in our sample of the most psychologically disturbed subgroup. Nonetheless, the pattern of findings reported here and elsewhere provides a strong mandate and direction for intervention with this vulnerable, disadvantaged group of young people.

REFERENCES

Allerton, M., Champion, U., Beilby, R., Butler, T., Fasher, M., Kenny, D., Murphy, M., & Vecchiato, C. (2003). *2003 NSW Young People in Custody Healthy Survey. Key Findings Report.* NSW Department of Juvenile Justice, New South Wales Government.

American Psychiatric Association (APA) (1994). *Diagnostic and Statistical Manual of Mental Disorder: Fourth Edition.* Washington, DC: American Psychiatric Association.

Andrews, G., & Slade, T. (2001). Interpreting scores on the Kessler Psychological Distress Scale (K10). *Australian and New Zealand Journal of Public Health, 25*(6), 494-497.

Australian Institute of Health and Welfare (2002). *2001 National Drug Strategy Household Survey: First Results.* AIHW Cat. No. PHE 35. Canberra: AIHW (Drug Statistics Series No. 9).

Australian Standard Geographical Classification (ASGC) (2005). Canberra: Australian Bureau of Statistics.

Aylward, R., & Bamford, E. (2000). A comparison of the ARIA (accessibility/remoteness index of Australia) and RRMA (rural, remote and metropolitan areas classification) methodologies for measuring remoteness in Australia [online discussion paper]. Department of Health and Aged Care and University of Adelaide.

Bailey, S., Doreleijers, T., & Tarbuck, P. (2006). Recent developments in mental health and screening assessment in juvenile justice systems. *Child Adolesc Psychiatric Clin N Am, 15*, 391-406.

Baumeister, R. F. (1990). Suicide as escape from the self. *Psychological Review, 97*, 90-113.

Belenko, S., & Dembo, R. (2003). Treating adolescent substance abuse problems in the juvenile drug court. *International Journal of Law and Psychiatry, 26*, 87-110.

Bernstein, D. P., & Fink, L. (1998). *Childhood Trauma Questionnaire: A Retrospective Self-Report.* San Antonio: Harcourt Brace and Company.

Bickel, R., & Campbell, A. (2002). Mental health of adolescents in custody: The use of the 'Adolescent Psychopathology Scale' in a Tasmanian context. *Australian and New Zealand Journal of Psychiatry, 36,* 603-609.

Bond, L., Thomas, L., Toumbourou, J., & Patton, G. (1998). *Adolescent Health and Wellbeing Survey Phase One Report.* Victoria: Report prepared for the Division of Youth and Family Services, Victorian Department of Human Services.

Brener, N. D. et al. (1995). Youth Risk Behaviour Questionnaire (YRBQ). Centres for Disease Control and Prevention. http://www.cdc.gov/HealthyYouth/YRBS/data/1995/yrbs1995.pdf.

Brown, P., & Butler, T. (1997). *Inmate Health Survey.* NSW: Corrections Health Service.

Butler, T., & Milner, L. (2003). *Inmate Health Survey.* NSW: Corrections Health Service.

Carroll, M. (2002). *Young Offender Risk and Protective Factor Survey.* Victoria: Department of Human Services.

Centres for Disease Control and Prevention (2001). *Youth Risk Behaviour Survey: Youth Risk Behaviour Surveillance System.* http://www.cdc.gov/HealthyYouth/YRBS/data/2001/yrbs2001.pdf.

Chitasbesan, P., & Bailey, S. (2006). Mental health, educational and social needs of young offenders in custody and in the community. *Current Opinion in Psychiatry, 19,* 355-360.

Cicchetti, D., & Rogosch, F. A. (2002). A developmental psychopathology perspective on adolescence. *Journal of Consulting and Clinical Psychology, 70,* 6-20.

Coffey, C., Veit, F., Wolfe, R., Cini, E., & Patton, G. (2003). Mortality in young offenders: Retrospective cohort study. *British Medical Journal, 326,* 1064-1068.

Davies, C., Martin, G., Kosky, R., & O'Hanlon, A. (2000). *The Australian Early Intervention Network for Mental Health in Young People* (AUSEINET).

De Leo, D., & Heller, T. S. (2004). Who are the kids who self-harm? An Australian self-report school survey. *Medical Journal of Australia, 181,* 140-144.

Dembo, R., Williams, L., Getreu, A., Genung, L., Schmeidler, J., Berry, E., Wish, D., & La Voie, L. (1991). A longitudinal study of the relationships among marijuana/hashish use, cocaine use, and delinquency in a cohort of high risk youths. *Journal of Drug Issues, 21,* 271-312.

Dixon, A., Howie, P., & Starling, J. (2004). Psychopathology in female juvenile offenders. *Journal of Child Psychology and Psychiatry, 45*(6), 1150-1158.

Evans, E., Hawton, K., Rodham, K., & Deeks, J. (2005). The prevalence of suicidal phenomena in adolescents: A systematic review of population-based studies. *Suicide and Life-Threatening Behavior, 35,* 239-250.

Gavazzi, S. M., Yarcheck, C. M., & Chesney-Lind, M. (2006). Global risk indicators and the role of gender in a juvenile detention sample. *Criminal Justice and Behavior, 33*(5), 597-612.

Goldston, D. B. (2003). *Measuring Suicidal Behavior and Risk in Children and Adolescents.* Washington, DC: American Psychological Association.

Gordon, M. S., Kinlock, T. W., & Battjes, R. J. (2004). Correlates of early substance use and crime among adolescents entering outpatient substance abuse treatment. *American Journal of Drug and Alcohol Abuse, 30,* 39-59.

Gorske, T. T., Srebalus, D. J., & Walls, R. T. (2003). Adolescents in residential centers: Characteristics and treatment outcome. *Children and Youth Services Review, 25(4)*, 317-326.

Grisso, T. (1999). Juvenile offenders and mental illness. *Psychiatry, Psycholology & Law, 6*(2), 143-151.

Grisso, T., Vincent, G., & Seagrove, D. (Editors) (2005). *Mental Health Screening and Assessment in Juvenile Justice.* New York, London: Guildford Press.

Hammersley, R., Marsland, L., & Reid, M. (2003). *Substance Use by Young Offenders: The Impact of the Normalization of Drug Use in the Early Years of the 21st Century.* Home Office Research Study 261, Development and Statistics Directorate, London: British Government.

Holloway, K., Bennett, T., & Farrington, D. (2005). The effectiveness of criminal justice and treatment programmes in reducing drug-related crime: A systematic review. *Home Office Online Report* 26/05: UK.

Howard, J., Lennings, C. J., & Copeland, J. (2003). Substance abuse and self-harm in a sample of young offenders. *Crisis, 24*(3), 98-104.

Kenny, D. T., Nelson, P., Butler, T., Lennings, C., Allerton, M., & Champion, U. (2006). *NSW Young People on Community Orders Health Survey 2003-2006: Key Findings Report.* The University of Sydney.

Kessler, R. C., Andrews, G., Colpe, L. J., Hiripi, E., Mroczek, D. K., Normand, S. L. T., Walters, E. E., & Zaslavsky, A. M. (2002). Short screening scales to monitor population prevalence and trends in non-speci˜c psychological distı ss. *Psychological Medicine, 32*, 959-976.

Kruger R. F., & Piasecki, T. M. (2002). Toward a dimensional and psychometrically-informed approach to conceptualizing psychopathology. *Behaviour Research and Therapy, 40*, 485-499.

Lennings, C. J. (1994). A cognitive understanding of adolescent suicide. *Genetic, Social and General Psychology Monographs, 27*, 269-278.

Lennings, C. J., Kenny, D. T., Howard, J., Arcuri, A., & Mackdacy, L. (in press). The relationship between substance abuse and delinquency in female adolescents in Australia. *Psychiatry, Psychology and the Law.*

Lennings, C. J., & Pritchard, M. (1999). Prevalence of drug use prior to detention among residents of youth detention centres in Queensland. *Drug and Alcohol Review, 18*, 145-152.

Loeber, R., & Farrington, D. P. (2001). Young children who commit crime: Epidemiology, developmental origins, risk factors, early interventions, and policy implications. *Development and Psychopathology, 12*, 737-762.

Moffitt, T. E. (1997). Adolescence-limited and life-course-persistent offending: A complementary pair of theories. In T. R. Thornberry (Ed). Developmental theories of crime and delinquency. *Advances in Criminology Theory*, 7, New Brunswick: Transaction Pub., pp. 11-54.

Newman, T. (1998). Young offenders, drugs and prevention. *Drugs, Education, Prevention and Policy, 5*, 233-243.

Prichard. J., & Payne, J. (2005). *Alcohol, Drugs and Crime: A Study of Juveniles in Detention.* Research and Public Policy Series, No. 67. Australian Institute of Criminology, Canberra, Australia.

Raphael, B. (2000). *Promoting the Mental Health and Wellbeing of Children and Young People.* National Mental Health Strategy, National Community Child Health Council, Canberra, Australia.

Reynolds, W. M. (2000). *Adolescent Psychopathology Scale – Short Form.* Florida: Psychological Assessment Resources Inc.

Richards, I. (1996). Psychiatric disorder among adolescents in custody. *Australian and New Zealand Journal of Psychiatry, 30,* 788-793.

Rohde, P., Seeley, J. R., & Mace, D. E. (1997). Correlates of suicidal behavior in a juvenile detention population. *Suicide and Life-Threatening Behavior, 27,* 164-175.

Sprott, J. B., Jenkins, J. M., & Doob, A. N. (2000). *National Longitudinal Survey of Children and Youth.* Quebec, Canada: Report prepared for the Applied Research Branch, Strategic Policy, Human Resources Development Canada.

The National Centre on Addiction and Substance Abuse at Columbia University (CASA) (2004). *Criminal Neglect: Substance Abuse, Juvenile Justice and the Children Left Behind.* William T. Grant Foundation, New York, NY.

Udry, J. R. (1998). *The National Longitudinal Study of Adolescent Health.* University of North Carolina: Carolina Population Centre. http://www.cpc.unc.edu/projects/addhealth.

Van Zeijl, J., Mesman, J., Van Ijzendoorn, M. H., Bakermans-Kranenburg, M. J., Juffer, F., Stolk, M. N., Koot, H. M., & Alink, L. R. (2006). Attachment-based intervention for enhancing sensitive discipline in mothers of 1- to 3-year-old children at risk for externalizing behavior problems: A randomized controlled trial. *Journal of Consulting and Clinical Psychology, 74*(6), 994-1005.

Wei, Z., Makkai, T., & McGregor, K. (2003). Drug use among a sample of juvenile detainees. *Australian Institute of Criminology Trends and Issues in Crime and Criminal Justice Number 258.* AIC, Canberra, Australia.

Whitmore, E. A., Mikulich, S. K., Thompson, L. L., Riggs, P. D., Aarons, G. A., & Crowley, T. J. (1997). Influences on adolescent substance dependence: Conduct disorder, depression, attention deficit hyperactivity disorder, and gender. *Drug and Alcohol Dependency, 47*(2), 87-97.

Zubrick, S. R., Garton, A. F., & Silburn, S. R. (1994). *Western Australian Child Health Survey.* Perth, Western Australia: Institute for Child Health Research.

AUTHORS' NOTES

Dianna T. Kenny, PhD, Christopher J. Lennings, PhD, and Paul K. Nelson, MAS, are affiliated the University of Sydney, Australia.

Address correspondence to Professor Dianna T. Kenny, Faculty of Health Sciences C42, University of Sydney, P.O. Box 170, Lidcombe NSW, Australia 1825 (E-mail: D.Kenny@usyd.edu.au).

This study was funded by a grant from the Australian Research Council, the NSW Department of Juvenile Justice and Justice Health NSW, Australia.

doi:10.1300/J076v45n01_10

Mental Health Issues in the Criminal Justice System. Pp. 149-165.
Available online at http://jor.haworthpress.com
© *2007 by The Haworth Press, Inc. All rights reserved.*
doi:10.1300/J076v45n01_11

Administrative Segregation
for Mentally Ill Inmates

MAUREEN L. O'KEEFE

ABSTRACT Largely the result of prison officials needing to safely and efficiently manage a volatile inmate population, administrative segregation or supermax facilities are criticized as violating basic human needs, particularly for mentally ill inmates. The present study compared Colorado offenders with mental illness (OMIs) to nonOMIs in segregated and non-segregated environments. OMIs committed a large portion of institutional misbehaviors, likely a symptomatic expression of their illness, causing them to be placed at a disproportionately high rate in segregation. Even when OMIs cannot be managed in a less restrictive setting, corrections officials must provide enhanced services to monitor their psychological well-being. doi:10.1300/J076v45n01_11 *[Article copies available for a fee from The Haworth Document Delivery Service: 1-800-HAWORTH. E-mail address: <docdelivery@haworthpress. com> Website: <http://www.HaworthPress.com> © 2007 by The Haworth Press, Inc. All rights reserved.]*

KEYWORDS Administrative segregation, offender characteristics, prevalence rates

INTRODUCTION

The rapid upsurge of modern supermax prisons across the country has only fueled the controversy that has existed since their earliest use. Prison officials, tasked with maintaining secure prisons that protect the safety of inmates and staff alike, have gravitated towards the supermax model whereby high-risk, dangerous inmates are centralized in a tightly controlled facility as opposed to dispersing them throughout the prison system (Hershberger, 1998; Riveland, 1999). The "last stop" in a system replete with many punitive and security options, supermax prisons offer relief to the rest of the correctional system by lessening rigid controls in the other prisons.

Yet, it has been argued that supermax is an overused management tool (Human Rights Watch, 2000; Metzner & Dvoskin, 2006; Toch, 2001). Although institutional behavior may serve as the basis for placements, supermax confinement is an administrative decision rather than a punitive one, relying on staff to predict an inmate's propensity to create disturbances and violence within prison. Herein lies one of the primary concerns–that it is too readily used for inmates who may be a nuisance rather than dangerous and violent (Human Rights Watch; King, 2000; Toch).

Supermax is known by many names–administrative segregation (AS), security housing units (SHU), intensive management unit, and extended control unit–but is characterized by long-term solitary confinement regardless of how it is called (Collins, 2004; Haney, 2003; King, 2000; Riveland, 1999). Most supermax facilities confine inmates to their cells for 23 hours per day, allowing just one hour for personal hygiene and exercise. Inmate movement is severely restricted, with multiple restraints placed on inmates before leaving their cell. Personal contact is kept to a minimum. Human rights advocates argue that these conditions are too harsh and inhumane with extremely long periods of isolation and little stimulation (Fellner & Mariner, 1997; Haney; Human Rights Watch, 1999, 2000; King; Kurki & Morris, 2001; Toch, 2001), in place for punishment rather than true safety reasons.

Perhaps the gravest concern of all is the placement of mentally ill offenders in supermax facilities, where psychiatric symptoms are thought to be exacerbated by the very setting itself (Abramsky & Fellner, 2003; Haney, 2003; Haney & Lynch, 1997; Human Rights Watch, 2000; King, 2000; Metzner & Dvoskin, 2006; Toch, 2001). The suffering of mentally ill persons that occurs as a result of solitary confinement is generally believed to be permanently disabling.

Effects of Supermax on Psychological Functioning

The literature addressing the psychological consequences of long-term solitary confinement is highly polemic, bent more towards the theoretical than the empirical. The largely political and sensitive nature of supermax confinement has no doubt exacerbated the traditional difficulties of conducting research in prisons, posing even greater obstacles to researchers interested in advancing systematic and independent knowledge in this area. Nonetheless, some elemental understanding of the psychological functioning of inmates in supermax and related theories can be gleaned from a review of the studies.

The same year that the Federal Bureau of Prisons opened the Marion, Illinois supermax facility, Grassian (1983) described the psychopathological features resulting from solitary confinement that he believed to form a clinical syndrome, later known as the SHU syndrome. He noted perceptual changes, affective disturbances, cognitive difficulties, disturbing thought content, and impulse control problems that immediately subsided following release from such confinement.

Since then, various qualitative accounts and case studies acquired through on-site observation and interviews with staff and inmates have been added to the literature (Benjamin & Lux, 1975; Fellner & Mariner, 1997; Human Rights Watch, 1999; King, 2000; Kurki & Morris, 2001). Case study and similar designs are perhaps most useful for developing theories that can be tested empirically. Nonetheless, there are serious empirical limitations to be considered. Small sample sizes, as are the norm in case studies, mean findings may not generalize to all, or even most, segregated offenders. Particularly concerning is that sampling procedures are often not discussed, suggesting that special care was not taken to select a representative sample. In the case of Dr. Grassian's 1983 study, the 14 study participants were plaintiffs involved in a class action lawsuit regarding their conditions of confinement and Dr. Grassian relayed how it was necessary for the interviewer to press the participants to endorse these symptoms after initially denying them.

Another shortcoming of these approaches is that they do not provide a relative comparison of the participants' behavior in other settings. Inmates who report serious psychological difficulties in segregation may experience those same problems in other prison settings or in the community at large. Even quantitative studies are subject to these same limitations when adequate comparison groups are not engaged. Haney (2003) found elevated symptoms of psychological trauma (e.g., anxiety, headaches, impending nervous breakdown, lethargy) and psychopathological features (e.g., ruminations, social withdrawal, irrational anger) among 100 SHU prisoners compared to national probability samples. However, it is not surprising that prisoners as a whole, not just those in segregation, differ dramatically from a non-clinical, non-incarcerated sample. Indeed, another study found that prisoners in general were different from standardized samples across multiple measures such as anxiety, depression, hostility and socialization (Seudfeld, Ramirez, Deaton, & Baker-Brown, 1982).

Several studies have compared segregated to non-segregated inmates. In one study, no differences were found between the groups (Seudfeld et al., 1982). In a study of Canadian offenders, the segregated group had more criminal justice system involvement, poor education, skills deficits, family dysfunction, antisocial attachments, chemical dependencies, thinking problems, and antisocial attitudes than randomly selected non-segregated offenders (Motiuk & Blanchette, 2001). Furthermore, segregated offenders had a higher recidivism rate than the non-segregated offenders. A third study found that severe mental disorders were higher among segregation populations than the general population, particularly schizophrenia and bipolar disorder (Hodgins & Cote, 1991). Major depression was lower in segregation than the general population, and suicide attempts were of equal proportion between samples.

Danish inmates in solitary confinement were compared to non-segregated offenders using a longitudinal research design (Andersen, Sestoft, Lillebaek, Gabrielsen, Hemmingsen, & Kramp, 2000), and the results indicated that psychiatric disorders were higher among offenders in solitary confinement than those not segregated. However, those disorders primarily included adjustment and depressive disorders rather than psychotic disorders. Because of releases and transfers from solitary confinement, the 228 participants at the beginning of the study declined to 14 within three months. In another longitudinal study, Zinger and his colleagues (2001) found that mental health and psychological functioning did not deteriorate over time in Canadian offenders, although segregated offenders had psychological indices that were often elevated over non-segregated offenders. This study was limited to a 60-day period, and it suffered a 40-44% refusal rate (depending on group) and a 56% attrition rate. The short durations in these two studies coupled with high attrition rates suggest that segregation in these foreign countries is perhaps more equivalent to punitive segregation found in the U.S. rather than AS.

Taken together, these findings suggest that inmates in AS are different from their peers in the general prison population, particularly in regards to their psychological functioning. What is still not known is if these differences are attributable to harmful effects of solitary confinement or if inmates with more serious psychological problems are being placed into AS at a disproportionately high rate.

Constitutionality of Supermax Prisons

To achieve a thorough understanding of the issues surrounding supermax confinement, one must review not only the literature but also case law. The absence of empirical evidence that supermax prisons either are or are not psychologically harmful, and for which individuals, has forced the courts to rely upon expert testimony. Cases concerning conditions of confinement, which fall under the Eighth Amendment's prohibition against cruel and unusual punishment, must consider whether conditions harm prisoners or pose a substantial risk of serious harm and whether officials have been deliberately indifferent to inmates' basic human needs (Collins, 2004).

Madrid v. Gomez (1995) was a landmark case that found California state officials in violation of the Eighth Amendment by housing mentally ill inmates in the Pelican Bay SHU. Although the SHU was not considered a violation for all inmates, the totality of conditions for certain subgroups in confinement over extended periods of time was. The unit in question was a modern forerunner of supermax prisons; unsanitary conditions or antiquated buildings were not in question. The court reasoned however: "For [mentally ill] inmates, placing them in the SHU is the mental equivalent of putting an asthmatic in a place with little air to breathe . . . Such inmates are not required to endure the horrific suffering of a serious mental illness or major exacerbation of an existing mental illness before obtaining relief." Not only was it ruled cruel and unusual punishment to place mentally ill inmates in the SHU, those at reasonably high risk of suffering mental illness as a result of SHU conditions were also restricted.

In another benchmark case regarding conditions of confinement (*Ruiz v. Johnson*, 1999), a Texas judge ruled that the "extreme deprivations and repressive conditions of confinement of Texas' administrative segregation units . . . violate the Constitution of the United States' prohibition against cruel and unusual punishment, both as to the plaintiff class generally and to the subclass of mentally ill inmates housed in such confinement." Although AS itself was not deemed unconstitutional, the deprivation of "even the most basic psychological needs" such as human contact, psychological stimulation, and human dignity was. Mentally healthy individuals would decompensate under such conditions; the symptoms and responses are aggravated for mentally ill inmates.

Similar to the *Ruiz v. Johnson* (1999) case, individual conditions in *Jones 'El v. Berge* (2001) did not constitute cruel and unusual punishment, but the totality of the circumstances did (e.g., cell temperatures, nocturnal lighting, lack of outdoor recreation). State officials agreed to a number of improved conditions, which included not placing severely mentally ill inmates in supermax as a routine procedure and providing adequate mental health services to ameliorate the effect of the setting on an inmate's illness.

Despite the case law, there has not been a unified definition of mental illness or even severe mental illness. Nor has it ever been deemed that all mentally ill offenders are excluded from solitary confinement. Various definitions have been used by the prison systems, but it is not known what types of offenders, if any, suffer psychological pain as a result of long-term solitary confinement.

Administrative Segregation in Colorado

Colorado was among the first states to adopt the supermax model by constructing an entire facility in 1993 for inmates classified as AS. Further expansion of this security level occurred when the Colorado Department of Corrections included AS units within three newer multi-custody facilities. Although considerably smaller, these additional facilities expanded the overall capacity and provided female and mentally ill offender segregation units.

The current study examined the prevalence of offenders with mental illness (OMIs) in AS relative to the general population (GP) to determine the frequency at which they are being held in this highly restrictive environment. Comparisons were made between OMIs and nonOMIs in both AS and GP in order to better understand the types of OMIs that are placed in AS. Finally, this study employed a logistic regression analysis to identify the offender characteristics that predict placement into AS confinement.

METHOD

Participants

Prevalence rates of OMIs were analyzed using the fiscal year-end inmate population for each of seven years. The 2005 population was used to profile inmates by OMI status and AS classification. Participants included 17,393 adult inmates, excluding 143 cases that had missing classification or mental health data. Inmates were 92% male with a mean age of 35.7 ($SD = 10.6$). Ethnic backgrounds were 46% Caucasian, 31% Hispanic, 20% African American, 2% Native American, and 1% Asian.

Inmates were coded into four groups: (1) OMIs in AS ($n = 443$), (2) OMIs in GP ($n = 3,802$), (3) nonOMIs in AS ($n = 766$), and (4) nonOMIs in GP ($n = 12,382$). Offenders were grouped according to their classification level rather than by their assigned facility due to long AS waitlists where offenders occupy a punitive segregation bed prior to an AS bed becoming available. Classification ratings are conducted at intake into prison and reevaluated every six months or more often as needed over the course of offenders' incarceration, although classification to AS uses a hearing process that incorporates due process procedures. Colorado prison security levels are minimum, minimum-restricted, medium, close, new/maximum, and AS.

Offenders were classified as OMI according to their psychological code, rated during the intake process and again later as warranted over the course of incarceration. A number of measures factor into an initial psychological code including assessments, previous inpatient and outpatient treatment, prescription for psychotropic medications, medical examinations, and prior successful "not guilty by reason of insanity" pleas. Following their initial rating, inmates are seen by mental health staff for a diagnosis and further categorization. For the purposes of this study, inmates with scores of 3 or higher on this 5-point scale, signifying the need for mental health services, were considered OMI regardless of their type of diagnosis.

Materials

The Culture Fair Intelligence Test (CFIT; Cattell & Cattell, 1973) is a non-verbal measure designed to assess general mental capacity in terms of fluid ability, meaning the ability to perceive relationships, to analyze, and to reason in abstract or novel situations. The goal of this measure is to use items which are free of cultural bias usually associated with language, cultural background, and educational level. Internal consistency reliability estimates vary between high .70s to .90s depending on the scale. Test-retest reliabilities run in the low .80s and equivalent-forms reliabilities range from .58 to .72 (Koch, 1992; Tannenbaum, 1965).

The CFIT's convergent validity with other intelligence tests has an average correlation of .70 (Koch).

The Level of Supervision Inventory–Revised (LSI-R; Andrews & Bonta, 1995) is a 54-item assessment conducted in a semi-structured interview format. It measures offender recidivism risk and can be utilized to determine the amount of supervision necessary for offenders in the community. The LSI-R is administered to all prison intakes as part of the diagnostic assessment and, using norms set for Colorado parolees, scores between 0 and 12 designate offenders as low risk, 13 to 25 as medium risk, and 26 to 54 as high risk.

The Brief Psychiatric Rating Scale (BPRS; Overall & Gorman, 1962) is a 24-item scale most commonly used to assess patients with psychiatric disorders. It is designed to allow for the rapid review of changing symptoms (Lukoff, Nuechterlein, & Ventura, 1986; Ventura, Lukoff, Nuechterlein, Liberman, Green, & Shaner, 1993). An 18-item version of the BPRS administered to supermaximum inmates in Washington produced a reliability coefficient of .75 and correctly identified inmates meeting criteria for serious psychosocial impairment (Cloyes, Lovell, Allen, & Rhodes, 2006). Research has also indicated that there are five factors to which the individual items are associated: thinking disorder, withdrawal, anxiety/depression, hostility/suspicion, and activity (Burger, Calsyn, Morse, Klinkenberg, & Trusty, 1997; Cloyes et al.; Hedlund & Vieweg, 1980).

Procedure

Offender data for this study was downloaded from the Department of Corrections' administrative database. Electronic offender records are received from the judicial system with mittimus data, and prison staff add demographic, assessment, classification, and behavioral data to offenders' official record. During the intake process, inmates are assessed through a variety of sources including official records, interviews, pencil and paper tests, and file reviews. Institutional behavior is monitored over the course of their incarceration and recorded in the administrative database. These variables include security threat group involvement and disciplinary violations including sanctions. One-way chi-square, one-way analysis of variance, and *t* tests were conducted between groups using an alpha level of .001 unless otherwise noted.

RESULTS

Prevalence rates of OMIs in AS versus GP were analyzed by fiscal year across a seven-year span (see Figure 1). OMIs were highly overrepresented in AS, with the disparity growing in 2002 and 2003. This increase coincided with an economic crisis in the state that resulted in significant budget cuts, which impacted prison program services the hardest.

Descriptive demographic data are presented in Table 1 for each group. Significant group differences were found for all demographic characteristics. Females were more likely than males to present with mental health issues but were less likely to be classified as AS. OMIs were more likely than nonOMIs to be Caucasian while inmates in AS were more likely than GP to be Hispanic. AS inmates were younger and completed less formal education than GP inmates. NonOMIs in GP had a higher intelligence score than both OMI groups, but all were well within normal bounds.

Criminal history and institutional behavior tended to distinguish AS inmates from those in the GP (see Table 2). Post hoc analyses found AS inmates were more violent and more involved in security threat groups, and had more disciplinary infractions, and more punitive segregations than GP. OMI inmates in AS had the highest LSI-R scores followed by

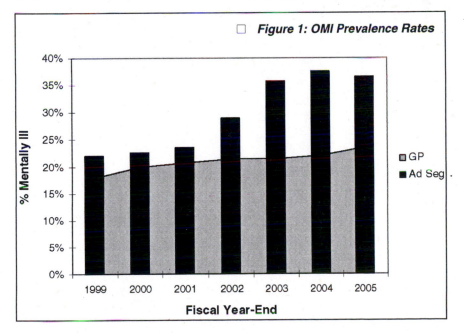

Figure 1: OMI Prevalence Rates

☐ **Table 1: Demographic Characteristics**

	OMI		nonOMI	
	AS	GP	AS	GP
Gender*				
Male	95%	82%	99%	94%
Female	5%	18%	1%	6%
Ethnicity*				
Caucasian	51%	61%	29%	42%
Hispanic	33%	21%	50%	33%
African American	13%	15%	18%	22%
Other	3%	3%	3%	3%
Degree/Certificate*				
0-8	21%	10%	17%	11%
9-11	65%	61%	69%	61%
12	9%	17%	9%	17%
Post secondary	5%	12%	5%	11%
Mean CFIT (*SD*)*	99.7 (13.3)	99.6 (13.5)	100.8 (13.3)	101.7 (13.1)
Mean age (*SD*)*	32.2 (8.3)	36.5 (10.2)	32.0 (8.4)	35.9 (10.8)

* $p < .001$

☐ **Table 2: Criminal and Institutional History**

	OMI		nonOMI	
	AS	GP	AS	GP
% with prior incarceration	30%	29%	28%	28%
% with violent crime*	60%	47%	62%	47%
% security threat group*	63%	23%	72%	26%
Mean # violations (*SD*)*	34.4 (37.1)	9.5 (14.9)	24.7 (22.8)	6.5 (10.6)
Mean # punitive seg (*SD*)*	11.0 (9.9)	4.1 (6.9)	8.6 (7.9)	2.5 (4.8)
Mean LSI-R (*SD*)*	34.1 (7.0)	32.4 (7.7)	32.2 (6.9)	28.8 (7.6)

* $p < .001$

OMIs in GP and nonOMIs in AS; nonOMIs in GP had the lowest LSI-R scores. Although AS accounted for some of the group differences on the number of disciplinary infractions and punitive segregations, OMI status also accounted for some of those differences. Higher frequencies were found for OMIs than nonOMIs in AS, as were for OMIs in GP when compared to nonOMIs in GP. Finally, OMIs were also less involved in security threat groups than nonOMIs.

Axis I diagnoses, as assigned by mental health clinicians, were grouped by category and examined for OMIs in AS and GP (see Figure 2). AS inmates had similar rank order of Axis I diagnoses, except for attention-deficit hyperactivity disorder and "other" disorders. Approximately one-third of other diagnoses were impulse control or intermittent explosive disorders and another third was physical abuse of a child, partner, or adult. Although substance abuse disorders are ranked as the top Axis I diagnoses among Colorado offenders, this is an underestimation of actual substance abuse problems. Because there is a separate assessment process to identify substance abusers, clinicians oftentimes do not assign a substance abuse diagnosis where one is warranted.

Mentally ill inmates are routinely assessed on the BPRS, typically at six-month intervals or more frequently. Table 3 lists mean BPRS scale and total scores for OMIs in AS and GP. *T*-test analyses showed that OMIs in AS had higher BPRS total, thinking disorder, hostility suspicion, and activity scale scores than OMIs in GP. This finding suggests that not only is mental illness more prevalent among AS inmates, but they exhibit the more severe psychopathology.

☐ **Table 3: Psychiatric Severity of OMIs**	AS	GP
BPRS Scale (*score range*)	M (SD)	M (SD)
Thinking disorder (*5-35*)*	6.9 (2.7)	6.2 (2.3)
Withdrawal (*6-42*)	7.7 (2.1)	7.6 (2.1)
Anxiety-depression (*5-35*)	10.0 (3.3)	9.6 (3.4)
Hostility suspicion (*3-21*)*	5.1 (2.4)	4.2 (1.8)
Activity (*5-35*)*	7.2 (2.3)	6.5 (2.0)
BPRS Total (*24-168*)*	36.9 (8.3)	34.2 (7.7)

* $p < .001$

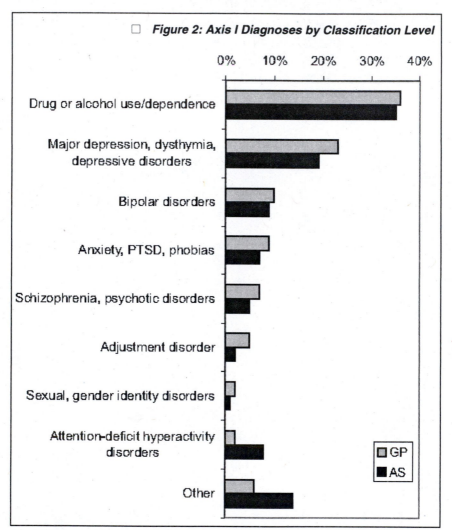

Figure 2: Axis I Diagnoses by Classification Level

A logistic regression was conducted to determine offender character-istics that might predict administrative segregation placements. The de-pendent variable was administrative segregation (yes, no). The following variables, which differentiated administrative segregation inmates from the general population in the univariate comparisons, were added to the logistic regression equation in two blocks: (1) gender (male, female), age, Hispanic (yes, no), high school completion (yes, no), and OMI (yes, no); and (2) LSI-R score, security threat group (yes, no), number of punitive segregations, number of disciplinary violations, and violent offender (yes, no).

Table 4 gives the results of the analysis; only variables found to be significant predictors at the .01 alpha level are listed. The equation correctly classified inmates at a rate of 74%. Security threat group was the strongest predictor; the odds ratio indicated that inmates with this involvement were 4.1 times more likely to be placed in administrative segregation than those with no involvement. Violent, Hispanic, and OMI male inmates had the greatest odds of such a placement rather than inmates without those traits.

Interestingly, Hispanic ethnicity remained a significant predictor even when accounting for both ethnicity and security threat group. It appears that Hispanic gang members are segregated at a greater rate than gang members of other cultures. Indeed, a review of gang affiliations showed increased placements for predominantly Hispanic gangs (Surenos-13, Gallant Knights) and fewer placements for African American (Bloods, Crips) and Caucasian (White Supremacists) gangs. This may reflect greater violence among Hispanic gangs, more visible activities, or a greater perceived threat.

DISCUSSION

Segregated offenders were discernibly different from their non-segregated peers, especially on criminal history indicators and institutional behaviors. In particular, offenders involved with security threat groups or engaged in gang-related activities were targeted for AS placements–at a rate 4.5 times of those who had no known involvement. Other factors known to correlate to higher risk and recidivism were related

☐ Table 4: Predicting AS Classification from Offender Characteristics

Variable	B	p	Odds Ratio
Security threat group	1.4	<.001	4.1
Male	0.7	<.01	2.0
Mentally ill	0.6	<.001	1.8
Violent	0.5	<.001	1.6
Hispanic	0.3	<.001	1.4
# disciplinary infractions	0.1	<.001	1.1
# punitive segregations	0.1	<.001	1.1

to AS classification, specifically younger males with less formal education.

OMIs in segregation were of special interest to this study, given the serious concerns about their ability to cope within a more isolated environment. Not only were OMIs found in AS at a disproportionately high rate, this disparity has grown over recent years in conjunction with severely restricted funding for program services. Mental health resources have become so reduced within Colorado prisons that staff have limited their services to assessment, medication monitoring, and crisis management. It seems likely that cutbacks have affected the prison system's ability to manage OMIs in less restrictive environments.

Mental illness was found to be the third strongest predictor of AS classification. Clearly, OMIs were responsible for a significant number of the disciplinary violations within the prisons, but mental illness was found a considerably better predictor of AS classification than disciplinary infractions. Indeed, OMIs are less likely to be identified with security threat groups, which suggests that their acting out may be directly related to symptomatic expression of their illness. This is supported by clinician ratings of OMIs as having more severe psychopathology paired with high activity levels and low impulse control.

The logistic regression model was limited by the availability of data that exist among official records. Although more extensive variables were used in research reported elsewhere (O'Keefe, 2005), these did little to improve the prediction equation. Colorado's administrative database is focused upon institutional *mis*behavior; tracking of victim-prone characteristics or even incidents is not recorded in a systematic way. Protective custody may account for some of the unexplained variance in the prediction model. Even though Colorado does not endorse protective custody, inmates can engage in certain behaviors to invoke the protections that solitary confinement offers.

Just as arrests occur when a mentally ill person's behavior exceeds society's limited tolerance for deviance (Abram & Teplin, 1991), so too may a lower tolerance exist for mentally ill persons within the prison system, thereby giving rise to increased segregation placements. Traditionally, prison security and mental health services have operated independently of each other. Whether the prevailing perspective that prison mental health services are ancillary changes to one where they are accepted as integral, or mental health training is brought to the front lines (i.e., security staff), prisons need to learn how to better manage their mentally ill inmates and protect them in less restrictive prison settings.

Optimally both scenarios would be in effect, where mental health clinicians work closely with line staff to employ the best management strategies.

In states where the courts have prohibited placement of mentally ill inmates in supermax confinement, prison systems have been forced to consider alternative solutions. This has given rise to secure mental health units or entire facilities where isolation is minimized and mental health services are enhanced. However, such units are resource-intensive, particularly in regards to mental health personnel and the physical plant to allow secure group interactions.

William Collins (2004, p. 8) concluded, "The fact that [administrative segregation's] extremely restrictive conditions place it at the very edge of what is constitutionally permissible suggests that, with properly developed policies and procedures, it can function in a constitutionally acceptable fashion." Based upon case law, Collins recommends prudent practices that establish criteria to exclude certain inmates from segregation and screen all inmates prior to segregation for these criteria. For inmates placed in segregation units, staff must continually monitor inmates to determine if or when they meet the criteria and subsequently transfer out those who do. Solely by definition, OMIs require more rigorous programming and treatment services than most. In addition to their mental health needs, this group presents with greater academic, vocational, rehabilitation, and medical needs (O'Keefe & Schnell, this volume) which can not be neglected on the basis of their administrative segregation placement.

REFERENCES

Abram, K.M., & Teplin, L.A. (1991). Co-occurring disorders among mentally ill jail detainees. *American Psychologist, 46,* 1036-1045.

Abramsky, S., & Fellner, J. (2003). *Ill Equipped: U.S. Prisons and Offenders with Mental Illness.* New York: Human Rights Watch.

Andersen, H.S., Sestoft, D., Lillebaek, T., Gabrielsen, G., Hemmingsen, R., & Kramp, P. (2000). A longitudinal study of prisoners on remand: Psychiatric prevalence, incidence, and psychopathology in solitary vs. non-solitary confinement. *Acta Psychiatr Scand, 102,* 19-25.

Andrews, D.A., & Bonta J.L. (1995). *LSI-R: The Level of Service Inventory–Revised.* Toronto: Multi-Health Systems.

Benjamin, T.B., & Lux, K. (1975). Constitutional and psychological implications of the use of solitary confinement: Experience at the Maine state prison. *Clearinghouse Review, 9,* 83-84.

Burger, G.K., Calsyn, R.J., Morse, G.A., Klinkenberg, W.D., & Trusty, M.L. (1997). Factor structure of the Expanded Brief Psychiatric Rating Scale. *Journal of Clinical Psychology, 53*, 451-454.

Cattell, R.B., & Cattell, H.E.P. (1973). *Measuring Intelligence with the Culture Fair Tests.* Champaign, IL: Institute for Personality and Ability Testing.

Cloyes, K.G., Lovell, D., Allen, D.G., & Rhodes, L.A. (2006). Assessment of psychosocial impairment in a supermaximum security unit sample. *Criminal Justice and Behavior, 33*(6), 760-781.

Collins, W.C. (2004). *Supermax Prisons and the Constitution: Liability Concerns in the Extended Control Unit.* Longmont, CO: US Department of Justice, National Institute of Corrections.

Fellner, J., & Mariner, J. (1997). *Cold Storage: Super-Maximum Security Confinement in Indiana.* New York: Human Rights Watch.

Grassian, S. (1983). Psychopathological effects of solitary confinement. *American Journal of Psychiatry, 140*, 1450-1454.

Haney, C. (2003). Mental health issues in long-term solitary and "Supermax" confinement. *Crime and Delinquency, 49*, 124-156.

Haney, C., & Lynch, M. (1997). Regulating prisons of the future: A psychological analysis of supermax and solitary confinement. *New York Review of Law and Social Change, 23*, 477-570.

Hedlund, J.L., & Vieweg, B.W. (1980). The Brief Psychiatric Rating Scale (BPRS): A comprehensive review. *Journal of Operational Psychiatry, 11*, 48-62.

Hershberger, G.L. (1998). To the max: Super-max facilities provide prison administrators with more security options. *Corrections Today, 60*, 54-57.

Hodgins, S., & Côté, G. (1991). The mental health of penitentiary inmates in isolation. *Canadian Journal of Criminology, 33*, 175-182.

Human Rights Watch (1999). Red Onion State Prison: Super-maximum security confinement in Virginia. *Human Rights Watch, 11*, 1-24.

Human Rights Watch (2000, February). Out of sight: Super-maximum security confinement in the United States. *Human Rights Watch, 12*(1), 1-9.

Jones 'El v. Berge, 164 F. Supp. 2d 1096 (W.D. Wisc. 2001).

King, R. (2000). The rise and rise of super-max: An American solution in search of a problem? *Punishment and Society, 1*, 163-186.

Koch, W.R. (1992). Culture Fair Intelligence Test. In D.J. Keyser & R.C. Sweetland (Eds.), *Test Critiques Vol. I.* (pp. 233-238). Austin, TX: Pro-ed.

Kurki, L., & Morris, N. (2001). The purposes, practices, and problems of supermax prisons. *Crime and Justice, 28*, 1-21.

Lukoff, D., Nuechterlein, K., & Ventura, A. (1986). Manual for the expanded brief psychiatric rating scale. *Schizophrenia Bulletin, 13*, 261-276.

Madrid v. Gomez, 889 F. Supp. 1146 (N.D. Cal. 1995).

Metzner, J., & Dvoskin, J. (2006). An overview of correctional psychiatry. *Psychiatric Clinics of North America, 28*, 761-772.

Motiuk, L.L., & Blanchette, K. (2001). Characteristics of administratively segregated offenders in federal corrections. *Canadian Journal of Criminology, 43*, 131-144.

O'Keefe, M.L. (2005). *Analysis of Colorado's Administrative Segregation.* Technical report. Colorado Springs, CO: Department of Corrections.

O'Keefe, M.L., & Schnell, M.J. (this volume). Offenders with mental illness in the correctional system. *Journal of Offender Rehabilitation.*

Overall, J.E., & Gorham, D.R. (1962). The brief psychiatric rating scale. *Psychological Reports, 10,* 799-812.

Riveland, C. (1999). *Supermax Prisons: Overview and General Considerations.* Longmont, CO: US Department of Justice, National Institute of Corrections.

Ruiz v. Johnson, 37 F. Supp. 855 (S.D. Tex. 1999).

Suedfeld, P., Ramirez, J., Deaton, J., & Baker-Brown, G. (1982). Reactions and attributes of prisoners in solitary confinement. *Criminal Justice and Behavior, 9,* 303-340.

Tannenbaum, A.J. (1965). Culture Fair Intelligence Test. In O.K. Buros (Ed.), *The Sixth Mental Measurements Yearbook* (pp. 721-723). Lincoln, NE: University of Nebraska Press.

Toch, H. (2001). The future of supermax confinement. *The Prison Journal, 81,* 376-388.

Ventura, J., Lukoff, D., Nuechterlein, K.H., Liberman, R.P., Green, M.F., & Shaner, A. (1993). *Training and Quality Assurance with the BPRS.* Los Angeles, CA: UCLA Department of Psychiatry and Biobehavioral Sciences.

Ward, D.A. (1999). Supermaximum facilities. In P.M. Carlson & J. S. Garrett (Eds.), *Prison and Jail Administration: Practice and Theory.* Gaithersburg, MD: Aspen.

Zinger, I., Wichman, C., & Andrews, D. A. (2001). The psychological effects of 60 days in administrative segregation. *Canadian Journal of Criminology, 43,* 47-88.

AUTHOR'S NOTE

Maureen L. O'Keefe, MA, is QA Officer, Rehabilitation Programs, Colorado Department of Corrections, 2862 South Circle Drive, Colorado Springs, CO 80906 (E-mail: Maureen.Okeefe@doc.state.co.us).

doi:10.1300/J076v45n01_11

Mental Health Issues in the Criminal Justice System. Pp. 167-188.
Available online at http://jor.haworthpress.com
© 2007 by The Haworth Press, Inc. All rights reserved.
doi:10.1300/J076v45n01_12

Preparing Communities for Re-Entry of Offenders with Mental Illness: The ACTION Approach

WENDY M. VOGEL
CHAN D. NOETHER
HENRY J. STEADMAN

ABSTRACT Approximately 900,000 people with active symptoms of serious mental illness are booked annually into U.S. jails. Of these, about three quarters have a co-occurring substance use disorder. When these people return to the community they have multiple, complex and interrelated treatment needs, which are often exacerbated by release into the community. This article presents an approach to cross-systems collaboration among the criminal justice, mental health and substance abuse systems to promote recovery of incarcerated people with co-occurring disorders re-entering into the community through *education, facilitated strategic planning* and follow-up *technical assistance*. The ACTION Approach is described, and results from process and outcome evaluations are presented and discussed. doi:10.1300/J076v45n01_12 *[Article copies available for a fee from The Haworth Document Delivery Service: 1-800-HAWORTH. E-mail address: <docdelivery@ haworthpress.com> Website: <http://www.HaworthPress.com> © 2007 by The Haworth Press, Inc. All rights reserved.]*

KEYWORDS Jail and prison, re-entry, cross-systems collaboration, co-occurring disorders

INTRODUCTION

Over two million individuals are currently incarcerated in U.S. jails and prisons, representing a 91% increase in the number of incarcerated individuals since 1990 (Harrison & Beck, 2006). At any given time an additional 4.9 million adult men and women are on probation or parole (Glaze & Bonczar, 2006). In total, more than 3% of all adults in the U.S. are under direct supervision of the criminal justice system at any given time.

Estimates of serious mental illness among the 13 million people booked annually into U.S. jails vary between 8% (Teplin, 1994; Teplin, Abram, & McClelland, 1996; National GAINS Center, 2004) and 16% (Ditton, 1999). This means that at least 900,000 people are booked into U.S. jails each year with acute mental illness. Moreover, approximately three quarters of these people have a co-occurring substance use disorder (Abram & Teplin, 1991).

As the number of inpatient psychiatric beds available in the public sector has been drastically reduced, correctional institutions have become primary "treatment" facilities in many U.S. communities. Due primarily to a lack of appropriate, comprehensive, and integrated treatment options in the community, as well as barriers to accessing services that are available, many people who have a mental illness come into contact with the criminal justice system, often recycling through its doors. The ever-increasing correctional population includes a large number of individuals with multiple, complex and interrelated treatment needs, which are often exacerbated upon release into the community.

Given the approximately seven million individuals released from local correctional facilities annually, and an additional 670,000 returning to the community from state prison systems (Hammett, Roberts, & Kennedy, 2001; Harrison & Beck, 2006), as well as the high rates of mental illness and co-occurring substance use disorders among these people, there is clearly a need for communities to take action and assume responsibility for addressing the issues facing these citizens. An appropriate response to these issues clearly requires, at a minimum, real collaboration among the criminal justice, mental health, substance abuse and social service systems.

Just how important post-release community interventions are has become evident in the research on modified therapeutic communities

(MTCs). Therapeutic communities are one of the few evidence-based treatment strategies that have been successfully adapted for use with justice system-involved populations in correctional settings. As adapted for use in jails and prisons, MTCs are integrated treatment program models that focus specifically on public safety outcomes for persons with mental health and substance use disorders (De Leon, 1993; Sacks, Sacks, De Leon, Bernhardt, & Staines, 1997). Research on the efficacy of the prison-based modified therapeutic community (MTC) approach definitively demonstrates that long-term maintenance of improvements attained while incarcerated, as well as subsequent treatment success, are almost completely dependent upon the provision of adequate and appropriate treatment services and supports when an offender re-enters the community.

In a recent study by Sacks and colleagues (2004), 236 male inmates in a Colorado correctional facility who had co-occurring serious mental illnesses and substance use disorders were randomly assigned to either a MTC or traditional mental health treatment program. Upon release from prison, offenders who completed the prison MTC program could enter a MTC aftercare program. The results of this study showed at 12 months post prison release that inmates who received treatment in the MTC program had significantly lower rates of re-incarceration as compared to those who received traditional mental health services (9% versus 33%). Further, the results showed an even greater difference in the rate of re-incarceration among the group that received MTC plus aftercare and the traditional mental health treatment group (5% versus 33%), with significant differences also reported in rates of criminal activity (42% versus 67%) and in rates of criminal activity related to drug and alcohol use (30% versus 58%).

Wexler, Melnick, Lowe, and Peters (1999) also found similar results in their study of a prison-based therapeutic community and aftercare program for substance abusers. Re-incarceration rates for those individuals who had received treatment services via in-prison therapeutic communities (ITCs), who had also completed an aftercare program following discharge in the community, had significantly lower rates of re-incarceration (27%) than those who had received no treatment (75%). Perhaps more striking in this study is that the rate of re-incarceration among those individuals who had completed the ITC program, but received no aftercare services, was higher (79%) than those who had received no treatment at all (75%). Further, reductions in re-incarceration rates of more than 40% at 12 months and more than 50% at 24 months after release from prison were found for subjects who completed ITC plus aftercare (Wexler, De Leon, Thomas, Kressel, & Peters, 1999). These improvements remained significant after controlling for client characteristics that have been identified as predictors of recidivism.

In a study of a multi-stage ITC treatment program for offenders in the Delaware correctional system, Incardi and colleagues (1997) found that those individuals whose treatment included a community aftercare component following release from prison had significantly lower rates of drug relapse and criminal recidivism, even when adjusted for other risk factors. Further, the rates of recidivism and drug relapse among those individuals who were in the ITC plus aftercare program were significantly lower (31% versus 45% for re-incarceration; 65% versus 73% for drug use) than those in the ITC only (no aftercare) group (Martin, Butzin, Saum, & Inciardi, 1999).

In a study of male inmates in the Texas correctional system who participated in an ITC treatment program, Hiller, Knight, and Simpson (1999) examined the impact of residential aftercare on recidivism following prison-based treatment for drug-involved offenders. They found that the rate of recidivism among subjects three years following re-entry into the community was significantly lower for those who received community-based treatment services and supports following release. Those who had completed the ITC aftercare program were significantly less likely to be re-incarcerated for new offenses (6%), as compared to those who had either never received treatment (19%) or had dropped out of the aftercare program prior to completion (22%). Further, among those offenders who had the highest level of symptom severity, three year re-incarceration rates were significantly lower (26%) for the group who had received treatment and completed the aftercare program, as compared to aftercare dropouts (66%) and those who received no treatment (52%) (Knight, Simpson, & Hiller, 1999).

All of these findings clearly support the efficacy of prison-based therapeutic communities coupled with community-based aftercare, in reducing re-incarceration rates among inmates treated for severe mental illnesses, substance use disorders or both. However, in their review of the array of services that jails typically provide, Steadman and Veysey (1997) found that transition planning is the least frequently provided mental health service within jail settings. In fact, the larger the facility, the less likely individuals diagnosed with mental illness are to receive transition planning. These results underscore the need for providing comprehensive and appropriate transitional services and community-based treatment and supports for offenders who are being released. Having demonstrated the value of these programs, key questions remain regarding

implementation and how to effectively bring together the often compet-
ing systems of criminal justice, mental health and substance abuse. The
ACTION approach, a product of the Adult Cross-Training Curriculum
(AXT) Project, is a proven approach to improving clinical practices for justice system-involved individuals in jail and in the community by promoting
positive organizational changes through cross-systems collaboration.

THE ADULT CROSS-TRAINING (AXT) PROJECT: PREPARING COMMUNITIES FOR OFFENDER RE-ENTRY

To successfully help people achieve recovery and resiliency from
co-occurring disorders and reduce recidivism, the mental health, substance abuse, criminal justice and social service systems must identify
ways to break down organizational barriers and collaborate to provide
coordinated and integrated co-occurring treatment services. System
transformation is possible when communities take action by establishing cross-systems partnerships that include consumers and other professionals at all levels of decision-making. Cross-systems collaboration
and coordination of integrated services result in efficient and effective
services, increased public and personal safety and a higher quality of life
for all community residents. This was the goal of the AXT Project. At its
core, the ACTION approach promotes partnerships and collaboration
across systems, directs communities toward exemplary practices, and
prepares communities to assess current services available to re-entering
offenders in the community.

For the criminal justice, mental health and substance abuse treatment
systems to improve their own processes or linkages, it is critical for each
system to understand the philosophies and service delivery processes of
the other systems with regard to justice system-involved individuals.
All too often clients who are encountered every day in each system are
bouncing between the three systems because their complex treatment
and service needs cannot be adequately addressed by any one system.
The ACTION approach is designed to facilitate such cross-systems education and identification of service gaps and untapped resources in the
community.

The objective of the AXT Project was to develop and pilot test a
cross-training curriculum to increase the capacity of communities to
provide essential services to persons with co-occurring mental illnesses
and substance use disorders in contact with the criminal justice system.
As a comprehensive five-module, two-day cross-training, it is designed

to bring disparate jurisdictions from varying "points of readiness" through an entire series of training exercises and materials that culminates in a self-directed action plan. The structure of the full cross-training curriculum consists of five modules (see Table 1).

The AXT Project, from which the ACTION approach was developed, included two distinct phases. During Phase I, a cross-training curriculum for professionals in the criminal justice, mental health and substance abuse systems was developed and tested at two sites: Spokane, WA and Orleans Parish, LA. In Phase II, the cross-training curriculum was revised and delivered at http://pra-axt.com/meet_sites.htm across the U.S. (see Table 2 below).

Intervention. Based upon *The Sequential Intercept Model* (Munetz & Griffin, 2006), the AXT curriculum, currently known as the ACTION approach, combines: (1) *education* about the fundamental principles and culture of each of the mental health, substance abuse, and criminal justice systems; (2) *facilitated strategic planning* to assist communities in

☐ Table 1: AXT Cross-Training Curriculum Modules	
Module 1	Background and Mapping the System
Module 2	Screening and Assessment
Module 3	Treatment and Strategic Intercepts: Issues and Strategies
Module 4	Jail Re-entry
Module 5	Systems Collaboration and Action Blueprint

☐ Table 2: AXT Project – Beta Pilot Test Sites	
Modular Training Combination	Beta Pilot Test Site
Cross-Training (Modules 1, 2, 3, 4, & 5)	Cuyahoga County, OH Skagit County, WA Mercer County, NJ Johnson County, IA
Systems Impact (Modules 1 & 5)	Penobscot County, ME Denton County, TX
Re-entry (Modules 1, 4, & 5)	Hillsborough County, FL DeKalb County, GA
Integrated Treatment (Modules 2 & 3)	Harford County, MD

developing a concrete action plan; and (3) *technical assistance* to plan, implement, and maintain cross-systems collaboration and systems change activities. Particular attention is paid to "mapping" the local system, focusing on the five strategic intercepts (see Table 3), or points of contact with the criminal justice system, where individuals with mental health and substance use disorders can be targeted for intervention.

Taking a multi-disciplinary approach, the ACTION approach works to build partnerships and facilitate cross-systems collaboration by: (1) leveling the playing field through education of administrators, service providers, front-line staff, policymakers and consumers about the issues faced by people who are justice system-involved and who have mental health and/or substance use disorders, highlighting the challenges faced by these individuals and discussing their service and treatment needs; (2) creating a local systems map and collectively identifying critical gaps and untapped resources in the service delivery systems at each intercept in which to intervene; and (3) facilitating the development of a comprehensive, realistic and strategic plan for action to address the implementation of the strategic system modifications identified through the systems mapping and consensus building exercises.

INTERVENTION PRODUCTS: THE LOCAL CROSS-SYSTEMS MAP, ACTION PLAN AND FOLLOW-UP TECHNICAL ASSISTANCE

The Local Cross-Systems Map. Common among all the AXT Project trainings, and a core component of the ACTION approach, is the development of a local cross-systems map. The systems map is created during a dynamic and interactive exercise, known as *The Systems Mapping Exercise* (National GAINS Center, 2006). Through this exercise, a

☐ **Table 3: Points of Contact Within The Sequential Intercept Model**	
Intercept 1	Law Enforcement/Emergency Services
Intercept 2	Arrest & Initial Detention/Initial Court Hearings (First Appearance Court)
Intercept 3	Jails (pre-trial)/Courts (Dispositional/Specialty)
Intercept 4	Re-entry (Jail/Prison)
Intercept 5	Community Corrections/Community Support (Probation/Parole)

flowchart that maps the process by which individuals move through the local criminal justice system is created, indicating points for intervention or diversion of people with mental illness and providing a visual depiction of the ways in which treatment systems interact with the local criminal justice system.

The Action Plan. Another key component of the ACTION approach, and the culminating event for each of the AXT Project trainings, is the development of a comprehensive, cross-systems community Action Plan. The Action Plan is a dynamic document, developed during the cross-training, that contains a mutually identified set of immediate, short-term next steps or "small wins" toward systems change, as well as concrete longer-term goals, each of which is geared toward addressing a particular issue or set of issues identified throughout the course of the cross-training and facilitated strategic planning session. The Action Plan includes a set of best known approaches to address the identified problems and a list of identified individuals who have agreed to pursue each action step.

Follow-up Technical Assistance. During the 12 months following the cross-training, four of the sites that participated in the Phase II pilot tests were targeted to receive one on-site, follow-up technical assistance visit designed to accomplish two primary goals: (1) to provide advice and assistance regarding additional next steps to build on the progress that had already been made toward achieving the goals of their Action Plan; and (2) to provide targeted technical assistance around key issues that needed to be addressed and/or core strategies that communities were seeking to implement to further accomplish the goals established during the initial facilitated strategic planning session.

RESEARCH METHODOLOGY

Study Sites. The nine Beta pilot test sites were selected from 52 applicants through a competitive solicitation process using the following criteria: (1) a local-level jurisdiction, (2) at an appropriate level of readiness for cross-systems collaboration, (3) geographically diverse (e.g., rural and urban), and (4) demographically diverse. In addition, individual applications were requested from key community stakeholders to demonstrate buy-in from key decision makers. Specifically, individual applications were requested from:

- Administrator from the local jail;
- Administrator from the local public mental health agency (such as the county mental health department);
- Administrator from the local public substance abuse agency;
- Administrator from the local city police and/or county sheriff's departments;
- Consumer representative (i.e., a person that identifies him/herself as a current or former recipient of mental health services)
- Judge

Cross-Training Facilitators. The AXT cross-training facilitation was done by two-person teams of experienced multidisciplinary professionals with a mix of systems: clinical, mental health, criminal justice, substance abuse, co-occurring disorders and cultural competence backgrounds. The two co-facilitators for each cross-training were selected on the basis of the site-specific interest areas and on an appropriate balance of clinical and systems-level expertise. The co-facilitators led the cross-training participants through each of the educational modules and exercises, and facilitated *The Systems Mapping Exercise* and action planning.

Research Design. A comprehensive process and outcome evaluation methodology was developed to assess the effectiveness and impact of the AXT Project cross-training curriculum for short-term and long-term impact at both the individual and systems levels. Of particular interest was the value added of receiving follow-up technical assistance. These questions required utilizing a multi-modal data collection strategy.

Often, training evaluation methodology is limited to a "customer satisfaction" survey (or so-called "reaction measures") administered to training participants upon completion of the training program. While these data are useful, they address only a small segment of the research questions. To fully understand the effectiveness of the community cross-training, as well as the short-term effects and long-term impact of a training session on its attendees and the systems in which they function, a much broader and more comprehensive methodology was applied using a modified version of the Kirkpatrick model (Kirkpatrick, 1979).

The Kirkpatrick model includes four levels of evaluation for training programs: reaction, learning, behavior, and results. The model was adapted for this study by adding an additional "needs assessment" level. The addition of this fifth level was necessary in order to provide the community-level context for the training, the results of which were used to tailor the cross-training to the community. The needs assessment was comprised of a pre-training site visit, facilitated by the co-facilitators, with the key community stakeholders who signed individual applications as part of the solicitation response. The purpose of the site visit was threefold: (1) to interact with the key decision makers and build rapport; (2) to visit one or more agencies or facilities (e.g., jail) to obtain a sense of the community context; and (3) to identify community-specific barriers and issues in advance so the cross-training curriculum could be tailored to hone in on the specific needs of the community.

Process Evaluation. All nine Beta pilot test sites were included in the cross-training process evaluation. The process evaluation was designed primarily to assess the reaction and learning components of the evaluation model. The process evaluation consisted of: (1) a post-training meeting evaluation; (2) a post-training focus group; and (3) a pre- and post-training knowledge questionnaire. The purpose of the post-training evaluation was to assess the overall strengths and weaknesses of the curriculum, as well as to obtain a short-term assessment of the curriculum content and process. The 11-item meeting evaluation form was administered to all training participants and the data was used to inform the post-training focus group.

A post-training focus group was conducted on site within two weeks following the cross-training event, and comprised a cross-section of six to eight individuals who participated in the entire training event. An experienced focus group facilitator conducted the groups at each site. The purpose of the focus group was to evaluate the content and delivery of the cross-training curriculum and the short-term perceptions of the training content and process, including the helpfulness of the cross-training at furthering collaboration and establishing realistic goals for the future.

To assess the participants' level of short-term learning in key content areas of the curriculum both *prior to* and *following* the training, a pre- and post-training knowledge questionnaire was administered to each focus group participant. The 30-item questionnaire was a compilation of the core concepts covered during each of the five modules of the training.

Outcome Evaluation. Eight of the nine Beta pilot test sites were selected to participate in the outcome evaluation. The site not included (Harford County, MD) was the site that received the Integrated Treatment cross-training. This site was not included since the Integrated

Treatment cross-training was conceptualized primarily as a clinical staff educational piece and not primarily focused on systems change.

The outcome evaluation was designed primarily to assess the behavior and results levels of the evaluation model. The outcome evaluation measures consisted of a two- and 12-month follow-up phone interview with a cross-section of participants identified by the sites in advance of the training, and a six- and 10-month site progress report from the key community stakeholders who participated in the initial site visit and the training. The purpose of the phone interviews was to get a short- and long-term behavioral assessment of the *person-level impact* of the training and the implementation of the action plan. The purpose of the site progress report was to conduct a short- and long-term results assessment of the *systems-level* impact of the training and the implementation of the action plan.

Value Added of Technical Assistance. Based on the National GAINS Center's (http://www.gainscenter.samhsa.gov) experience of providing technical assistance to nearly 200 communities nationwide regarding issues concerning people with mental illness and co-occurring disorders involved in the criminal justice system, it was hypothesized that enhancing the cross-training effectiveness with follow-up technical assistance within six months of the training event would significantly enhance positive systems change within the community. To assess the impact of follow-up technical assistance, similar sites were paired on demographic and geographic dimensions, with one site in each pairing receiving follow-up technical assistance. Technical assistance sites and non-technical assistance sites were compared for differences in the level of systems change (outcomes) achieved.

FINDINGS

Process Evaluation

The process evaluation of the AXT cross-training yielded several significant learning and reaction findings from the nine participating sites. First, the total number of correct responses on the knowledge questionnaire across all nine sites increased by 36% following the cross-training showing an overall increase in participants' knowledge. Second, both quantitative and qualitative analyses were conducted on the 11-item post-training evaluation form. The opportunity to network and to convene key decision makers and representatives from each of the core systems in the community was the most frequent response to the open-ended question, What did you like most about the cross-training? The lack of adequate representation of key players in the community who are important to the action planning and decision-making process was the most frequent response to the open-ended question, What did you like least about the cross-training? All four sites that received the two-day training reported that it was difficult for key decision makers to commit two full days of time, especially judges and law enforcement. Overall, it was clear that a critical component to the systems change process was providing the opportunity for participants to network across systems and ensuring that the right people from all relevant systems were represented to facilitate this process.

Participants reported a high level of satisfaction with the overall curriculum content and process, with overall mean scores on a 4-point scale of 3.72 and 3.81, respectively. All nine sites reported a high level of satisfaction with the modular content. In addition, the results of the content analsysis of recommended changes to the curriculum showed five of nine sites suggested the addition of a module on barriers to information sharing (e.g., The Health Insurance Portability and Accountability Act of 1996 [HIPAA]). Sites viewed the addition of this module as a means by which myths could be dispelled, paving the way for the sharing of critical information that could greatly facilitate the transition planning process. Another recommendation from four of nine sites was to emphasize that the AXT cross-training is not simply training, but is really a facilitated strategic planning session with a more traditional educational/training component included as part of the partnership building and collaboration process. Other salient findings from the process evaluation included providing more opportunity for participation and reducing the length of the training from two to one-and-one-half days.

Outcome Evaluation

As a direct result of participating in the AXT cross-training, the eight communities included in the outcome evaluation implemented an array of systems-level changes over the 10-month follow-up period following the cross-training. In addition, sites that received follow-up technical assistance reported a greater level of achievement as a result of the additional targeted technical assistance provided by the project. A qualitative analysis of the telephone interview and progress report data was conducted, and individual and system-level changes reported by communities were primarily associated with (1) transition planning; (2) community preparedness for offender re-entry; and (3) effective collaboration strategies for responsive offender re-entry into the community.

Transition Planning. Effective multi-agency transition planning, involving consumers in the planning process, is critical for breaking the cycle of recidivism and promoting recovery for people with co-occurring mental health and substance use disorders transitioning from the criminal justice system into the community. During the 10 months following the training, six out of eight counties reported creating funded positions for individuals who would serve as "boundary spanners" (Steadman, 1992) or liaisons between the jail and the community provider agencies to facilitate transition planning for people with mental illness and co-occurring disorders in the jail. One county funded liaison positions for five of the largest mental health providers. Another county created three funded boundary spanner positions and used follow-up technical assistance offered by the AXT project to train the boundary spanners. One local mental health provider created a forensic case worker position for in-reach into the jail and one county jail hired a social service supervisor to facilitate and coordinate transition planning. Another county developed a pilot project to create an intervention specialist position to divert inmates and connect them to community services. Finally, one county funded an entire jail transition project involving case management, strategic planning and the creation of a transition team. Most of these liaison positions were created by shifting dollars–no new funding was applied.

To facilitate transition planning among boundary spanners and liaisons, the AXT cross-training suggested the use of the National GAINS Center's *Re-Entry Checklist* (National GAINS Center, 2005), a unique tool to assist in the development of responsive transition planning procedures. The checklist includes the essential components to successful re-entry of offenders into the community, including mental health services, psychotropic medications, housing, substance abuse services, health care, health care benefits, income/support benefits, food/clothing, and transportation. During the 10 months following the cross-training, one participating county was able to pilot test and implement the *Re-Entry Checklist*, which was completed by the county's five jail liaisons in the jail, in order to improve service coordination in the community. The jail was instrumental in facilitating the use of the form via weekly staff case review meetings convened to review the treatment and service needs of inmates with mental illness in the jail.

An important treatment issue among inmates, while in jail and upon release into the community, and a key component of the *Re-Entry Checklist*, is continuity of psychotropic medications. Maintaining continuity of psychotropic medications upon release of an inmate into the community is a critical component to health and recovery (Council of State Governments, 2002). Three out of eight counties reported positive systems-level changes regarding continuity of medication provision. One county developed a contract with the jail mental health provider to provide prescription medications to inmates with mental illness upon release. Another used jail in-reach to expedite obtaining medications in the community setting. Finally, one county allotted three hours per week for jail psychiatrists to conduct medication follow-ups with individuals in the community post-release. This example of following up with offenders in the community is one of many ways in which the participating counties prepared the community-based service system for receipt of inmates exiting their jails.

Community Preparedness. A core component of effective transition planning and aftercare of inmates is the preparedness of the community to appropriately identify, stabilize, and divert people with mental illness away from the justice system into coordinated, integrated and appropriate services in the community setting. Although many communities have been successful at developing and executing jail diversion programs for people with mental illness (GAINS/TAPA Center, 2007), most still have first responders who are untrained in mental health issues, limited or no crisis stabilization capacity, and fragmented and uncoordinated service delivery systems to which offenders are linked as part of the diversion program. These non-integrated approaches often result in poorer outcomes for people who are justice system-involved (Council of State Governments, 2005).

During the 10 months following the training, all eight AXT Project sites achieved a number of successes in regard to community preparedness, both at the front door and at the back door of the criminal justice process. A key goal of the AXT Project at the front door of the process (Intercepts 1 and 2 of *The Sequential Intercept Model* (Munetz & Griffin, 2006)), is training first responders to identify and appropriately refer people with mental illness to services or into a jail diversion program. Crisis Intervention Team (CIT) training for first responders (e.g., law enforcement officers) is an evidence-based practice that gives first responders the skills to appropriately identify and refer to services people with mental illness whose offenses are non-threatening to the community. Three counties reported new or additional CIT training activities for law enforcement in the 10 months following the training. Regarding crisis stabilization, four communities identified untapped resources, such as detoxification beds and crisis stabilization locations, which could be reserved for diversion.

The use of specialty courts, such as mental health courts and drug courts, is a rapidly expanding approach to diverting people with mental illness and substance abuse problems away from the justice system and into treatment. One county created a pilot mental health court following the cross-training. Utilizing the technical assistance offered as part of the AXT project, this community was able to begin planning for an integrated treatment court, combining their existing drug court and pilot mental health court program.

A key goal of the AXT Project at the back door of the process (Intercepts 3-5 of *The Sequential Intercept Model* (Munetz & Griffin, 2006)), is reducing or eliminating major barriers to successfully engaging offenders in treatment by reestablishing social services and disability benefits and solidifying affordable housing upon release. One county developed a pilot project to allow individuals with mental illness convicted of drug possession to participate in treatment for co-occurring disorders and receive benefits immediately rather than wait the six months that had traditionally been the standard. Three counties identified new housing resources and ways to obtain additional funding or resources, including purchasing software to locate housing through a web-based housing inventory. Another county incorporated housing into the transition plan, whereas previously housing had been excluded.

Additionally, in order to prepare for inmate re-entry, one county provider allotted time and service slots solely for inmates. Another county identified a community advocate to train county staff on how to increase effective engagement of clients whose illnesses involve resistance to treatment. A third county developed a similar pilot program among the jail, the hospital, probation and DHHS to divert probationers with co-occurring disorders, who were identified as being at high risk for re-incarceration, from getting re-arrested. Although no counties reported making positive changes toward integrating mental health and substance abuse services in the community, because of the complex nature of integrating services and systems that have traditionally been adversarial, this could possibly be a longer-term outcome of the partnerships and community collaboration established during the AXT project. Since the key to service system integration in any community begins with effective cross-systems collaborations and all of the participating AXT Project

sites reported increases in cross-systems coordination and improved relationships, the stage is set for such systems change to be realized.

Cross-Systems Collaboration. In order to successfully help people
achieve recovery and resiliency from co-occurring disorders, the mental
health, substance abuse, criminal justice and social service systems
must identify ways to break down organizational barriers and collaborate to provide coordinated and comprehensive co-occurring treatment
services for offenders who are re-entering into the community from jail.
The ACTION approach promotes a number of effective cross-systems
collaboration strategies for responsive offender re-entry, including a
shared vision and direction, developing an action plan that includes low
cost, short-term attainable action steps, and cross-systems information
sharing and the use of electronic data.

A requirement of the AXT Project was that communities develop a
cross-systems Task Force prior to the cross-training. This Task Force
would agree upon a shared vision and be responsible for oversight of the
action plan developed during the cross-training. All eight sites reported
that their Task Force was still intact at six months following the
cross-training. By 10 months following the training three of eight sites
reported that their Task Force still met regularly. Three other sites reported that their Task Force members had moved on to other new initiatives related to the same issues, but also reported that the work on the
AXT Action Plan positively informed the new roles of the original Task
Force members. One site reported that several of their Task Force members had moved into new, unrelated positions and the few remaining
members disbanded. One of the three sites whose Task Force stayed intact received follow-up technical assistance for the purpose of further
refining their Action Plan by developing specialized subcommittees.
This site used the Task Force and subcommittee model to successfully
implement many positive changes that assisted their community in
successfully obtaining two new grants to fund their work.

A common challenge to cross-systems collaboration faced by communities is compliant data sharing. Specifically, trying to decipher all of
the Federal, state and local data sharing laws designed to protect individuals' private information has proven to be problematic. HIPAA and
similar legislations have been a platform for resistance regarding the
sharing of information, and a tremendous obstacle for effective collaboration by hampering the ability to clearly identify target populations and
create appropriate programming. Most of the participating counties expressed concerns about information sharing during the cross-training

event. Specifically, sites were concerned about the regulatory restrictions of sharing private health information across agencies, yet expressed the need for the sharing of individual level data across systems in order to provide appropriate, expeditious and comprehensive services. Following the cross-training, two of the counties requested and received technical assistance regarding the myths surrounding HIPAA and other regulations that have created significant barriers for cross-systems information exchange. In addition, two of the counties fine-tuned their information systems and identified ways to share information about booking data in "real time" to providers in order to instigate jail in-reach and maintain continuity of care. One county reported increased information sharing at "higher levels" in the county structure.

Technical Assistance Results in Implementation

Three of four targeted technical assistance sites received follow-up technical assistance during the six months following the cross-training. One site was unable to overcome political obstacles and was thus unable to coordinate a technical assistance visit within the six-month timeframe. Compared to similar non-technical assistance sites, the three sites that received technical assistance confirmed the hypothesis that positive systems change is substantially enhanced when follow-up technical assistance is received within a reasonably short period of time following the cross-training. In sum, the technical assistance sites were able to move beyond the cross-systems education and planning aspects of their action plan and actually implement a portion of their identified action steps.

All of the three technical assistance sites were able to take one or more of their action steps beyond planning and coordination to implementation as a direct result of the technical assistance provided. As mentioned earlier in the findings, one of the sites reported creating three paid boundary spanner positions. While the cross-training provided an opportunity for a common understanding about the importance of boundary spanners in transition planning, and the systems mapping and action planning process helped the participants identify how to use existing resources to fund these positions, this site used follow-up technical assistance to support this effort even further. A boundary spanner training, led by an outside expert, was held shortly following the training to reinforce the concept for agency administrators and to launch these positions quickly. Often communities without the resources or local expertise for this type of training would not be able to execute the idea without first identifying additional resources to pay for an outside expert. These fiscal restraints often create barriers that slow or quash cross-systems change efforts.

The second technical assistance site received an information sharing and data collection consultation from two expert consultants. The community was facing significant cross-systems collaboration barriers as a result of fear of sharing client data across systems. As discussed previously, a common challenge faced by communities is compliant data sharing. Myths and misunderstanding regarding the sharing of information about justice system-involved individuals have been a huge obstacle for effective collaboration. In this county, a legal expert convened a small group of agency administrators from each of the core systems to educate the group about the reality and myths of information sharing regulations (e.g., HIPAA). Although the cross-training curriculum does address the importance of information sharing as an effective collaboration strategy, it does not go into detail on the topic. The community reported that the technical assistance on compliant information sharing helped them overcome these barriers and implement a cross-systems database for sharing booking data with provider agencies in real time. In addition, the site reported using their shared data to obtain two additional grants to continue the work of their Action Plan.

Finally, as a result of the targeted technical assistance provided, the third technical assistance site reported engaging in advanced planning and being in the early stages of implementing an integrated treatment court. Prior to the cross-training, this site had a pilot mental health court project and a separate fully-functioning drug court. As a result of participating in the cross-training, a common understanding about the prevalence of co-occurring disorders was reached and a group of key decision makers decided to strategize about how to effectively combine the two courts. Consequently, the site used their technical assistance to bring in two outside experts, one nationally recognized in the field of co-occurring disorders and another who works directly with a highly functioning integrated treatment court, to consult about developing an integrated court. At 12 months, the site was well into the planning phase and preparing to launch the court in the following year.

LIMITATIONS

This outcome evaluation was limited to the implementation of the AXT cross-training curriculum and its impact on positive individual and systems-level change toward cross-systems collaboration to improve integrated service delivery. An excellent follow-up to this investigation would be an examination of offender outcomes such as recidivism and improved access to mental health and substance abuse treatment in the community.

SUMMARY AND RECOMMENDATIONS

Recovery from mental illness and co-occurring substance use disorders, as well as increased public safety and reduced rates of recidivism, are possible when communities take action by forming cross-systems partnerships and identify a mutually identified set of action steps to promote continuous, appropriate, and integrated treatment services in the community for justice system-involved citizens. Given the nearly eight million people re-entering the community from jails and prisons each year (Hammett, Roberts, & Kennedy, 2001; Harrison & Beck, 2006), it is evident that community transition planning and aftercare is essential. Research on the Modified Therapeutic Community treatment model proves that providing coordinated aftercare in the community is the key component to maintaining and improving outcomes for justice system-involved individuals upon release from correctional facilities into the community. However, transition planning results will only be as good as the correctional-behavioral health care partnership in the community (Osher, Steadman, & Barr, 2002). The path to positive systems-level change is through effective cross-systems collaboration, the key concept upon which the ACTION approach is based.

Providing further validation of the efficacy of the ACTION approach, the U.S. Department of Justice, through its Office of Justice Programs' Bureau of Justice Assistance, has espoused the ACTION approach through its Justice and Mental Health Collaboration Program (JMHCP). This program was created by the Mentally Ill Offender Treatment and Crime Reduction Act of 2004 (Public Law 108-414) in response to requests from state government officials to recommend improvements to the criminal justice system's response to people with mental illness. The purpose of the program is to increase public safety by facilitating collaboration among the criminal justice, juvenile justice, mental health treatment and substance abuse systems in order to increase access to treatment for this unique group of offenders. Through its FY2006 and FY2007 JMHCP grant announcements, Bureau of Justice Assistance required states and communities to demonstrate familiarity with the ACTION approach and *The Sequential Intercept Model* (Munetz &

Griffin, 2006). As a core aspect of the JMHCP, this approach is fundamental to furthering the goals of the program and essential to successfully facilitate collaboration among systems.

The ACTION approach,[1] as developed during the AXT Project, is a unique approach for stimulating community change that goes beyond classic training or cross-training to promote cross-systems collaboration and coordinated integrated treatment methods for people with co-occurring disorders in contact with the criminal justice system. The ACTION approach demonstrates that positive systems change is possible through *education* about the fundamental principles and culture of each of the mental health, substance abuse, and criminal justice systems, and *facilitated strategic planning* to assist communities in developing a concrete action plan. Added value can be attained with follow-up *technical assistance* to plan, implement, and maintain cross-systems collaboration and systems change activities. At its core, this systems change approach reflects a blending of shared information and action planning activities designed to launch local communities beyond informal communication and cooperation into formal cross-systems collaboration efforts, promoting transformation at the interface of the mental health, substance abuse and criminal justice systems within a community.

NOTE

1. For information on ACTION training, contact (518) 439-7415; training@prainc.com; www.prainc.com.

REFERENCES

Abram, K. M., & Teplin, L. A. (1991). Co-occurring disorders among mentally ill jail detainees. *American Psychologist, 46*(10), 1036-1045.

Council of State Governments (2002). *Criminal justice / mental health consensus project*. New York, NY: Author.

Council of State Governments (2005). *Report of the re-entry policy council: Charting the safe and successful return of prisoners to the community*. New York, NY: Author.

De Leon, G. (1993). Modified therapeutic communities for dual disorders. In J. Solomon, S. Zimberg, & E. Shollar (Eds.), *Dual diagnosis: Evaluation, treatment, training, and program development*. New York, NY: Springer-Verlag New York, LLC.

Ditton, P. M. (1999). *Mental health and treatment of inmates and probationers* (NCJ Publication No. 174463). Washington, DC: U.S. Department of Justice, Office of Justice Programs, Bureau of Justice Statistics.

Glaze, L. E., & Bonczar, T. P. (2006). *Probation and parole in the United States, 2005* (NCJ Publication No. 215091). Washington, DC: U.S. Department of Justice, Office of Justice Programs, Bureau of Justice Statistics.

Hammett, T. M., Roberts, C., & Kennedy, S. (2001). Health-related issues in prisoner reentry. *Crime & Delinquency, 47*(3), 390-409.

Harrison, P. M., & Beck, A. J. (2006). Prison and jail inmates at midyear 2005 (NCJ Publication No. 213133). Washington, DC: U.S. Department of Justice, Office of Justice Programs, Bureau of Justice Statistics.

Hiller, M. L., Knight, K., & Simpson, D. D. (1999). Prison-based substance abuse treatment, residential aftercare and recidivism. *Addiction, 94*(6), 833-842.

Inciardi, J. A., Martin. S. S., Butzin, C. A., Hooper, R. M., & Harrison, L. D. (1997). An effective model of prison-based treatment for drug-involved offenders. *Journal of Drug Issues, 27*, 261-278.

Kirkpatrick, D. L. (1979). Techniques for evaluating training programs. *Training and Development Journal, 33*(6), 78-92.

Knight, K., Simpson, D. D., & Hiller, M. L. (1999). Three-year reincarceration outcomes for in-prison therapeutic community treatment in Texas. *The Prison Journal, 79*(3), 337–351.

Martin, S. S., Butzin, C. A., Saum, C. A., & Inciardi, J. A. (1999). Three-year outcomes of therapeutic community treatment for drug-involved offenders in Delaware: From prison to work release to aftercare. *The Prison Journal, 79*(3), 294-320.

Munetz, M. R., & Griffin, P. A. (2006). Use of The Sequential Intercept Model as an approach to decriminalization of people with serious mental illness. *Psychiatric Services, 57*, 544-549.

National GAINS Center (2004). *The prevalence of co-occurring mental illness and substance use disorders in jail.* Fact Sheet Series. Delmar, NY: Author.

National GAINS Center (2005). *GAINS re-entry checklist for inmates identified with mental health service needs.* Delmar, NY: Author.

National GAINS Center (2006). *The Systems Mapping Exercise.* Delmar, NY: Author.

Osher, F., Steadman, H. J., & Barr, H. (2002). A best practice approach to community re-entry from jails for inmates with co-occurring disorders: The APIC model. Delmar, NY: The Center for Mental Health Services' National GAINS Center.

Sacks, S., Sacks, J., De Leon, G., Bernhardt, A. I., & Staines, G. L. (1997). Modified therapeutic community for mentally ill chemical "abusers": Background; influences; program description; preliminary findings. *Substance Use and Misuse, 32*(9), 1217-1259.

Sacks, S., Sacks, J. Y., McKendrick, K., Banks, S., & Stommel, J. (2004). Modified TC for MICA offenders: Crime outcomes. *Behavioral Sciences & the Law, 22*(4), 477-501.

Steadman, H. J. (1992). Boundary spanners: A key component for the effective interactions of the justice and mental health systems. *Law and Human Behavior, 16*(1), 75-87.

Steadman, H. J., & Veysey, B. (1997). *Providing services for jail inmates with mental disorders.* Research Brief. Washington, DC: U.S. Department of Justice, Office of Justice Programs, National Institute of Justice.

Teplin, L. A. (1994). Psychiatric and substance abuse disorders among male urban jail detainees. *American Journal of Public Health, 84*(2), 290-293.

Teplin, L. A., Abram, K. M., & McClelland, G. M. (1996). Prevalence of psychiatric disorders among incarcerated women. *Archives of General Psychiatry, 53*, 505-512.

Wexler, H. K., De Leon, G., Thomas, G., Kressel, D., & Peters, J. (1999). The Amity prison TC evaluation: Reincarceration outcomes. *Criminal Justice and Behavior, 26*(2), 147-167.

Wexler, H. K., Melnick, G., Lowe, L., & Peters, J. (1999). Three-year reincarceration outcomes for amity in-prison therapeutic community and aftercare in California. *The Prison Journal, 79*(3), 321-336.

AUTHORS' NOTES

Wendy M. Vogel, MPA, is Research Associate, Policy Research Associates, 345 Delaware Avenue, Delmar, NY 12054 (E-mail: wvogel@prainc.com).

Chanson D. Noether, MA, is Division Manager for Criminal Justice, Policy Research Associates, 345 Delaware Avenue, Delmar, NY 12054 (E-mail: cnoether@prainc.com).

Henry J. Steadman, PhD, is President, Policy Research Associates, 345 Delaware Avenue, Delmar, NY 12054 (E-mail: hsteadman@prainc.com).

This project has been funded in whole with Federal funds from the National Institute of Mental Health, National Institutes of Health, Department of Health and Human Services, under Contract #N44MH32055 from NIMH. The contributions of Eliot Hartstone, PhD, of Spectrum Associates in designing, running and analyzing the focus groups, are gratefully acknowledged.

doi:10.1300/J076v45n01_12

Mental Health Issues in the Criminal Justice System. Pp. 189-206.
Available online at http://jor.haworthpress.com
© 2007 by The Haworth Press, Inc. All rights reserved.
doi:10.1300/J076v45n01_13

Costs, Control or Just Good Clinical Practice? The Use of Antipsychotic Medications and Formulary Decision-Making in Large U.S. Prisons and Jails

BONITA M. VEYSEY
VANJA STENIUS
NOEL MAZADE
LUCILLE SCHACHT

ABSTRACT Medications are central to the psychiatric armamentorium in U.S. jails and prisons. Psychiatric medications are used both to stabilize acute symptoms as well as maintain mental health once symptoms are reduced. Both jails and prisons rely heavily on traditional antipsychotics, but both have a full array of atypical medications in their formularies. The heavy reliance on cheaper traditional medications when alternatives are present suggests that cost remains a factor. The fact that psychiatrists prescribe off the formulary and are more influenced by demonstrated efficacy in formulary decision-making, in contrast, supports the notion that they are indeed concerned with good practice. doi:10.1300/J076v45n01_13 *[Article copies available for a fee from The Haworth Document Delivery Service: 1-800-HAWORTH. E-mail address: <docdelivery@haworthpress.com> Website: <http://www.HaworthPress.com> © 2007 by The Haworth Press, Inc. All rights reserved.]*

KEYWORDS Mental health, psychiatry, antipsychotic, medications, jail, prison

INTRODUCTION

The number of persons in U.S. jails and prisons exceeded 2.2 million at mid-year 2005 (Harrison & Beck, 2006). State and federal prisons housed 1.5 million inmates at mid-year while jails held nearly 750,000 (Harrison & Beck, 2006). Accompanying increases in the jail and prison populations is a growing number of inmates and jail detainees with mental health problems. An estimated 16 percent of state prisoners and jail inmates had mental disorders in 1998 (Ditton, 1999); prevalence rates for severe mental illness (schizophrenia, bipolar depression and major depression) within a jail population have been found to exceed that in the general population by two to three times (Teplin, 1990, 1994); and state prisoners typically have higher rates than jails (Veysey & Bichler-Robertson, 2002). A recent study of prison and jail inmates based on self-report suggests that 56 percent of prisoners and 64 percent of jail inmates have had a recent treatment episode or received a clinical diagnosis. Even assuming the lowest estimates, this means that approximately 231,400 state prison inmates and 119,600 jail inmates/detainees have a mental disorder in need of treatment on any given day.

Even in the absence of growth in the percent of inmates with mental illness, the sheer number poses burdens for corrections administrators and state and local governments trying to cover the costs of treatment. In the array of possible treatments for mental illnesses, medications remain the mainstay in correctional facilities (Beck & Marushack, 2001). At the same time, psychiatric medications represent a significant proportion of pharmacy budgets, second only to HIV medications (Wolff & Veysey, 2001). Despite the high level of need and use of psychiatric medications within corrections, relatively little is known about the selection and use of various medications. This paper explores the provision of antipsychotic medications within large prisons and jails and the factors that go into formulary decisions and the adoption of new medications.

Provision of Mental Health Services in Correctional Facilities

Correctional institutions have a Constitutional duty to provide both safe custody and to insure inmates' health and well-being. Case law, such as *Estelle v. Gamble* and *Bowring v. Goodwin*, established the requirement to provide a least minimal medical and psychiatric care (Cohen & Dvoskin, 1992). Case law and statutes typically do not clearly define what constitutes adequate care within correctional facilities;

however, professional organizations and accrediting agencies have a general agreement as to minimum care standards. According to the American Psychiatric Association, jails and prisons should provide mental health screening and evaluation, crisis intervention and short-term treatment (usually medication), access to inpatient services, and discharge/release planning (American Psychiatric Association, 1989).

While most prisons and jails provide some mental health care, many fail to provide comprehensive services. In 2000, 89 percent of state public and private prisons reported that they provide mental health services to inmates. Seventy-three percent reported offering psychotropic medications to inmates (Beck & Marushack, 2001). Similarly, most U.S. jails with 50 or more detainees offer at least one mental health service, but few provide a comprehensive range of services (Steadman & Veysey, 1997). Of the jails that provide a fairly comprehensive range of services (i.e., inpatient psychiatric programs, screening, evaluation, special housing, and psychotropic medication), most have a rated capacity of 1,000 or more (Steadman & Veysey, 1997). While a national weighted estimate places the percent of jails that provide psychiatric medications at 42 percent, all of the jails with a capacity of 1,000 or more report offering this service (Steadman & Veysey, 1997).

In terms of service usage, a large number of inmates with mental illness do not receive services. Of the 56 percent of prison inmates who have had recent mental health problems, only 34 percent report having received some form of mental health treatment during their incarceration (James & Glaze, 2006). Reported service receipt is lower in jails with only 18 percent of those with a self-reported mental illness having received mental health services (James & Glaze, 2006).

Incarceration of persons with mental illnesses creates unique problems within a correctional setting. Correctional staff often lack the training to deal with the behaviors and needs of this population, creating management problems. Persons with acute psychiatric symptoms often have difficulty conforming to rules and following directions. They may behave in ways that increase security risk through the escalation of dangerous behavior, disturbing other inmates, or through increased vulnerability to victimization. Creating calmer environments through the stabilization of inmates is essential to correctional security. Separation into specialized housing units also helps. Medication, case management and one-on-one therapy all serve to stabilize individuals. In jails and prisons the cheapest, most cost-effective intervention that meets the standards of good practice remains medication. In fact, medication may be over-prescribed to sedate, and therefore control, rather than to stabilize.

Large facilities, particularly prisons, are better understood as whole communities where a full array of inpatient and outpatient care is available. Many large prisons have a continuum of housing from psychiatric inpatient to transitional or long-term specialized housing to general population, and use a principle of least restrictive setting. Persons arrive in the prison usually from the jail. They have had time to stabilize. People with mental illnesses in prisons have acute and stable phases, like those in the community. Like the free community, individuals may be prescribed medication in any setting. Other supports may also be offered to help each person function at his/her highest level.

Large jails are similar to large prisons in their capacity to provide a wide range of mental health supports, but differ in their primary mandate and population. Unlike prisons, where individuals arrive largely stabilized, jails are often the setting where people in acute states are held. Often persons arrive in jail having stopped medications and are actively psychotic and sometimes suicidal. The jail's primary psychiatric mandate is to stabilize. Prison inmates serve long sentences; jail detainees, on the other hand, may remain only a few days. In fact, the single day jail census is misleading. Jails typically process 10 times the census number over the course of a year. The relatively short stay of jail inmates limits the potential for long-term planning and treatment (American Psychiatric Association, 2000; Veysey et al., 1997), while the acute nature of the conditions requires jails to focus on high impact, short-term interventions.

Traditional vs. Atypical Antipsychotic Medications

The provision of mental health services helps alleviate problems for the institution in addition to treating the inmate or detainee with psychiatric needs. Medications represent a primary means of providing this treatment and dealing with problematic and potentially violent behavior of which antipsychotic agents are a large part. However, the use of antipsychotics is not without controversy. The use of medications, whether traditional or atypical, is a matter of research and debate both within general psychiatric practice and within correctional settings where formulary restrictions and costs place additional constraints on prescriptions.

Within community-based practice, atypical antipsychotic medications are rapidly replacing the traditional agents (Worrel et al., 2000; Leslie & Rosenheck, 2002). The newer agents are at least equally effective compared to traditional and have fewer adverse effects (Brown et al., 1999; U.S. Department of Health and Human Services, 1999), and reductions in adverse effects have been postulated to result in increased

compliance with prescribed medication regimens and improved therapeutic outcomes (Brown et al., 1999). This does not necessarily mean
that atypical agents are a better choice since efficacy varies by drug
(Markowitz et al., 1999; Koro et al., 2002) as well as by individual.
Also, emerging research suggests that atypical antipsychotics may play
an important role in increased body mass index (BMI) and type II diabetes
(Metzer, 2005). While most prescription changes involving the two
classes switch from traditional to atypical, in some cases prescriptions
revert back to traditional medications (Leslie & Rosenheck, 1992)
suggesting that atypical agents are not necessarily the best choice for all
persons receiving antipsychotic medications.

While developed and indicated for the treatment of schizophrenia
and other psychotic disorders, the use of atypical antipsychotics extends
beyond the intended usage. In addition to the treatment of psychotic disorders, atypical agents are used for other conditions including mania
(Glick, 2001; Worrel et al., 2000), depression and aggression (Worrell
et al., 2000), with study findings suggesting that the atypical agents may
be useful in treating these conditions and behavior (Glick, 2001; Worrel
et al., 2000). The efficacy and use of atypical medications for aggression
are of particular significance within a correctional environment where
violence and aggressive behavior by inmates present a major security
risk, especially among those with mental illnesses (Ditton, 1999).

Costs and Formulary Restrictions

Correctional agencies attempt to contain costs, particularly volatile
ones, through several different strategies. Medical and psychiatric costs
take up large proportions of correctional budgets. The costs of maintaining expensive infrastructures (i.e., staffing, space and equipment),
medications and supplies are skyrocketing. Agencies attempt to control
costs through contract services. Many jails and prisons contract with
for-profit companies to provide medical, including psychiatric, care and
pharmacy services. These companies in turn attempt to maximize profit
by limiting services and restricting formularies. Even in the absence of
contract services, corrections administrators may instruct medical directors to reduce costs, particularly by encouraging the use of generic or
older medications.

The costs of atypical antipsychotics are higher than those for traditional agents. While atypical agents potentially create cost-savings
through prevention, the upfront cost poses a barrier to use. Acquisition
costs for atypical medications can be several thousand dollars per year

compared to a few hundred dollars for traditional medications (Worrel et al., 2000). Cost reductions through relapse prevention, decreased hospitalization, and lower treatment costs associated with adverse effects of traditional agents may ultimately lead to cost savings (Brown et al., 1999). However, available research is fraught with problems and yields mixed results, with some indicating costs-savings while other studies find significant cost increases (Worrel et al., 2000). It appears that atypical antipsychotics present a high acquisition cost with uncertain future cost reduction. This may be especially true in jails where inmates or detainees may not remain in the facility long enough for it to realize direct cost-savings.

In the past, adopting atypical agents within the correctional system meant both formulary expansion and a willingness on the part of correctional psychiatrists to change their prescribing practices. Under normal conditions these factors can be problematic. Introduction of a new drug during an era of cost containment in which expensive therapies were subjected to considerable scrutiny by managers of public and private correctional facilities, and mental health systems more generally, further limited the availability and use of atypical agents within prisons and jails. The lag between the availability of newer agents and their inclusion in facility pharmacy formularies has now come to the attention of managers, patients, the courts, and payers (Gabriele, 1998; Hyman, 1998; Richardson, 1998; Richardson, 1999).

METHODS

This study[1] consists of a mail survey submitted to all identified U.S. prisons and jails with a rated capacity of 1,000 or more. The study addresses the degree to which the correctional environment or auspice inhibit or enhance: (1) continuity of care, (2) identification and treatment of psychiatric disorders, (3) range of available interventions, and (4) ability of the psychiatric staff to meet professional standards of care. Prison and jail mailings were sent out separately.

Prisons were identified through an extensive search process. State facilities were identified by searching the Department of Corrections website for each state and selecting all facilities with a rated capacity of 1,000 or more. Federal and private facilities were similarly identified via the internet. State Department of Corrections, the Federal Bureau of Prisons and private prison companies were contacted for clarifications.

Surveys were mailed to 321 facilities in late 1999, with a follow-up in early 2000.

Jails eligible for the study were identified in a similar fashion. Using the most recent version of the *Who's Who in Jail Management* published by the American Jail Association, all jails with rated capacities of 1,000 or more were selected. In counties with more than one facility the size criterion was determined by the combined rated capacity. In these counties, the respondents were asked to combine the population characteristics of the multiple facilities into single estimates. Two rounds of surveys were mailed to 90 facilities in spring of 2000.

Of the 321 prisons that met the criteria for inclusion, 48 individual facilities responded and six states provided statewide aggregates for a total of 54 completed surveys. The states that responded (California, Alabama, Oregon, Pennsylvania, Texas, and Alaska) reflect information from a total of 188 individual facilities or 67 percent of all identified prisons. Combined, the data captures 82 percent of the prisons. Twenty-two of the 90 jails returned the surveys for a response rate of 24 percent. The findings reported here reflect the responses by individual prisons and jails; statewide prison aggregates were excluded to improve comparability across types of facilities. Respondents were asked to provide estimates for the year 1998.

Potential Bias

Statewide aggregates create a potential issue in the characterization of facilities. Six completed surveys reflect the sum of 188 separate facilities. Any variation between facilities, in terms of services, population characteristics, or decision-making, is eliminated by aggregation. The state-level data are relevant in terms of cross-state contrasts. However, the few states that submitted surveys ($n = 6$) limit the generalizability of the findings. These aggregate responses have been excluded from the following analyses.

Of more critical concern is the possibility of response bias. That is, the facilities that responded may be significantly different from non-respondents in a systematic way. There are several possible ways these differences could manifest. First, facilities that respond may have a greater number of persons with mental illnesses, or may be designated facilities for the treatment of persons with mental illnesses in comparison to those that did not respond. Second, in comparison to non-respondents, facilities that respond are more satisfied with the services they provide. Third, facilities currently under investigation or under court-order may be unlikely to complete a survey that provided incriminating evidence. Fourth, certain types of facilities may not be as likely to respond (e.g., federal facilities or smaller facilities) as others. When the respondents differ in a systematic way from non-respondents, the findings of the study cannot be assumed to apply to the non-respondents unless the nature of the bias is known. Under the current circumstances, the nature is not known and therefore findings must be carefully interpreted.

RESULTS

Facility Characteristics

In this sample, large prisons had a one-day census of 2,117 inmates and a relatively low turnover with 2,630 new admissions in the previous year (see Table 1). While the large jails had a lower census of 1,540 inmates, the number of individuals processed and held far exceeded that of prisons at 23,638 admissions. Similarly, the number of prison inmates receiving mental health services in prisons was larger than the number in jails (265 vs. 218), but jails served over three times the number of persons as prisons over the course of a year.

□ Table 1: Facility Characteristics (n = 63)

	Prison	Jail
	Mean (sd)/%	Mean (sd)
# Bookings/admissions during 1998	2630 (4773)	23,638 (18,399)
# inmates currently housed	2117 (1211)	1540 (642)
# of inmates receiving MH treatment in 1998	1198 (1698)	3760 (3579)
# of inmates currently under psychiatric care	264.9 (214.5)	218.4 (149.2)
Annual expenditures for mental health care	$960,699 ($1,286,157)	$636,086 ($1,007,146)
Operation of psych services*		
% corrections department	68.8	35.0
% for-profit contract	43.8	55.0
% local/regional/state MH agency	6.3	50.0

* Exceeds 100%. Psychiatric and psychological staffs in individual facilities are often employed by different agencies.

The average annual expenditure for mental health care for these facilities was $960,699, while the average annual expenditure in jails is $636,086; about one third lower than prisons. The figures provided do not necessarily include medications costs as some facilities include these costs with medical expenses. The department of corrections and contracted services operate mental health services in prisons. Corrections department staff operate services in 69 percent of prisons. Almost half of the prisons provide services through contracts with for-profit correctional medical and behavioral health companies. Seventeen percent of prisons use both corrections department resources and contracted services. A state mental health authority operates services in 6 percent of prisons. None of the prisons have services operated by a local mental health agency or county or regional mental health authority. More than half of the jails rely on contracted services and about one third use corrections department staff. Jails also use local mental health agencies and a county or regional mental health authority.

Prevalence of Mental Health Problems

Both the prisons and jails deal with a considerable number of inmates with identified mental health needs. In 1998, prison staff identified 19.0 percent of inmates as needing mental health treatment upon admission into the facility. Another 10.6 percent of inmates from the general prison population had new or previously unidentified mental health treatment needs. Combined, about 30 percent of prison inmates needed mental health treatment. At the time of the survey 12.6 percent of inmates were receiving care. The prevalence of mental health issues was higher in jails although the percent currently receiving treatment was approximately the same. Jail staff identified 32.1 percent of new jail admissions and 16.2 percent of individuals from the general population as having mental health treatment needs. At the time of the survey, 13.8 percent of jail detainees were receiving mental health care. The difference between the percent of inmates with identified mental health needs and the percent receiving care at any one time potentially suggests that many of those with identified needs did not receive care. The difference may also be attributable to changing needs as inmates/detainees stabilize and are no longer in need of treatment or leave the facility. Many inmates, notably in jails where suicide and depression present greater problems upon intake, may be in need of acute, but temporary services.

Distribution of Diagnoses

Schizophrenia and major depression make up the majority of Axis I diagnoses (excluding substance use disorders) and account for about half of all inmates who were receiving psychiatric care in prisons and jails (see Table 2). Substance abuse and dependence represents the most common diagnosis affecting 71.9 percent of the prison inmates and 69.0 percent of jail detainees receiving care, almost all of whom also have another Axis I or Axis II diagnosis. This corresponds to roughly 1 in 11 inmates or detainees. Note that these diagnoses are only for inmates *currently* receiving care.

Formulary Contents and Medication Use

All correctional facilities that provided mental health services in this sample have the ability to prescribe antipsychotic medication (9% of prisons do not house inmates with mental illnesses and provide no services). On average, 219 prison inmates and 182 jail detainees per facility received psychiatric medications in the 30 days preceding the survey. In both prisons and jails, this corresponds to 83 percent of those receiving psychiatric care at the time of the survey.

□ **Table 2: Distribution of Diagnoses for Inmates/Detainees Currently Receiving Care in Large Prisons and Jails (n = 63)**

Diagnosis	Prison			Jail		
	%	SD	Pop. Rate	%	SD	Pop. Rate
Schizophrenia/other psychotic disorder	24.8	21.8	1:29	27.4	17.3	1:28
Major depression	26.6	15.7	1:28	22.3	17.3	1:36
Bipolar disorder	11.5	7.5	1:57	16.8	9.3	1:45
PTSD	5.2	5.7	1:123	6.6	6.0	1:128
Other anxiety disorder	8.9	10.8	1:104	8.3	5.7	1:85
Substance abuse/dependence	71.9	23.8	1:11	69.0	23.2	1:10
Mental retardation/developmental disability	3.9	5.5	1:201	6.1	5.2	1:118
Other Axis I disorders	19.7	17.9	1:53	6.1	5.8	1:100
Axis II personality disorders	47.5	33.6	1:16	37.4	23.4	1:20
Axis I or II & substance-related disorder	71.4	23.2	1:11	69.0	22.6	1:10

Both prisons and jails have a range of medications available in their formularies and are similar in specific drug availability. While all facilities had traditional antipsychotics, only approximately 70 percent have atypicals as well (see Table 3). The availability of specific atypical antipsychotics varies from a low of 27 percent for Clozapine in prisons to a high of Risperidone in jails. In all cases in both settings, psychiatrists are allowed to prescribe off formulary. The percent of facilities that use specific medications always exceeds the percent of facilities that have the medication in its formulary. This suggests that clinical practice may overrule cost considerations in some cases.

However, there remains a heavy reliance on traditional antipsychotics. Both jails and prisons use traditional agents more frequently than atypical ones. This is particularly true of high potency medications. Moreover, jails are significantly more likely than prisons to rely on any traditional antipsychotic (73% vs. 52%, p < .05) and particularly high potency ones (77% vs. 49%, p < .05).

Among atypical agents, the medication of choice varies by facility. Prisons and jails primarily keep Risperidone and Olanzapine in their formularies. Jails, however, tend to have a greater range of atypical agents in their formularies and use them with greater frequency. Both prisons and jails use Olanzapine and Risperidone more frequently than

☐ Table 3: Use of Antipsychotics in Large Prisons and Jails (n = 63)						
	% In Formulary		% In Use		% Used Frequently	
	Prison	Jail	Prison	Jail	Prison	Jail
Any Traditional Antipsychotic	91.3	100.0	100.0	100.0	52.2	72.7*
High potency	91.3	100.0	100.0	100.0	48.8	76.5*
Medium Potency	85.4	100.0	92.9	100.0	26.2	35.3
Low Potency	87.0	94.4	97.6	94.1	35.7	35.3
Any Atypical Antipsychotic	71.7	72.7	90.2	90.0	39.1	50.0
Clozapine	26.8	47.4	40.0	57.9	0	5.3
Olanzapine	59.5	57.9	75.0	84.2	27.5	31.6
Quetiapine	31.0	50.0	41.5	70.6	7.3	11.8
Risperidone	67.4	70.0	90.2	82.4	24.4	52.6

* p < .05.

Clozapine or Quetiapine. Although most facilities have atypical medications, many use them only after trying a traditional medication first. More than half of the facilities (55.6% of prisons and 57.9% of jails) that use atypical antipsychotics require the demonstration of treatment failure of traditional antipsychotics before prescribing an atypical agent.

Formulary Decision-Making

Prisons and jails differ in terms of who is responsible for establishing the formulary. In prisons, a state or regional corrections authority figures highly in establishing the formulary, doing so in 38.1 percent of the prisons. The facility pharmacy or medical director (23.8%) and contracted health or behavioral health care company (26.2%) are also important. In jails, the facility pharmacy (47.6%) or a contracted behavioral health or health care company (42.9%) typically sets the formulary. In some facilities more than one body decides what medications will be in the formulary. Note that a state or regional corrections authority does not set the formulary in any of the jails. These differences reflect the local nature of jails and reliance on private service providers in the provision of services.

Jails and prisons differ somewhat in the factors that determine formulary decisions (see Table 4). In jails, the top five factors in determining the frequency of use of antipsychotic agents in order are: (1) personal clinical experience, (2) research-demonstrated efficacy, (3) FDA-approved indications, (4) trainings received through continuing education or professional meetings, and (5) cost. In prisons, the top five factors are: (1) FDA-approved indications, (2) personal clinical experience, (3) accreditation or professional standards, (4) research-demonstrated efficacy, and (5) trainings received through continuing education or professional meetings. Both prisons and jails shared four of their top five. Significant differences in ratings between jails and prison emerge for the availability of an injectable formulation and availability of programs to facilitate ease of use. Jails rate the availability of an injectable version as more important than prisons do (p < .01). Jails also rated the availability of programs to facilitate ease of use as more important (p < .05). Prisons rated this as the least important factor. For jails, local or state health care policies were the least important factors.

A second analysis contrasted facilities (jails and prisons) that use atypicals frequently to those that use them infrequently or not at all (see Table 5). Three factors influencing formulary decisions varied significantly and this difference existed only in prisons. Specifically, personal

☐ **Table 4: Factors Influencing Frequency of Use of Anti-Psychotic Medications in Large Prisons and Jails (n = 63)**

Factor	Prison Mean (sd)	Jail Mean (sd)
Local or state health care policies	3.68 (2.10)	3.57 (2.09)
Accreditation requirements of professional standards of care	5.32 (2.08)	4.91 (1.93)
Facility correctional policies	4.24 (2.26)	3.81 (2.09)
Financing or cost	4.29 (1.90)	5.00 (1.45)
Personal clinical experience	5.54 (1.40)	5.91 (1.15)
Research-demonstrated efficacy	5.27 (1.66)	5.55 (1.63)
FDA-approved indications	5.27 (1.70)	5.41 (1.59)
Availability of liquid formulation	2.98 (1.54)	4.00 (2.16)
Availability of injectable formulation**	3.46 (1.43)	4.91 (1.80)
Adoption or use of treatment guidelines	4.60 (1.58)	4.73 (1.45)
Trainings received through continuing education or professional meetings	5.22 (1.35)	5.09 (1.77)
Availability of programs to facilitate ease of use from pharmaceutical companies*	2.61 (1.52)	3.82 (2.04)

1 = not at all, 7 = extremely
* $p < .05$, ** $p < .01$

clinical experience ($p < .05$), research-demonstrated efficacy ($p < .05$), and FDA-approved indications ($p < .01$) were rated significantly more important in facilities that used atypicals frequently compared to facilities that did not. In general, facilities with full formularies always rated decision-making factors more highly than facilities with restricted formularies. This suggests that facilities that do not have or do not value comprehensive care will not be influenced by typical factors in redressing their deficits.

CONCLUSION

Jails and prisons serve different missions and different individuals. The burdens of one cannot be assumed for the other. Essential to both, however, is the need to provide psychiatric care to those in need. Medications are central to the psychiatric armamentorium. Psychiatric medications are used both to stabilize acute symptoms as well as maintain mental

☐ **Table 5: Factors Influencing Formulary Decisions by Frequent Use of Atypical Antipsychotics in Large Prisons and Jails (n = 63)**

Factor	Frequent Use Mean (SD)	No Use/ Infrequent Use Mean (SD)
Local or state health care policies		
Prison	3.88 (2.06)	3.54 (2.17)
Jail	3.80 (2.15)	3.36 (2.11)
Accreditation requirements of professional standards of care		
Prison	5.44 (1.90)	5.25 (2.23)
Jail	5.64 (1.50)	4.18 (2.09)
Facility correctional policies		
Prison	4.00 (2.21)	4.42 (2.32)
Jail	4.30 (2.11)	3.36 (2.06)
Financing or cost		
Prison	4.00 (1.50)	4.50 (2.15)
Jail	4.91 (1.54)	5.09 (1.45)
Personal clinical experience		
Prison*	6.06 (1.09)	5.17 (1.49)
Jail	6.00 (0.78)	5.82 (1.47)
Research-demonstrated efficacy		
Prison*	5.94 (1.20)	4.79 (1.79)
Jail	5.36 (1.63)	5.73 (1.68)
FDA-approved indications		
Prison**	6.63 (0.92)	5.08 (1.909)
Jail	5.64 (1.57)	5.18 (1.66)
Availability of liquid formulation		
Prison	2.88 (1.73)	3.04 (1.43)
Jail	4.55 (2.08)	3.45 (2.21)
Availability of injectable formulation		
Prison	3.29 (1.40)	3.58 (1.47)
Jail	5.18 (1.72)	4.64 (1.91)
Adoption or use of treatment guidelines		
Prison	4.71 (1.53)	4.52 (1.65)
Jail	5.09 (1.58)	4.36 (1.29)
Trainings received through continuing education or professional meetings		
Prison	5.71 (1.26)	4.88 (1.33)
Jail	5.09 (1.45)	5.09 (2.12)
Availability of programs to facilitate ease of use from pharmaceutical companies		
Prison	2.65 (1.66)	2.58 (1.44)
Jail	3.73 (2.01)	3.91 (2.17)

1 = not at all, 7 = extremely
* $p < .05$, ** $p < .01$

health once symptoms are reduced. Jails commonly face the former, while prisons must be prepared for both. Antipsychotic medications are used primarily to treat schizophrenia, but may also be used to treat other conditions as indicated. Approximately 25 percent of inmates on mental health roles have a diagnosis of schizophrenia, underscoring the pressing need for good clinical practice. As one of the most disabling and disruptive disorders, assisting inmates to recover their day-to-day functioning is important both from a humanitarian as well as security standpoint.

Psychiatrists now have a meaningful choice in the medications they prescribe for inmates with schizophrenia. They have an array of traditional antipsychotics, such as Thorazine, Stellazine and Haldol, as well as newer atypical medications, such as Clozapine and Risperidone. Both classes are effective. Both come with side-effects. Neither the older nor the newer medications work for everyone in every episode. Good practice requires that a treating psychiatrist has the freedom to work with each inmate to explore what works best for him or her. However, correctional psychiatrists work within substantial constraints, including the absolute need for security and cost containment. Both classes of medications sedate patients, but the atypicals are more expensive.

In general, prison and jail prescription practices are more similar than they are different. Both jails and prisons rely heavily on traditional antipsychotics, but both have a full array of atypical medications in their formularies. More importantly, psychiatrists appear to be able to prescribe off the formulary when necessary.

Jails and prisons differ in only a few notable ways. Jails are more likely to use traditional, particularly high potency, antipsychotics than prisons. In comparison to prisons, jails are also more likely to be influenced to choose a specific medication if the medication comes in an injectable form and whether programs are available through pharmaceutical companies to facilitate ease of use. This suggests that jails are indeed more concerned about the ability to administer a fast-acting agent to control acute symptoms than prisons.

In terms of formulary decision-making, both jails and prisons are influenced most by personal clinical experience, research-demonstrated efficacy, FDA-approved indications, and exposure through continuing education or professional meetings. Cost is not among the most important factors, but also is not among the least important.

Overall, it appears that psychiatric staff in jails and prisons must balance good clinical practice with costs. The heavy reliance on cheaper medications, when alternatives are present, suggests that cost remains a factor. The fact that psychiatrists prescribe off the formulary and are more influenced by demonstrated efficacy, in contrast, supports the notion that they are indeed concerned with good practice. If one assumes that the more chaotic the environment, the greater the likelihood a facility will use all methods at their disposal to control, and therefore sedate, inmates, jails should differ from prisons in many ways. There is some evidence to suggest that this might be true, but this question must remain unanswered for the time being. Further investigations are warranted to explore the complex pressures facing psychiatric staff in providing the best services in a very difficult environment.

NOTE

1. This study, "Psychiatric Practices in U.S. Jails and Prisons," was conducted under the guidelines of federal human subjects procedures and approved by the Rutgers University Institutional Review Board (E99-371).

REFERENCES

American Psychiatric Association (1989). *Psychiatric Services in Jails and Prisons.* Washington, DC, American Psychiatric Association.

American Psychiatric Association (2000). *Psychiatric Services in Jails and Prisons, 2nd Edition.* Washington, DC, American Psychiatric Association.

Beck, A.J. & Maruschak, L.M. (2001). Mental health treatment in state prisons, 2000. *Bureau of Justice Statistics Special Report.* Washington, DC, US Department of Justice.

Brown, C.S., Markowitz, J.S., Moore, T.R. & Parker, N.G. (1999). Atypical antipsychotics part II: Adverse effects, drug interactions, and costs. *The Annals of Pharmacotherapy, 33,* 210-17.

Cohen, F. & Dvoskin, J. (1992). Inmates with mental disorders: A guide to law and practice. *Mental and Physical Disability Law Reporter, 16,* 339-346, 462-470.

Ditton, P.M. (1999). Mental health treatment of inmates and probationers. *Bureau of Justice Statistics Special Report.* Washington, DC, US Department of Justice.

Glick, I.D., Murray, S.R., Vasudevan, P., Marder, S.R. & Hu, R.J. (2001). Treatment with atypical antipsychotics: New indications and new populations. *Journal of Psychiatric Research, 35,* 187-91.

Harrison, P.M. & Beck, A.J. (2006). Prison and jail inmates at midyear, 2005. *Bureau of Justice Statistics Bulletin* (NCJ213133). Washington, DC, US Department of Justice.

James, D.J. & Glaze, L.E. (2006). Mental health problems of prison and jail inmates. *Bureau of Justice Statistics Special Report* (NCJ213600). Washington, DC, US Department of Justice.

Koro, C.E., Fedder, D.O., L'Italien, G.J., Weiss, S., Magder, L.S., Kreyenbuhl, J., Revicki, D & Buchanan, R.W. (2002). An assessment of the independent effects of Olanzapine and Risperidone exposure on the risk of hyperlipidemia in schizophrenic patients. *Archives of General Psychiatry, 59,* 1021-26.

Leslie, D.L. & Rosenheck, R.A. (2002). From conventional to atypical antipsychotics and back: Dynamic processes in the diffusion of new medications. *American Journal of Psychiatry, 159*(9),1534-40.

Markowitz, J.S., Brown, C.S. & Moore, T.R. (1999). Atypical antipsychotics, part I: Pharmacology, pharmacokinetics, and efficacy. *The Annals of Pharmacotherapy, 33,* 73-85.

Mazade, N., Glover, R. & Hutchings, G. (2001). Environmental scan, 2000: Issues facing state mental health agencies. *Administration of Policy in Mental Health, 27*(4), 167-81.

Meltzer, H.Y. (2005). The metabolic consequences of long-term treatment with olanzapine, quetiapine and risperidone: Are there differences? *"http://journals.cambridge. org/action/displayAbstract;jsessionid=8CB00B197FA7391E9B2A88FCA126344A. tomcat1?fromPage=online&aid=298616"\/"#"8,* 153-56.

Steadman, H.J. & Veysey, B.M. (1997). Providing services for jail inmates with mental disorders. *National Institute of Justice: Research in Brief.* Washington, DC, US Department of Justice.

Teplin, L.A. (1990). The prevalence of severe mental disorder among male urban jail detainees: Comparison with the Epidemiologic Catchment Area Program. *American Journal of Public Health, 80*(6), 663-669.

Teplin, L.A. (1994). Psychiatric and substance abuse disorders among male urban detainees. *American Journal of Public Health, 84*(2), 290-93.

US Department of Health and Human Services (1999). *Mental Health: A Report of the Surgeon General-Executive Summary.* Rockville, MD, US Department of Health and Human Services.

Veysey, B.M. & Bichler-Robertson, G. (2002). Prevalence estimates of psychiatric disorders in correctional settings. In *Health Status of Soon-To-Be Released Inmates. Report to Congress, Vol. 2.* Chicago, National Commission on Correctional Health Care.

Veysey, B.M., Steadman, H.J., Morrissey, J.P. & Johnsen, M. (1997). In search of the missing linkages: Continuity of care in US jails. *Behavioral Sciences and the Law, 15,* 383-397.

Wolff, N. & Veysey, B.M. (2001). *Correctional health care in New Jersey jails: Briefing paper.* New Brunswick, NJ, Institute for Health, Health Care Policy and Aging Research.

Worrel, J.A., Marken, P.A., Beckman, S.E. & Ruehter, V.L. (2000). Atypical antipsychotic agents: A critical review. *American Journal of Health Systems Pharmacy, 57,* 238-255.

AUTHORS' NOTES

Bonita M. Veysey, PhD, is affiliated with the School of Criminal Justice, Rutgers University, 123 Washington St., Newark, NJ 07102.

Vanja Stenius, PhD, is affiliated with the School of Criminal Justice, Rutgers University, 15 Washington St., Newark, NJ 07102.

Noel Mazade, PhD, is Executive Director, NRI, 66 Canal Center Plaza, Suite 302, Alexandria, VA 22314.

Lucille Schacht, PhD, is affiliated with NRI, 66 Canal Center Plaza, Suite 302, Alexandria, VA 22314.

This study, "Psychiatric Practices in U.S. Jails and Prisons," was supported by funds from Pfizer, Inc.

doi:10.1300/J076v45n01_13

Mental Health Issues in the Criminal Justice System. Pp. 207-225.

Available online at http://jor.haworthpress.com

© 2007 by The Haworth Press, Inc. All rights reserved.

doi:10.1300/J076v45n01_14

Co-Occurring Mental Disorders Among Incarcerated Women: Preliminary Findings from an Integrated Health Treatment Study

DOREEN D. SALINA

LINDA M. LESONDAK

LISA A. RAZZANO

ANN WEILBAECHER

ABSTRACT There is a growing awareness of the incidence of mental disorders among women involved in the criminal justice system. Two hundred and eighty-three women were participants in a federally-funded study and all met *DSM-IV* criteria for at least two Axis I disorders, including one substance abuse diagnosis. Posttraumatic Stress Disorder (chronic) was the primary mental health diagnosis for 75% of the sample. Based on findings, the need for rigorous and accurate diagnostic evaluation for women in criminal justice settings is discussed; specific recommendations include: · providing evidence-based, integrated, trauma-informed treatment, and designing comprehensive gender-specific programs to improve outcomes for incarcerated women. doi:10.1300/J076v45n01_14 *[Article copies available for a fee from The Haworth Document Delivery Service: 1-800-HAWORTH. E-mail address: <docdelivery@haworthpress.com> Website: <http://www.HaworthPress. com> © 2007 by The Haworth Press, Inc. All rights reserved.]*

KEYWORDS Posttraumatic stress disorder, HIV prevention, co-occurring disorders, incarcerated women, correctional health, PTSD

INTRODUCTION

The rates of women entering the criminal justice system are increasing at an alarming pace. Many women enter and exit the criminal justice system with treatable disorders that have impacted their involvement in criminal activities. Many of these same women who have substance abuse or dependence diagnoses also have at least one additional treatable mental diagnosis (BJS, 2006). This pattern is reflected in the high rates of substance abuse and mental health disorders in published studies examining samples of incarcerated women (Teplin, Abram, & McCleland, 1996, 1997; Parsons, Walker, & Grubin, 2001). Drug-related crimes also are cited as the most frequent reason for female incarceration (NIDA, 2006). The majority of detained women have had little or no past involvement with mental health and substance use professionals, and when they do, the existing resources are often inadequate to properly identify and treat them.

Addressing serious mental disorders among detained individuals in jail or diversion programs also makes psychological, practical and fiscal sense. If women are accurately assessed while simultaneously under the jurisdiction of criminal justice and receiving effective integrated treatment, and subsequently linked to comprehensive community services, the possibility of reducing the multiple burdens among women with mental illness increases. Moreover, the multiple issues that these women present for jails and prisons, and the communities to which they continually return, also may benefit.

In a ground breaking study examining the relationship between mental disorders and incarceration, Teplin, Abram and McClelland (1996) measured the prevalence of mental illness in women detained in Cook County Jail, the largest single site jail in the nation. When examining the prevalence of lifetime mental disorders, Teplin and colleagues found that 81% of the women surveyed ($n = 1272$) had at least one serious, diagnosable mental disorder in their lifetime. Of these, 33.5% experienced Post-Traumatic Stress Disorder (PTSD). Almost two-thirds (64%) of the female sample were diagnosed with drug abuse or dependence. However, this study also documented that more than 70% of women in Cook County jail, regardless of charge, also met diagnostic criteria for at least one serious mental disorder in the last six months (Teplin, Abram, & McClelland, 1996).

Published studies also have demonstrated that rates of history of physical and sexual abuse among incarcerated women are extremely high, with chronic abuse often beginning in young childhood (Klein & Chao, 1995; Najavits, Weiss, & Shaw, 1999; Silbert & Pines, 1983). Trauma is a common occurrence to most incarcerated women; many have lost children to death, witnessed violent deaths, or have been used as sexual objects by multiple people throughout their lives. The individual and collective impact of these experiences has devastating consequences to girls' and women's sense of self and their ability to function adaptively in the community. As a response to these traumas, symptoms of Post-Traumatic Stress Disorder (PTSD) frequently develop, with most women meeting formal criteria for a psychiatric diagnosis (*DSM-IV*, 2000). As noted in the *DSM-IV*, PTSD is characterized by persistent cognitive intrusions of the traumatic event(s), chronic physiological arousal and avoidance of any aspect related to the event. Individuals with PTSD generally exhibit a numbing of general responsiveness and often report reexperiencing the trauma, commonly known as flashbacks, which they describe as distressing, intrusive and frightening (*DSM-IV*, 2000).

Without appropriate intervention and supports, chronic mental disorders, including PTSD, contribute to decreased adaptive and psychological functioning, substance use and abuse, poor decision-making, all of which have been shown to be associated with increased recidivism (Hobfoll, 1998). Research has indicated that the initiation of substance abuse frequently occurs in an attempt to avoid or reduce psychological symptoms, or in an attempt to cope with them (Covington, 1999; Schilling, El-Bassel, Schinke, Gordon, & Nichols, 1991). Thus, studies must identify evidence-based tools and methods that can be used to accurately assess women's needs within criminal justice systems, as well as to provide effective rehabilitation and to efficiently use scarce institutional resources. In addition, published research cites the need to implement and continue to expand gender-responsive treatment for female detainees in order to promote recovery and successful re-entry (Blitz, Wolff, Pan, & Pogorzelski, 2005).

Published estimates document that more than half the individuals with substance use disorders also have mental disorders (Volkow, 2003). In mental health services, rigorous research has documented integrated treatment for dual diagnoses (IDDT) as the EBP for individuals with co-occurring disorders (Drake, Goldman, Leff et al., 2001; Osher,

Steadman, & Barr, 2003). Recently, there has been growing empirical evidence supporting the simultaneous treatment of both substance abuse and PTSD in particular (Najavits, Weiss, & Shaw, 1999; Najavits, 2002). Najavits and her colleagues (1999) documented that women with co-occurring disorders experience more severe psychological symptoms and are more likely to engage in criminal behaviors. Through a series of studies, Najavits and her colleagues developed and empirically validated a behaviorally-based intervention, which consistently lowered symptoms associated with PTSD. The curriculum, entitled, *Seeking Safety* (2002), clarifies the link between substance abuse and trauma-related mental disorders for women in a variety of life circumstances. These include incarcerated women, women in drug treatment and inner city women. The curriculum builds on Judith Herman's theory of trauma treatment (Herman, 1992) of creating a safe psychological space within which to learn behavioral skills related to coping, substance abuse triggers and behavior change. This curriculum consists of 25 independent modules that can be implemented based on the requirements of the site.

Since early psychiatric deinstitutionalization and further closing of many inpatient psychiatric facilities, increasing numbers of individuals, including higher numbers of women with mental health disorders, have been incarcerated (Blitz, Wolff, Pan, & Pogorzelski, 2005; Draine & Solomon, 1999; Lurigio & Schwartz, 2000; Perez, Leifman, & Estrada, 2003). Previous research supports that the majority of these women are not adequately assessed for mental disorders within the community due to diminished community mental health resources and lack of facilities. In addition, other barriers to community success for women, such as under- or unemployment, minimal economic resources, and co-occurring substance abuse, generally go unaddressed as well. Criminal justice settings, including jails and diversion programs, represent an opportunity to adequately assess accurate diagnoses, provide short-term mental health services, and community linkages in an effort to reduce recidivism. Collectively, these services comprise the foundation of psychiatric rehabilitation and recovery. Furthermore, continuity of rehabilitation services upon returning to the community has been identified as an important component of successful re-entry (Haimowitz, 2004).

The present paper provides a summary of data collected from 283 women diagnosed with co-occurring mental and substance use disorders involved in a jail-based diversion program. This research, funded by the National Institute on Drug Abuse (NIDA), was specifically designed to integrate programming to simultaneously address mental health, substance use, and HIV/STI risk behaviors (D.D. Salina, PI). Data demonstrate the types and frequency of mental and substance use disorders in this sample, as well as examine co-occurring medical conditions, psychosocial impairments, and level of functioning. These indicators have been shown to be significantly associated with relapse and recidivism. Results also outline the need for valid and reliable methods for diagnostic assessment, identify the under-reported prevalence of PSTD among women with other mental and substance use disorder, and provide recommendations for criminal justice and community rehabilitation programs which provide services for this population, such as providing multidimensional assessment upon entry and re-entry to identify the specific domains that affect adaptive functioning, and successful community recovery.

METHODS

Study Site

The Cook County Sheriff's Department of Women's Justice Services (DWJS) is a diversion treatment program which was created to treat non-violent drug using women involved in the criminal justice system. This program has been highlighted as a pioneering effort to provide gender-specific treatment to women offenders (Berman, 2006). Women in DWJS programs are jurisdictionally under the Cook County Sheriff's Department in order to receive treatment in one of their three programs. DWJS is developing an effective community alternative to jail for non-violent women. It provides gender-specific programs and services to facilitate successful community re-entry. The program continues to develop gender-specific treatment for women. DWJS' approach includes an explicit understanding of the additional barriers present for women because of gender. Women within DWJS are generally pre-trial detainees, and may be receiving mandated treatment services prior to sentencing or case disposition. These programs are intended to divert women with substance abuse and other mental health disorders from the criminal justice system to appropriate treatment and comprehensive services within their communities. These programs include the *MOM's Program,* which provides residential treatment to pregnant drug abusing women and enables drug-free births; the Sheriff's Female Furlough Program (SFFP), which is a day reporting treatment center; and the Women's Residential Program, which provides integrated residential treatment within the walls of Cook County Jail. This sample was identified from the Women's Residential program.

Detainee Selection for DWJS Residential Treatment Programs

In order to participate in DWJS programming, women must first be processed through the Cook County Department of Corrections (Cook County Jail or CCJ). Upon arrival, all women in the jail are processed by security risk factors including severity of charges, escape attempts, court ordered conditions, etc. Medical staff also screen women for physical and mental health conditions. In general, individuals with overt psychotic symptoms and those with other serious medical conditions are assigned to one of several other special populations units. All other women are assigned to general population, which houses detainees who have a variety of charges and security risks.

Women in DWJS programs are identified in two ways: (1) pre-trial court mandate by the presiding criminal judge; or (2) database screening by security personnel. Women who are involved specifically in the County drug court are usually mandated to DWJS, but other justices are becoming more aware of DWJS programs and have increased the number of women mandated to services. DWJS officers also screen the jail census daily and attempt to identify women with specific criteria, such as non-violent crimes and/or drug-associated charges. There are several other correctional conditions, such as level (amount) of bond, posing a flight risk, etc., that prevent women from being eligible for treatment programming. However, the majority of women held for trial in the Cook County Jail are eligible. Women who meet the correctional criteria are approached by a DWJS officer and offered voluntary treatment through DWJS. All appropriate legal protections, including detainees' informed consent, are required. Women who agree are subsequently transferred to DWJS and placed in one of three drug treatment programs. Other women who receive DWJS services are court mandated to treatment via drug court, usually for a designated number of days prior to sentencing, or in lieu of sentencing to the penitentiary.

Sample

Participants with co-occurring disorders were identified within the Women's Residential Program through the DWJS Mental Health Program. All women receive preliminary mental health screening and symptomatic women were further assessed. Clinical referrals that were made to the mental health program by substance abuse counselors, the woman herself, or were the subject of an on-call crisis call were also used to identify potential participants. Staff responses include a number of different levels of assessment or the provision of acute psychological services, including transfer to psychiatric units or hospitals. Staff are comprised of clinical psychology externs (primarily Psy.D. students) completing their year-long practicum for clinical psychology. All staff have IRB approval through Northwestern University and were rigorously trained in assessment and research procedures by the first and fourth author. Each staff member received individual supervision on his/her assessments where errors were corrected and refined. There were also weekly staff meetings during which particularly complex cases were discussed. Regularly assigned meetings served as fidelity checks that all examiners were using standardized procedures and project decision rules to yield the *DSM-IV* diagnoses.

Diagnostic Specificity. From the beginning of the study, it was expected that accurate diagnoses would be essential to understanding the findings about women with co-occurring disorders. The research acknowledged the importance of rigorous assessment procedures. In response to clinical services, we provided a standardized assessment of the women. Each staff received at least 20 hours of group training on the SCID. All research staff were required to complete a competency certification SCID prior to recruiting study participants. As a further check for accuracy, senior staff reviewed each SCID for errors or mistakes. Thus, the results presented in this article were subjected to intense scientific rigor to ensure that the results and the conclusions drawn from them are based on accurate assessments. If there were indications that the woman displayed a mental health disorder, the staff member conducted a full assessment including a mini-mental status examination, a comprehensive psychosocial history and Structured Clinical Interview for *DSM-IV* (SCID).

Structured Clinical Interview for DSM-IV-Research Version (SCID). The Structured Clinical Interview for DSM-IV Axis I Disorders (SCID-I) is a semi-structured interview for making the major DSM-IV Axis I diagnoses. Reliability and validity of the SCID have been established in multiple studies, including those conducted with individuals with substance use disorders (Kranzler et al., 1996). Furthermore, psychometric properties for the SCID have been determined with longitudinal assessment designs, ratings from trained mental health clinicians, and triangulated data sources. Previous studies (Basco et al., 2000; Kranzler et al., 1996) using procedures such as these have demonstrated superior validity of the SCID over standard clinical interviews at intake. This translates to increased accuracy in mental illness diagnoses and, by extension, increases treatment accuracy and improved outcomes.

DSM-IV Diagnoses. The SCID can utilize all five DSM-IV axes. AXIS I identifies clusters of psychological symptoms for a set period of time that are usually treatable if properly identified; AXIS II, Personality disorders, were deferred in this sample; Axis III notes medical conditions that may influence psychological functioning; Axis IV identifies psychosocial stressors within the last year; AXIS V, Global Assessment of Functioning (GAF), measures the individual's overall level of occupational, vocational and social functioning. The research team made a decision to collect a maximum of two substance abuse/dependence diagnoses and two other axis one diagnoses for a maximum of four Axis I diagnoses after reviewing the first several research waves. Even with the rigorousness of the SCID instrument, some women received more than four diagnoses. For clarity's sake, it was decided that the two most problematic diagnoses would be listed in order of clinical severity. The Project Director was also a licensed clinical psychologist who reviewed SCID scoring and diagnostic conclusions on all participants. Given the trauma-informed interventions of the study, it also was decided that with all other aspects of the assessment being equal, that Post Traumatic Stress Disorder (PTSD) would always be considered the primary diagnosis. This decision was made based on the effects of the severe symptoms associated with this disorder, and multiple evaluation and diagnostic methods were used to ensure that each participant would be correctly diagnosed.

Criteria for Diagnoses. In order to provide psychiatric diagnoses, *DSM-IV* criteria and the multiaxial system were used to classify all mental disorders for women in this sample. This strategy was used for several reasons. First, women were evaluated using the SCID, which uses *DSM-IV* criteria in the diagnostic evaluation. Next, by applying these *DSM-IV* criteria, the sample would be evaluated, and subsequently diagnosed, using strict, standardized symptomatology (i.e., illness type and severity) and length of illness (i.e., duration). In addition, use of the multiaxial system allows for the identification of other persistent conditions that affect the mental health and level of functioning of individuals. All of these factors are relevant to the degree of impairment and the potential for recovery and community integration for detained clients.

RESULTS

The target sample in this study consists of 283 women diagnosed with co-occurring Axis I psychiatric and substance use disorders using the SCID. The majority of the sample was African American (75%), followed by white/Caucasian women (18%), Latinas (5%), and women who identified their race/ethnicity as "Other" (2%). The majority of women (60%) had completed less than a high school education. Seventy-five percent reported being single/never married, yet 83% reported having children and 92% reported at least one past pregnancy. Approximately 36% reported that they had been hospitalized and received inpatient treatment for mental health in the past, with 31% reporting use of outpatient mental health services. Forty-four percent of women in the sample reported witnessing violence or murder; on average, women were 23 years old at the time they witnessed violence. These demographics are summarized in Table 1.

☐ **Table 1: Sample Demographic Characteristics**

Participant Characteristic	% (N = 283)*
Race/Ethnicity	
African American/Black	75% (210)
Caucasian/White	18% (50)
Latina	5% (15)
Other	2% (6)
Education Level	
8th Grade or less	10% (27)
Some High School	50% (114)
High School Graduate/GED	21% (58)
Some College	17% (49)
College Graduate	2% (7)
Marital Status	
Single	75% (210)
Married	7% (19)
Separated	8% (23)
Divorced	7% (19)
Widowed	3% (9)
Currently In a Relationship	< 1% (1)
Proportion Who Have Been Pregnant in the Past	92% (257)
Proportion with Children	83% (163)
Average Number of Children = 3.0*	
Proportion Who Have Been Hospitalized for Inpatient Mental Health Treatment	36% (100)
Proportion Who Have Received Outpatient Mental Health Treatment	31% (87)
Proportion Who Have Witnessed Violence or Murder	44% (125)
Average Age When Witnessed = 23 yrs.	
Range = 56; Min/Max 2-58 yrs. old	

Axis I: Primary and Secondary Axis I Mental Disorders. Overall, results from the SCID evaluations revealed that the Axis I mental health condition identified among the largest proportion of women was Post-Traumatic Stress Disorder (PTSD). More then 75% of women in this sample were diagnosed with primary Axis I PTSD. Upon further investigation, it also was determined that among women with a diagnosis of PTSD, their symptoms met criteria for chronic, rather than acute, diagnosis of the disorder. The second most frequent primary Axis I mental health diagnosis was major depressive disorder (14%), followed by Bipolar Disorder (3%). Other primary Axis I mental health diagnoses, including Mood Disorder Not Otherwise Specified (NOS) and Schizophrenia Spectrum Disorders, were observed among less than 1% of the sample.

SCID results also revealed that 60% of the sample had a secondary Axis I mental health condition. Approximately 41% had symptoms that met criteria for a secondary Axis I diagnosis of major depression. In addition, other secondary Axis I diagnoses included: 8% with secondary Bipolar Disorder; 4% with Mood Disorder NOS; 2% with PTSD; and less than 1% with dysthymia and other secondary disorders. A complete summary of primary and secondary Axis I mental health diagnoses are presented in Table 2.

Axis I: Primary and Secondary Substance Disorders. In addition to Axis I mental disorders, SCID evaluations also revealed that women in the sample experienced symptoms that met *DSM-IV* criteria for substance disorders. These disorders are characterized by *DSM-IV* in two ways: substance dependence and substance abuse. Substance dependence, the more severe manifestation, is characterized by a "cluster of cognitive, behavioral, and physiological symptoms indicating that the individual continues use of the substance despite significant substance-related problems" (*DSM-IV*, 1994; 2000; p. 192). Dependence also is characterized by a pattern of behaviors related to repeated self-administration, generally resulting in increased levels of tolerance, risk for withdrawal, and in some cases, compulsive drug-using behaviors. Substance abuse refers to a "maladaptive pattern of substance use manifested by recurrent and significant adverse consequences related to the repeated use of substances" (*DSM-IV*, 2000; p. 194). However, substance abuse does not include relevance of tolerance, withdrawal, or compulsive use.

The most frequent diagnosis for primary Axis I substance disorder was Sedative-Opioid Dependence (52%), followed by Cocaine Dependence (24%), and Alcohol Dependence (12%). Primary Marijuana Dependence was reported by only 4% of the sample. With regard to secondary Axis I substance disorders, the most frequent diagnosis was

□ Table 2: Summary of Primary and Secondary Axis I Mental Health Disorders

Diagnosis (N = 283)	Primary Mental Health (%/n)	Secondary Mental Health* (%/n)
PTSD	75% (211)	2% (5)
Major Depression	14% (40)	41% (117)
Bipolar Disorders	3% (8)	8% (25)
Mood Disorder	< 1% (2)	4% (12)
Sedative-Induced Anxiety	< 1% (1)	
Anxiety NOS	< 1% (2)	—
Schizophrenia Spectrum	< 1% (1)	—
Psychotic NOS	< 1% (1)	—
Dysthymia	< 1% (1)	1% (4)
Obsessive-Compulsive	—	1% (4)
Dissociative	—	< 1% (1)
Agoraphobia	—	< 1% (1)

* Among those with diagnoses, primary and secondary mental health disorders; %...100

secondary Cocaine Dependence (38%), followed by Alcohol Dependence (13%), and Marijuana Dependence (7%). Approximately 71% of the sample met criteria for secondary substance disorders. All SCID findings regarding primary and secondary substance use disorders are summarized in Table 3. In addition, it is clear from the data in Table 3 that the majority of substance-related disorders met the more intense criteria for substance dependence than those for substance abuse.

Axis III: General Medical Conditions. The SCID provides information for each axis in the *DSM-IV* multi-axial system. Axis III is for reporting of general medical conditions that could have relevance to individuals' primary mental health symptoms and functioning (*DSM-IV*, 2000). Further, as noted in the *Manual*, "Some general medical conditions may not be directly related to the mental disorder but nonetheless have important prognostic or treatment implications. . . ." (*DSM-IV*, 2000, p. 30). Overall, 55% of the women reported at least one physical health or medical condition at the time they completed their SCID. In addition, this sample of women reported a wide range of clinically relevant general medical conditions, several with clinical significance. In particular, among those with Axis III medical conditions, 25% reported chronic health problems

Table 3: Summary of Primary and Secondary Axis I Substance Disorders		
Substance (N = 283)	Primary Substance Use (%/n)	Secondary Substance Use (%/n)
Sedative-Opioid Dependence	52% (145)	3% (8)
Cocaine Dependence	24% (67)	38% (106)
Alcohol Dependence	12% (33)	13% (37)
Marijuana Dependence	4% (12)	7% (21)
Amphetamine Dependence	< 1% (1)	—
Hallucinogen Dependence	1% (2)	1% (4)
Marijuana Abuse	1% (2)	2% (5)
Cocaine Abuse	1% (2)	2% (7)
Alcohol Abuse	1% (3)	2% (8)
Sedative-Opioid Abuse	—	1% (3)
Amphetamine Abuse	—	< 1% (1)

*Among those with diagnoses, primary and secondary substance use disorders; %...100

related to asthma; 19% were living with severe, chronic hypertension; 11% had a diagnosis of a chronic health condition (e.g., chronic pain, fractures); 10% reported having seizure disorders; 7% had arthritis; 6% were anemic; and 6% were infected with hepatitis C. Smaller proportions of the sample also reported other medical conditions, including but not limited to: chronic thyroid problems (5%); brain injuries (4%); heart murmurs (3%); and migraines (3%). Three percent of the sample also were women living with HIV infection.

Axis IV: Social and Occupational Functioning. Axis IV allows for the classification of problems related to psychosocial and environmental stability that may affect the diagnosis, treatment options, and prognosis for recovery for Axis I mental disorders. These factors are characterized in nine different categories relating to problems with: (1) primary support group; (2) social environment; (3) education; (4) occupation and employment; (5) housing; (6) economic resources; (7) health care services; (8) legal system/criminal justice; and (9) other psychosocial and environmental problems (*DSM-IV*, 2000). Results from the SCID evaluations indicate that women in the sample have multiple issues related to community psychosocial and environmental functioning, with the entire sample characterized by problems related to the legal/criminal justice system. In addition, however, 60% of the sample also was determined to have at least one (or more) relevant factor on Axis IV. In particular, close to half (45%) also were determined to have clinically significant impairments in employment and occupational functioning (category #4) and over a quarter (26%) have clinically relevant disruptions with social/community support (category #1). A complete summary of the results for Axis IV is presented in Table 4.

Axis V: Global Assessment of Functioning. Following the specific SCID guidelines, Axis V was assessed to determine participants' values on the Global Assessment of Functioning (GAF). The GAF allows clinicians to rate individuals' overall functioning, and to use this information to guide treatment planning and evaluate treatment impact (*DSM-IV*, 2000). Scores on the GAF are assigned in categories with 10-point ranges, starting with 1 to 10, 11 to 20, 21 to 30, and so on through 91 to 100. Each categorical range characterizes functioning related to mental disorders, without taking into account medical conditions (Axis III) or other psychosocial limitations (Axis IV). A score of 0 can be assigned in cases were inadequate information related to an individuals' level of

□ **Table 4. Summary of Axis IV Psychosocial and Environmental Problems**

Axis IV Category*	Participants (N = 283)
Problems with Primary Support Group (1)	26% (n = 74)
Problems related to Social Environment (2)	16% (n = 45)
Educational Problems (3)	21% (n = 59)
Occupational Problems (4)	45% (n = 125)
Housing Problems (5)	18% (n = 51)
Economic Problems (6)	20% (n = 56)
Problems with Access to Health Care (7)	8% (n = 22)
Interactions with Legal System/Criminal Justice (8)	100% (n = 283)
Other Psychosocial Problems (9)	3% (n = 8)
Criminal Justice Axis IV Category Only	40% (n = 114)
Multiple Axis IV Categories	60% (n = 169)

* Participants could be assessed for multiple types of impairments; proportions will not equal 100%.

functioning is available. Lower scores on the GAF represent lower levels of functioning. For example, scores of 1 to 10 reflect "Persistent danger of severely hurting self or others (e.g., recurrent violence) OR persistent inability to maintain minimal personal hygiene OR serious suicidal act with clear expectation of death" (*DSM-IV*, 2000, p. 34).

Results of the SCID evaluations indicate a substantial amount of impairment among women in this group; the average GAF score for the sample was 49, with a median of 50, a minimum score of 30 and a high score of 69. This average score of 49 reflects a level of functional impairment categorized as "some impairment in reality testing or communication (e.g., speech is at times illogical, obscure, or irrelevant) OR major impairment in several areas, such as work or school, family relations, judgment, thinking, or mood ..." (*DSM-IV*, 2000, p. 34). The majority of the sample (42%) had GAF scores within the range of 41 to 50, denoting significant impairments. At best, functioning among women in the sample was characterized within the 61 to 70 range (i.e., a high score of 69), suggesting milder levels of impairment; however, only 8% of the sample was determined to be functioning at this higher level. Ninety-two percent had functional impairments classified as "moderate" or more severe based on the GAF category definitions in the *DSM-IV*.

SUMMARY AND CONCLUSIONS

Women who are incarcerated for crimes related to substance abuse and are selected for diversion programming are overwhelmingly afflicted with at least two diagnosable and treatable Axis I disorders. They also frequently tend to have co-morbid physical diseases and medical conditions, as well as psychosocial stressors that influence successful diversion treatment and community re-entry. Despite the severity of this sample's documented co-occurring disorders, which were communicated to the judges through psychological treatment summaries and recommendations, almost 15% of the enrolled study sample was sent to the penitentiary as a result of their most recent incarceration. Almost half had been there before, averaging 2.5 stays. Methods must be found to effectively and economically treat women with co-occurring disorders while involved in the criminal justice system if the human and financial costs are to be contained and rehabilitation efforts are to be successful.

Women involved in the criminal justice system have very high rates of co-occurring disorders. In this sample, 75% of these women also demonstrated symptoms of PTSD. This finding is noteworthy because while incarcerated women are presumed to have rates this frequently related to the experience of trauma, few studies measure the disorder's presence with such a rigorous, standardized procedure. This suggests that appropriate assessment for PTSD symptoms should be a required part of service delivery and community re-entry efforts. The effects of the symptoms of this disorder are pervasive and contribute to the failure of other types of treatment, which do not take the traumatic experiences into account. Many of the women had had at least one encounter with a health professional for psychiatric reasons, including emergency room visits, psychiatric hospitalizations or using medical resources within the criminal justice system. The women reported a plethora of mental health diagnoses, many of which proved to be inaccurate when the participant was assessed using standardized instruments and appropriate history taking.

Since incarcerated settings have high rates of detainees with substance abuse and mental disorders, they are an ideal place to interrupt this destructive cycle. However, pretrial charge status generally leaves only a short timeframe within which to intervene. But if valid and comprehensive assessments are conducted with a high level of rigor during this time, information derived from them can be employed to accurately identify the complex psychological disorders that influence drug use and psychiatric recovery. In addition, addressing women's needs surrounding adaptive functioning, and helping them and providers to prioritize services relevant for their multiple needs will further promote their success upon re-entry. While women are still actively involved in the criminal justice system, additional focus should be placed on obtaining accurate, comprehensive substance abuse and mental health diagnoses and developing multi-dimensional treatment planning that includes relevant data on all five axes of the *DSM-IV*. This multi-axial diagnosis is how the current DSM classification process was designed, specifically to understand the complexities of mental disorders. A brief interview or a measure without documented validity may yield information relevant to Axis I symptoms or general diagnostic categories, but they are generally ineffective in accurately classifying women overall, as well as determining the impact of co-occurring disorders. Use of all axes can inform both the appropriate treatment strategies and the expected prognosis and outcomes if all factors identified on the multi-axial format are considered and incorporated in discharge planning. The use of a valid instrument, such as the SCID, provides this level of accuracy, with multidimensional diagnostic information. Use of the instrument also can be accomplished in approximately 1.5 hours. This is not an excessive amount of time considering the amount of time and resources devoted to the repeated use of scarce psychological resources within both criminal justice and community agencies over time, and repeat incarcerations when treatment plans are indistinct and poorly informed to address women's specific mental health and substance use needs.

Accurate psychological assessment, early in the process of incarceration and which generates a multidimensional treatment plan, is key to identifying the most severe disorders. Use of multiple *DSM-IV* axes will clarify the complexities of the mental health problems and identify areas of functioning that impact the effectiveness of any forms of treatment. Through proper assessments, the most problematic of symptoms and disorders may be addressed within an integrated, multidisciplinary format and the impact of trauma-related symptoms might be reduced. As a result, linkages to appropriate community agencies and sharing the assessment and treatment recommendations (with the participants' permission) will result a higher level of continuity of care, and as a result, improve outcomes of both substance abuse interventions and adaptive functioning. These improvements can reasonably be considered as factors that may reduce recidivism. Information from assessments such as the SCID can guide community re-entry efforts and improve continuity of care for the many issues faced among women detainees, by identifying key personnel within community agencies who can utilize this information and make more informed treatment recommendations aimed to improve outcomes and assist in continued rehabilitation efforts.

This type of services planning, when designed for women with co-occurring disorders, must specify the provision of (or the linkage to) trauma-informed, integrated treatment within the community, using the current evidence-based practice. Currently, DWJS has extended the use of this model in collaboration with a local community-based hospital outpatient psychiatric department. While still under the jurisdiction of the diversion program, women in the day reporting diversion program (a furlough program) are assessed and then linked for psychological services at the community hospital. Detainees are able to see a psychiatrist for medication evaluation, receive appropriate medication and medical testing and then participate in a psychotherapeutic group focusing on depression, trauma and recovery. While some women are already en-rolled in entitlement programs (i.e., Medicaid), those who are not are as-sisted by hospital staff so that this collaboration does not unduly stress the resources of the community agency. Gender-specific treatment maxi-mizes the interventions as it is relevant to the women and promotes strength-based approaches. Women are encouraged to continue receiving services once released from the criminal justice jurisdiction.

The answer lies, in part, in providing additional funding to diversion programs that can provide appropriate treatment. This treatment must include standardized diagnostic assessment, and short-term mental health treatment services that promote more adaptive coping simultaneously with substance abuse treatment. In concert with evidence-based practice services, community linkage after release from the criminal justice system can improve access to longer-term treatment to address the long-term effects of trauma and substance use (Bond, Salyers, Rollins, Rapp, & Zipple, 2004). Finally, proper assessment while incarcerated also can allow for limited treatment resources to be utilized more effectively.

Diversion programs that provide appropriate assessment and integrated treatment hold much promise for reducing substance abuse and psychological symptoms in incarcerated women. Effective interventions can utilize this framework to interrupt the recurring cycle of substance abuse, incarceration and returning to the community without adequate treatment and resources.

REFERENCES

Basco, M.R., Bostic, J.Q., Davies, D. et al., (2000). Methods to improve diagnostic accuracy in a community mental health setting. *American Journal of Psychiatry, 157*, 1599-1605.

Berman, J. (2006). Responding to women offenders: The Department of Women's Justice Services in Cook County, Illinois. Washington, DC: National Institute of Justice.

Blitz, C.L., Wolff, N., Pan, K., & Pogorzelski, W. (2005). Gender-specific behavioral health and community releases patterns among New Jersey prison inmates: Implications for treatment and community reentry. *American Journal of Public Health, 95*(10), 1741-1746.

Bond, G.R., Salyers, M.P., Rollins, A.L., Rapp, C.A., & Zipple, A.M. (2004). How evidence-based practices contribute to community integration. *Community Mental Health Journal, 40*(6), 569-588.

Bureau of Justice Statistics [BJS] (2006). *Census of Local Jails*. Washington, DC. Bureau of Justice Statistics, NCJ 121101: U.S. Department of Justice.

Covington, S.S. (1999). *Helping Women Recover*: A program for treating substance abuse (special addition for use in the criminal justice system). San Francisco: CA: Jossey-Bass.

Diagnostic and Statistical Manual of Mental Disorders, 4th ed-revised (2000). Washington, DC: American Psychiatric Association.

Diagnostic and Statistical Manual of Mental Disorders, 4th ed (1994). Washington, DC: American Psychiatric Association.

Draine, J. & Solomon, P. (1999). Describing and evaluating jail diversion services for persons with serious mental illness. *Psychiatric Services, 50*(1), 56-61.

Drake, R., Goldman, H., Leff, H., Lehman, A., Dixon, L., Mueser, K., & Torrey, W. (2001). Implementing evidence-based practices in routine mental health service settings. *Psychiatric Services, 52*, 179-182.

Haimowitz, S. (2004). Slowing the revolving door: Community re-entry of offenders with mental illness. *Psychiatric Services, 55*(4), 373-375.

Herman, J.L. (1992). Complex PTSD: A syndrome in survivors of prolonged and repeated trauma. *Journal of Traumatic Stress, 5*(3), 377-391.

Hobfoll, S.E. (1998). Ecology, community, and AIDS prevention. *American Journal of Community Psychology, 26*(1), 133-144.

Klein, H. & Chao, B.S. (1995). Sexual abuse during childhood and adolescence as predictors of HIV related sexual risk during adulthood among female sexual partners of injection drug users. *Violence Against Women*, 55-76.

Kranzler, H.R., Kadden, R.M., Babor, T.F., Tennen, H., & Rounsaville, B.J. (1996). Validity of the SCID in substance abuse patients. *Addiction, 91*(6), 859-868.

Lurigio, A.J. & Swartz, J.A. (2000). Changing the contours of the criminal justice system to meet the needs of persons with serious mental illness. *Criminal Justice, 3*, 45-108.

Najavits, L.M. (2002). *Seeking Safety: A Treatment Manual for PTSD and Substance Abuse*. New York, NY: Gilford Press.

Najavits, L.M., Weiss, R.A., & Shaw, S.R. (1999). A clinical profile of women with PTSD and substance dependence. *Psychology of Addictive Behaviors, 13*, 98-104.

Osher, F.C., Steadman, H.J., & Barr, H. (2003). A best practice approach to community reentry from jails for inmates with co-occurring disorders: The APIC Model. *Crime & Delinquency, 49*(1), 79-96.

Parsons, S., Walker, L., & Grubin, D. (2001). Prevalence of mental disorder in female remand prison. *Journal of Forensic Psychiatry, 12*(1), 194-202.

Perez, A., Leifman, S., & Estrada, A. (2003). Reversing the criminalization of mental illness. *Crime & Delinquency, 49*(1), 62-78.

Schilling, R.F., El-Bassel, N., Schinke, S.P., Gordon, K., & Nichols, S. (1991). Building skills of recovering women drug users to reduce heterosexual AIDS transmission. *Public Health Report, 106*, 297-303.

Silbert, M.H. & Pines, A.M. (1983). Early sexual exploitation as an influence in prostitution. *Social Work*, 285-289.

Teplin, L.A., Abram, K.M., & McClelland, G.M. (1996). Prevalence of psychiatric disorders among pretrial jail detainees. *Archives of General Psychiatry, 53*, 505-512.

Teplin, L.A., Abram, K.M., & McClelland, G.M. (1997). Mentally disordered women in jail: Who receives services? *American Journal of Public Health, 87*, 604-609.

Volkow, N.D. (2003). The dual challenge of substance abuse and mental disorders. In *NIDA NOTES, 18*(5), 3-4.

AUTHORS' NOTES

Doreen D. Salina, PhD, is affiliated with Northwestern University, Feinberg School of Medicine, 333 N. Michigan Ave., Suite 1801, Chicago, IL 60601 (E-mail: d.salina@horthwestern.edu).

Linda M. Lesondak, PhD, is Director of Evaluation, STD/HIV/AIDS Program, Chicago Department of Public Health, 333 S. State St., 2nd Floor, Chicago, IL 60604 (E-mail: Lesondak_Linda@cdph.org).

Lisa A. Razzano, PhD, is Associate Professor of Psychiatry, UIC Center on Mental Health Services Research & Policy, 1601 W. Taylor St., M/C 912, Room 488, Chicago, IL 60612 (E-mail: Razzano@psych.uic.edu).

Ann Weilbaecher, PsyD, is a affiliated with Northwestern University, Feinberg School of Medicine, 333 N. Michigan Ave., Suite 1801, Chicago, IL 60601 (E-mail: annweill@sbcglobal.net).

The authors are grateful to the Cook County Sheriff's Department of Women's Justice Services (DWJS) for their support of and contributions to this project.

This work was funded by NIH/NIDA grant # R21 DA019247-01 *Integrated health treatment for women drug users*. This project would not be possible without the established collaboration with the Cook County Sheriff's Department of Women's Justice Services and the participants themselves.

This research was funded under Research Grant Programs of the National Institutes of Health (NIH), National Institute on Drug Abuse (NIDA), Bethesda, MD, R21-DA019247. The views expressed herein are those of the authors and do not necessarily reflect the policy or position of any Federal agency or the collaborating service organization.

doi:10.1300/J076v45n01_14

Mental Health Issues in the Criminal Justice System. Pp. 227-247.
Available online at http://jor.haworthpress.com
© 2007 by The Haworth Press, Inc. All rights reserved.
doi:10.1300/J076v45n01_15

Modified Therapeutic Community Treatment for Offenders with Co-Occurring Disorders: Mental Health Outcomes

CHRISTOPHER J. SULLIVAN
STANLEY SACKS
KAREN MCKENDRICK
STEVEN BANKS
JOANN Y. SACKS
JOSEPH STOMMEL

ABSTRACT This paper examines outcomes 12 months post-prison release for offenders with co-occurring disorders (n = 185) randomly assigned to either a mental health control treatment (C) or a modified therapeutic community (E). Significant between-group differences were not found for mental health measures, although improvements were observed for each group. Reductions in criminal behavior were associated more with substance use than improvements in mental health symptoms, supporting the primacy of substance abuse treatment in affecting recidivism. Additional study of this population is needed to describe the relationships among diagnostic subgroups, as well as change in substance use and in mental health symptoms. doi:10.1300/J076v45n01_15 *[Article copies available for a fee from The Haworth Document Delivery Service: 1-800-HAWORTH. E-mail address: <docdelivery@haworthpress.com> Website: <http://www.HaworthPress. com> © 2007 by The Haworth Press, Inc. All rights reserved.]*

KEYWORDS Modified therapeutic community, co-occurring disorders, mental health treatment outcomes, severe mental disorder, substance use disorder

BACKGROUND

The Problem

Offenders have a high rate of substance use and of crime related to substance use (Mumola, 1999; Belenko & Peugh, 2005; Harrison & Beck, 2005), as well as a higher prevalence of mental disorders than is found in the general population (Fazel & Danesh, 2002; O'Brien, Mortimer, Singleton, & Meltzer, 2003). A recent Bureau of Justice Statistics report stated that roughly 56% of state prison inmates either had a history of mental health problems or exhibited symptoms of mental health disorders (James & Glaze, 2006). Rates of alcohol and/or drug dependence and abuse are considerably higher among those with a mental health problem; whereas 74% of inmates with mental health problems cited substance dependence or abuse, compared to only 56% of their counterparts without mental problems. Reports from the Colorado Department of Corrections (DOC) chronicle a five-fold increase over the past 15 years in the proportion of inmates with serious mental disorders (mainly schizophrenia, bipolar disorders, and major depression), from 4% in 1991 to 14% in 2001 (Kleinsasser & Michaud, 2002), to 20% in 2006 (J. Stommel, personal communication, November 20, 2006). Among the 20% of inmates with serious mental disorders, three quarters were estimated to have a co-occurring substance use disorder. Given some degree of skepticism about the capacity of treatment to effect change in offenders (e.g., Farabee, 2005; Martinson, 1974; c.f., Cullen, 2005), it is essential to consider the viability of treatment modalities that are specifically designed to deal with emergent issues presented by certain offender populations. This study focuses on modified therapeutic community (MTC) and mental health treatment for a correctional population with co-occurring disorders.

Prisoners with mental disorders generally adapt less well to the complexity of prison life (Morgan, Edwards, & Faulkner, 1993), frequently face stigmatization or isolation from other prisoners, have high rates of victimization (Correctional Association of New York, 2004), and are more likely to be written up in incident reports during their first three months of incarceration (DiCataldo, Greer, & Profit, 1995), and to serve their full sentences (AISHealth.com, 2001). Recent increases in the number of individuals who have been incarcerated and who are re-entering the community from prison heighten concerns relating to mentally ill inmates whose problems may have been inadequately remedied and who may have difficulty acclimating to community life (Petersilia, 2000). Most offenders now rejoin the community with the same problems (e.g., substance addiction, psychological symptoms, lack of education) that they had when they entered prison (Taxman, Young, & Byrne, 2002), problems that impede their prosocial adjustment (Visher, LaVigne, & Travis, 2004) and that sustain the risk they pose to public safety.

These issues may be compounded for offenders with substance use disorders co-occurring with mental disorders, typically termed "co-occurring disorders." Hartwell (2004) reports that offenders with co-occurring disorders tend to have more trouble adjusting to the community upon release and are at higher risk for recidivism and reincarceration than those showing evidence of substance use disorders alone. In a study of residential substance abuse treatment for offenders as an alternative to prison, those who had a history of mental disorder were twice as likely to drop out of treatment (Lang & Belenko, 2000). Similarly, in a study of probationers, a prior history of mental disorder was associated with shorter lengths of stay in substance abuse treatment, as were higher levels of depression and anxiety (Hiller, Knight, & Simpson, 1999). In jails, compared to inmates who did not have histories of mental disorder, offenders with mental disorders were more likely to fail to complete treatment by ratios of nearly 2:1 (National Institute of Justice, 1997) and 3:1 (Brady, Krebs, & Laird, 2004).

Substance Abuse, Mental Health, and Crime

Although many studies have established a relationship between substance abuse and crime (e.g., National Center on Addiction and Substance Abuse, 1998), the relationship between mental health and crime has not been studied as consistently as substance use; however, research has increased during the last decade.

Perhaps the foremost source for empirical evidence on the relationship between mental illness and criminal behavior is the MacArthur Risk Study. Early studies reported that 27% of male and female patients released from psychiatric hospitals reported at least one violent act within an average of four months from release (Monahan, 1993). Yet, compared to other relevant variables (e.g., gender, age, socioeconomic status), the risk of violence for persons with mental illness is modest, which brings into question the use of mental health status as a marker for potential violent behavior. Later, Steadman and colleagues (1998) found that clients with mental disorders released from hospital facilities demonstrated a similar risk of violent behavior as others in the community, yet those with co-occurring substance use disorders had a higher risk of violent behavior than those with major psychiatric disorders alone (Steadman et al., 1998). More recently, Monahan and colleagues (2000) found that it was important to consider the specific diagnosis in determining the risk of violent behavior; that is, a diagnosis of schizophrenia was related to a reduced likelihood of later violence, but personality and adjustment disorders were related to greater risk (Monahan et al., 2005). A recent analysis of the Macarthur risk data showed that the prevalence of violence climbed from 15% to 26% to 29% for subjects classified as "no drug use," "little drug use," or " met criteria for substance abuse" (Melnick, Sacks, & Banks, 2005). The corresponding figures for alcohol were 14%, 23%, and 32%.

A combination of higher drug use and greater mental health problems has recently been associated with higher levels of criminal behavior for some offense types (Fletcher, Lehman, Wexler, & Melnick, 2007), although the interactive effects of substance use and mental health "were not straightforward" (p. 24). Such studies suggest the importance of considering the interrelationship between substance use, mental health disorders and change and crime outcomes.

All in all, offenders with co-occurring mental and substance use disorders demonstrate a diminished capacity to respond to traditional treatment (Fletcher et al., 2007). Recent reviews have uncovered few specialized treatment models for these clients that have been subjected to rigorous evaluation (Sacks & Pearson, 2003; Chandler, Peters, Field, & Juliano-Bult, 2004); one exception is the modified therapeutic community.

Rationale for the Current Study

The modified therapeutic community was designed specifically to address both substance use and mental disorders (Sacks, Sacks, & De Leon, 1999) and contains interventions (e.g., psycho-educational classes, dual recovery mutual self-help groups) that consider and attend to both disorders (Sacks, Sacks, & Stommel, 2003). Two previous papers reported that, compared to a randomly assigned mental health treatment group (C), modified therapeutic community treatment (E) resulted in significantly better outcomes on measures of crime (criminal activity, reincarceration rates) and substance abuse (declines in alcohol and drug use) for offenders with co-occurring substance use and mental disorders, 12 months post-prison release (Sacks, Sacks, McKendrick, Banks, & Stommel, 2004; Sullivan, McKendrick, Sacks, & Banks, 2006). This paper, drawn from the same study as the two previous reports, examines the effectiveness of modified therapeutic community treatment on mental health measures. In addition, this paper takes advantage of the opportunity afforded by the available study data to report on change in mental health measures for the combined groups and examines the relationship between mental health symptom change, substance abuse change, and criminal activity/recidivism.

METHODS

Research Design

The study randomly assigned male inmates with co-occurring disorders (N = 185) to one of two treatment groups, either E, a Modified Therapeutic Community (MTC) or C, a control group which received standard mental health treatment within the Colorado correctional system (see Sacks et al., 2003, 2004 for a full discussion of the study design and crime outcomes, and Sullivan et al., 2006 for a report on substance abuse outcomes). This paper continues the evaluation of the effectiveness of the modified therapeutic community, analyzing the same study sample with an emphasis on mental health measures (symptom change, medication use, or involvement in treatment services). The analytic plan involves an intent-to-treat analysis of the entire sample, and predicted significantly better results for E versus C on mental health measures 12 months post-prison release.

Experimental (E) Group: MTC Program

The MTC model involves three essential alterations to the traditional therapeutic community (TC) approach to respond to mental disorders occurring in conjunction with substance use disorders. The three modifications are: increased flexibility in programming to provide more choices in the daily regimen; decreased emotional intensity for better communication in interpersonal interactions; and greater individualization of work activities to achieve a better match of offender abilities to task assignments. The MTC, like all TC programs, seeks to develop a culture where clients, individually and collectively, can achieve behavior change with mutual support, and the encouragement associated with community affiliation. From this base, the MTC prison program incorporated further adaptations for the offender population with co-occurring disorders–a programmatic emphasis on criminal thinking and behavior; recognition and understanding of the interrelationship of substance abuse, mental illness, and criminality (triple recovery); adjustments to comply with facility security guidelines; and inclusion of security personnel on the treatment team. The MTC prison program included psycho-educational classes, dual recovery mutual self-help groups, cognitive behavioral protocols, vocational activities, medication and other therapeutic interventions (e.g., conflict resolution group). Psycho-educational classes help inmates with co-occurring disorders to deal with both their substance abuse and mental health problems more effectively. Cognitive behavioral elements help the offender to examine efforts to rationalize behaviors and justify criminal acts, and provide the offender with the tools to recognize and alter these patterns. After release from prison, those in the MTC group entered a six-month MTC aftercare program, receiving outpatient mental health services from community-based treatment agencies to assist with their community re-entry (see Sacks et al., 2003 for a complete description of the program).

The study employed a training and supervision regimen, administered under the direction of the first author and a co-author (Dr. Jo Ann Sacks), which consisted of three days of intensive training in the MTC approach, regular training sessions (monthly) using a manual and curriculum developed for the project team, and weekly consultation/supervision for the program director, clinical supervisor and program staff. A clinically trained Program Director with experience delivering TC programs provided site leadership, and a system-wide TC coordinator supplied monthly oversight of the MTC program. Previous publications describe the technical assistance protocols in more depth (cf. Sacks, De Leon, Bernhardt, & Sacks, 1997; Sacks et al., 1998, 1999).

Control (C) Group: Mental Health Treatment

The control group received psychiatric services consisting of medication, weekly individual therapy and counseling, and a cluster of discrete mental health and substance abuse interventions. The mental health interventions included a mandated cognitive behavioral core curriculum, anger management therapy and education, a focus on domestic violence, and parenting. Mental health status was monitored daily, and the type and dosage of medication were evaluated weekly. Substance abuse services consisted of a 72-hour cognitive behavioral curriculum focused on substance abuse education and relapse prevention (see Sacks et al., 2003 for a complete description of the program).

The MTC and Control programs were alike in their dual focus on mental and substance abuse disorders, in their use of medication, and in their application of cognitive behavioral elements to address criminal thinking; the main difference was the MTC program's use of the community as the healing agent and its reliance on mutual peer self-help. Upon release from prison, Control group subjects were typically referred to community-based treatment agencies to receive outpatient mental health and substance abuse services. The investigators confirmed the differential service provision within the two conditions through an inspection of program service logs and formal service utilization forms that the prison requires and maintains. This independence of programming can be attributed to three factors: each program is conducted in a distinct, self-contained unit; assigned staff are dedicated to only one program; and each program's design and schedule contain distinctive service elements.

Sample

Every offender, on entry to prison, undergoes a comprehensive assessment to determine eligibility for special services. The assessment consists of the *Colorado Standardized Offender Assessment* (Colorado DOC, 2004)–which captures lifetime and current mental and substance abuse problems, mental health and substance abuse treatment history, criminal history, substance use related crimes, and legal status; the *Brief Psychiatric Rating Scale* (Ventura, Green, Shaner, & Liberman, 1993)– which assesses the immediate need for psychiatric services; and a clinical interview, informed by a review of records for previous diagnoses, history of psychiatric hospitalization and medication. Offenders who are eligible for services are required by the State to participate in specialized treatment programs (available at facilities throughout the State), and are monitored regularly. Inmates with the most serious mental disorders (mainly schizophrenia and other psychotic disorders, bipolar disorders, major depression, cluster A personality disorders, and post traumatic stress disorders) are assigned to San Carlos Correctional Facility in Pueblo, which was constructed in 1995 specifically for male offenders with psychiatric disorders; the inmates assigned to San Carlos who had co-occurring disorders were placed in an eligibility pool for random assignment to one of the two study conditions: MTC (Experimental, E) or a mental health treatment program (Control, C).

The sample for this study consisted of 185 subjects who were randomly assigned to either E (MTC; n = 92) or C (n = 93). Retrieval rates for 12-month follow-up data were 75% (139/185) overall; 82% (75/92) for the MTC group, and 69% (64/93) for the C group, which constitutes the sample used in the analyses described in this paper.

Calculation of demographic characteristics (not shown) indicated that half of the study sample was Caucasian (49%), with African-Americans (30%) and Hispanic offenders (16.5%) comprising most of the remainder. The mean age of offenders in the sample was 34.3 years, and their first illegal activity and incarceration were at 10.8 and 19.1 years, respectively, on average. The sample completed an average 10.6 years of school; 37% were unemployed in the year prior to criminal justice contact. Profiles for substance use and criminal history show early onset for both types of behavior; inmates were an average of 13.5 years (SD = 5) at first alcohol use and 14 years (SD = 5) at first drug use.

All offenders in the study had received a Colorado DOC diagnosis of serious mental disorders. Research interviews using the *Diagnostic Interview Schedule* (Robins, Cottler, Bucholz, & Compton, 1995) found high rates of lifetime substance use and mental disorders in the study sample as shown in Table 1. Nearly all offenders (90%) were diagnosed

□ **Table 1: Diagnostic Profiles (Lifetime) of Study Subjects**

Diagnosis	Total (n = 139) %	MTC (n = 75) %	MH (n = 64) %
Substance Use or Dependence	90	89	91
Drug	77	79	75
Alcohol	63	68	58
Any Mental Disorder	77	79	75
Serious Mental Disorder	63	68	56
Schizophrenia	26	29	22
Bipolar	43	37	47
Major Depression	53	53	53
Other Mental Disorders			
Antisocial Personality Disorder	38	32	45
Phobia	28	29	27
PTSD	31	35	28
Dysthymia	29	29	29
Panic	22	20	25
General Anxiety	12	12	11
Obsessive/Compulsive	7	4	9
Gambling	7	8	5
Schizophreniform		1	2

with an Axis I Substance Abuse or Dependence disorder, and slightly more than three quarters (77%) were diagnosed with any mental disorder. About six in 10 received a diagnosis of serious mental disorder (schizophrenia, bipolar disorder or major depression), and over one-third (38%) met criteria for antisocial personality disorder. Table 1 also shows prevalence rates separately for alcohol and drug abuse and dependence disorders, as well as for an array of other mental disorders. No differences between E and C were evident for any of these diagnostic categories (not shown).

Data Collection. Data were collected using standardized self-report instruments (described below), administered individually by a trained interviewer to all study clients, and were obtained from the Colorado DOC computerized record information system. Interviews were conducted at baseline (on entry into treatment) and 12 months post-prison release. Baseline measures assessed activity during the 12 months prior to incarceration. The 12-month follow-up data assessed activity during the 12 months following release from prison.

Measures

Mental Health

This paper reports mental health data obtained from standardized symptom measures that reflect the 30-day period before they were assessed and from items on medication and service use that were selected from a larger interview protocol. Three standardized instruments were utilized in the analysis of mental health outcomes. The *Beck Depression Inventory-II* (BDI) is a self-report assessment focusing on depressive disorders identified in the DSM-IV (Beck, Steer, & Brown, 1996). The *Brief Symptom Inventory* (BSI), a condensed version of the *Symptom Checklist 90*, is used as a global measure of symptomatology (Derogatis, 1993). The fifty-three item inventory taps nine domains of psychiatric symptomatology, and includes a summary global severity index. The nine BSI subscales capture symptoms such as paranoid ideation, psychoticism, and hostility. A 20-item version of the *Manifest Anxiety Scale* (MAS) was also used as an outcome measure (Taylor, 1953), and two other measures looked specifically at medication use and psychological services received in the last 12 months. This service use was considered to be positive; mental disorders are generally acknowledged to reoccur, and continuing care is widely understood to be necessary to optimize treatment outcomes for this population (Center for Substance Abuse Treatment, 2005). (The limitations section of this paper discusses this issue in more detail.)

Substance Use

Substance use was self-reported by study participants. The "any substance use" measure employed combined both alcohol and drug use into one measure to examine relapse or success. A single dichotomous variable was scored "0" for no use and "1" if the subject used drugs or "alcohol to intoxication" during the 12-month post-prison period.

Criminal Activity

Crime outcome data were collected via self-report and, whenever available, checked against Colorado DOC records. The analysis employed two crime measures, "any criminal activity" and "reincarceration," which refer to activity or status during the first 12 months following release from prison and only to new crimes committed. This refers specifically to a return to an institutional facility. Parole or technical violations were omitted from the analysis, since all subjects were under parole supervision during follow-up and such heightened surveillance conditions result in disproportionately high detection of parole and technical offenses (Taxman et al., 2002), and to maintain consistency with previous reports of the investigators (Sacks et al., 2004; Sullivan et al., 2006). The individual crime types included property (e.g., fraud, forgery, fencing, burglary), violent (e.g., robbery, rape, violence against persons), and public order (e.g., vagrancy) offenses.

Analytic Plan

Analyses proceeded in three main steps. First, multivariate regression analyses were conducted to test the hypothesis of significantly better mental health outcomes for the MTC compared to the C group. Three covariates were used (i.e., age, employment, and number of residences), which had been used historically in other analyses and studies. Ordinary least squares regression equations were run for continuous outcome measures on standardized variables (BSI, BDI, MAS),[1] while multivariate logistic regression models were utilized with dichotomous mental health measures (medication use, or involvement in treatment services).

Next, the analysis examined changes for both the E and C groups combined on measures of mental health symptoms, medication use, and involvement in treatment services from baseline and follow-up. Inspection of the bivariate data indicated considerable pre-post change for both E and C, warranting further investigation of these changes for both groups combined. This step consisted of the application of paired sample t-tests for the symptom measures and McNemar tests for the treatment utilization and medication items.

Finally, analyses were conducted to examine the relationship between substance use change, changes in mental health symptoms, and criminal behavior and criminal justice involvement. Previous analyses of the investigators had found positive effects of the MTC model for crime and substance abuse (reported separately, i.e., Sacks et al., 2004; Sullivan et al., 2006), warranting an examination of potential interactions of substance abuse, mental health and crime outcomes. These analyses utilized multivariate regression and were conducted as a means of assessing the degree to which changes in substance use and changes in mental health symptoms were associated with reduction in criminal activity or reincarceration.

RESULTS

Differential Treatment Effects on Mental Health Outcomes

Table 2 shows that no significant differences were apparent between the groups from baseline to follow-up on measures of symptom change (BSI, BDI or MAS).[2] Table 2 also shows that no significant differences were evident between the groups on measures of medication use or treatment involvement. Compared to the C group, MTC clients tended toward a greater likelihood of treatment involvement and medication utilization at follow-up ($p = 0.09$).

Table 3 shows significant decreases in symptom scores found for the BSI global severity index (44.7 to 40.9) for both groups combined from baseline to follow-up and for the majority of BSI subscales (paranoid ideation, hostility, somatization, obsessive-compulsive, interpersonal sensitivity and anxiety). No significant changes were reported for the BDI total score or for the MAS. Table 3 also depicts significant increases

☐ **Table 2: E (MTC) vs. C Outcomes, 12 Months Post Prison Discharge**

	Model Nagelkerke/ Adj. R^2 (p)	Logit/ Unstd. B	MTC vs. MH Odds Ratio	p
BSI-Global Severity Index	0.01 (ns)	−1.75	0.760	0.47
BDI	0.05 (ns)	−3.23	0.615	0.37
MAS	0.08 (ns)	−0.72	0.770	0.54
Psychiatric Medication	0.15 (.01)**	0.72	0.487	0.09
Psychological Treatment	0.16 (.01)**	0.67	0.512	0.09

*p < 0.05, **p < 0.01, ***p < 0.001

☐ **Table 3: E (MTC) and C Outcomes, 12 Months Post Prison Discharge**

Mental Health Measures	Baseline Mean (sd) %		12-month Follow-up Mean (sd) %		t	p
Symptom Scales						
BSI-Global Severity Index	44.7	(11.1)	40.9	(10.1)	2.63	0.01**
BDI	12.8	(10.2)	12.7	(12.5)	.05	0.96
MAS	9.4	(5.0)	8.7	(5.2)	.99	0.32
BSI Subscales						
Psychoticism	48.1	(10.1)	45.8	(9.0)	1.77	0.08
Paranoid Ideation	50.8	(9.0)	47.1	(8.7)	3.25	0.00***
Phobic Anxiety	47.3	(8.6)	46.8	(7.9)	.40	0.69
Hostility	46.0	(8.9)	43.3	(8.4)	2.20	0.03**
Somatization	49.0	(9.1)	46.5	(8.8)	2.13	0.04*
Obsessive-Compulsive	43.6	(9.8)	41.0	(8.5)	2.05	0.05*
Interpersonal Sensitivity	45.5	(9.1)	41.1	(8.4)	3.58	0.00***
Depression	45.0	(9.6)	43.3	(8.8)	1.45	0.15
Anxiety	42.9	(10.5)	40.2	(9.4)	2.00	0.05*
Psychiatric Medication						
Yes	47.5		82.7		—	0.00***
Psychological Treatment						
Yes	36.7		66.2		—	0.00***

*p < 0.05, **p < 0.01, ***p < 0.001

in medication use (47.5 to 82.7%) and treatment involvement (36.7 to 66.2%) for the same period.

The Impact of Mental Health Symptoms and Substance Use on Crime

Table 4 indicates that relapse to substance use is a significant predictor of criminal activity ($p < 0.01$) and reincarceration ($p < 0.01$) during follow-up. Specifically, those clients who report relapse to alcohol and/or illicit drug use have nearly twice the odds (OR = 1.95) of self-reported criminal activity than those who did not. Similarly, those who relapsed had 2.11 times greater odds of reincarceration. Table 4 also shows that change in mental health symptoms, measured by the difference between follow-up and baseline BSI scores, did not exhibit a significant effect on either self-reported criminal activity or reincarceration, although lower levels of symptom improvement and/or worsening were associated with poorer crime outcomes. A variable reflecting the interaction of mental health symptom improvement and substance use relapse did not add significantly to the prediction of crime outcomes (not shown).

☐ **Table 4: Multivariate Analysis of Mental Health Change, Substance Use, and Recidivism (n = 95)**

	Model Nagelkerke R^2(p)	Logit (p)		Odds Ratio
Any Criminal Activity	0.30 (0.01)			
Any Substance Relapse (f/u)		0.67	(0.005)	1.95
Change in BSI (f/u-bl)		0.20	(0.46)	1.22
Any Reincarceration	0.32 (0.01)			
Any Substance Relapse (f/u)		0.75	(0.013)	2.11
Change in BSI (f/u-bl)		0.47	(0.15)	1.60

f/u = status at 12-month follow-up
f/u – bl = change score computed by subtracting the baseline score from the follow-up score
*p < 0.05, **p < 0.01, ***p < 0.001

DISCUSSION

Summary of Findings

Modified TC (E) vs. Mental Health (C)

No significant differences were detected between the E and C groups from baseline to follow-up on any measures of symptom change (BSI, BDI or MAS) or on measures of medication use or treatment involvement, but both groups showed significant improvements on some symptom measures. It may be difficult to demonstrate differential effects in studies such as this where medication was widely used among offenders in both experimental and comparison conditions. Overall, the study provides some evidence for the effectiveness of both study conditions on mental health measures, but does not confirm a differential advantage of MTC treatment on mental health measures. Because the MTC model is designed for persons with co-occurring disorders, it is important to strengthen the mental health features of the model and to demonstrate significant mental health effects.

As indicated in the section describing the MTC treatment, the program contained several elements traditionally employed in the treatment of mental disorders (e.g., medication, psycho-educational classes, vocational activities, self-help groups). One way the model might be strengthened would be to increase the focus on one of these (i.e., vocational activities) that has a considerable research base (Drake, Becker, & Bond, 2003) and, perhaps, the most direct bearing on successful transition to the community.

In a prison population, trauma symptom severity can complicate response to treatment and the recovery process (Brown, Recupero, & Stout, 1995; Brown, Read, & Kahler, 2003). Another approach that might prove fruitful would be to increase the MTC model's emphasis on trauma and trauma interventions. A recent study of the MTC treatment model, which incorporated trauma-informed addiction treatment, produced significantly better psychological outcomes for an outpatient MTC group of men and women, many with a history of criminal justice involvement, as compared to standard outpatient substance abuse treatment (Sacks, McKendrick, Sacks, Banks, & Harle, in press).

Substance Abuse, Mental Health and Crime

The findings indicated that, although mental health and substance use-related improvements for both groups in this study were associated with lower prevalence of self-reported criminal activity and reincarceration, greater and significant improvements in crime were related more to preventing drug and alcohol relapse than to improving mental health symptoms. This is not surprising given the typically high association observed between criminal activity and substance use; nonetheless, the finding supports a continued focus on providing substance abuse treatment to reduce criminal recidivism. The focus on substance use allows us to reduce the threat offender clients pose to public safety and the risks they run for future incarceration. Whatever the benefits mental health services have for offenders, they offer little or no apparent effect on the risk offenders pose to public safety as they reenter the community. Still, in a co-occurring disorders population, it is important to provide mental health treatment, and some evidence supports a small relationship to crime outcomes.

Limitations

The first limitation has to do with factors that might be affecting the capacity of this study to demonstrate positive mental health effects. At the outset, the mental health symptom scales employed, although measured at "baseline" for this study, may have underestimated the true level of psychiatric symptomatology in these offenders, since nearly half (47%) reported taking psychiatric medication in the six months prior to entering prison treatment. Second, as described above, *differential* symptom change may be difficult to assess in situations such as this where medication was widely used in both experimental and comparison conditions. Third, the sample size was relatively small, especially for the psychological measures, which limited the power of these analyses to demonstrate significant change. Future research should examine mental health outcomes across an array of measures (symptom change, medication compliance, improved self-esteem or sense of psychological well-being) and on larger samples in which baseline severity has not already been influenced by treatment services received prior to initiating the study.

A second limitation concerns increasing medication use and involvement in treatment services as indicators of positive outcome, although significant findings have not been reported for these variables. Using these services was perceived as being positive, since mental disorders are generally considered to be reoccurring or chronic conditions, and the need for continued care is widely acknowledged to be necessary to achieving optimal treatment outcomes in this population (Center for

Substance Abuse Treatment, 2005). Still, these results could either represent or be seen as being negative outcomes, since they reflect the impact of persistent problems that require costly services. At a minimum, future studies would need to determine that the use of these services was consonant with a post-prison release plan.

A third limitation is that, predominantly as a consequence of the small sample, tests of the relationship of mental health to substance abuse and crime outcomes focused on broad measures of symptoms and did not examine the relationships between diagnostic subgroups, specific mental health symptoms, substance abuse and crime outcomes. Future research should also examine mental health outcomes for particular diagnostic categories or groupings (e.g., schizophrenia, post-traumatic stress disorder, severe vs. any mental disorder). Studies can also disaggregate symptom measures by symptom type (e.g., anxiety, depression, paranoid ideation) to determine more accurately which subgroups in this population are most at risk and whether or not particular reductions in symptoms are related to crime outcomes.

CONCLUDING NOTE

The analyses reported in this paper did not confirm the hypothesis that MTC treatment would result in better mental health outcomes as compared to the control group. Still, significant improvements were noted for both the E and C groups, suggesting that the treatment conditions were equally effective in producing significant change on mental health symptoms. Future research and programming should emphasize boosting and evaluating MTC treatment for mental health. Nevertheless, given the need for research-based approaches, program and policy planners should consider the MTC when designing programs for co-occurring disorders, since previous study has demonstrated significantly better outcomes on the critical variables of crime and substance use. Furthermore, research to determine the relative cost-effectiveness of MTC programming has confirmed its value in treating a co-occurring disorders population, demonstrating that the total and average cost of MTC treatment was similar to the cost of standard services (French, Sacks, De Leon, Staines, & McKendrick, 1999; McGeary, French, Sacks, McKendrick, & De Leon, 2000), while every dollar spent on MTC treatment produced six dollars of benefit (French, McCollister, Sacks, McKendrick, & De Leon, 2002).

Additional analyses indicated that reductions on crime variables (criminal activity, reincarceration) were related more to decreases in substance use than to improvements on broad measures of mental health symptoms for both groups combined, indicating the primacy of drug treatment in relation to crime outcomes. To contain the risk the individual poses to his own and to the community's well-being, it is essential to make a first investment in responding to the offender's substance use problems. In an offender population with co-occurring disorders, however, additional study is needed to delineate the relationships between diagnostic subgroups, substance abuse change, change in specific mental health symptoms, and crime outcomes.

NOTES

1. Regression estimates for the control variables are available from the corresponding author by request.
2. Due to a late start, data for standardized psychological symptom measures were available on a smaller sample (i.e., BSI = 93, BDI = 93, MAS = 63) as reported in Table 2, Table 3, and Table 4; the full sample of 139 was available for all other variables shown in these tables.

REFERENCES

AISHealth.com (2001). Managed Care Adviser: Texas considers algorithm project to cut prison mental health costs. *Managed Care Week*, June 24, 2001.

Beck, A.T., Steer, R.A., & Brown, G.K. (1996). *Beck Depression Inventory–Second Edition (BDI-II) Manual.* San Antonio, TX: The Psychological Corporation.

Belenko, S., & Peugh, J. (2005). Estimating drug treatment needs among state prison inmates. *Drug and Alcohol Dependence, 77*(3), 269-281.

Brady, T.M., Krebs, C.P., & Laird, G. (2004). Psychiatric comorbidity and not completing jail-based substance abuse treatment. *American Journal of Addictions, 13*(1), 83-101.

Brown, P.J., Recupero, P.R., & Stout, R.L. (1995). PTSD substance abuse comorbidity and treatment utilization. *Addictive Behaviors, 20,* 251-254.

Brown, P.J., Read, J.P., & Kahler, C.W. (2003). Comorbid PTSD and substance use disorders: Treatment outcomes and role of coping. In P.C. Ouimette & P.J. Brown (Eds.), *Trauma and substance abuse: Causes, consequences, and treatment of comorbidity* (pp. 171-190). Washington, DC: American Psychological Association.

Center for Substance Abuse Treatment (2005). *Substance abuse treatment for persons with co-occurring disorders. Treatment Improvement Protocol (TIP)* series, Number 42. S. Sacks, Chair & R. Reis, Co-Chair, Consensus Panel. DHHS Pub. No.

(SMA) 05-3992. Rockville, MD: Substance Abuse and Mental Health Services Administration.

Chandler, R.K., Peters, R.H., Field, G., & Juliano-Bult, D. (2004). Challenges in implementing evidence-based treatment practices for co-occurring disorders in the criminal justice system. *Behavioral Sciences & the Law* (special edition), *22*(4), 431-448.

Colorado Department of Corrections (DOC) (2004). *Colorado Standardized Offender Assessment* (SOA). Denver, CO: Colorado DOC.

Correctional Association of New York (2004). *Mental health in the house of corrections: A study of mental health care in New York State prisons.* New York, NY: Correctional Association of New York, 135 E 15 Street, NY, NY 10003.

Cullen, F.T. (2005). The twelve people who saved rehabilitation: How the science of criminology made a difference. *Criminology, 43*, 1-42.

Derogatis, L.R. (1993). *Brief Symptom Inventory Administration, Scoring, and Procedures Manual* (third edition). National Computer Systems, Inc., Minneapolis.

DiCataldo, F., Greer, A., & Profit, W.E. (1995). Screening prison inmates for mental disorder: An examination of the relationship between mental disorder and prison adjustment. *Bulletin of the American Academy of Psychiatry Law, 23*, 573-585.

Drake, R.E., Becker, D.R., & Bond, G.R. (2003). Recent research on vocational rehabilitation for persons with severe mental illness. *Current Opinion in Psychiatry, 16*(4), 451-455.

Farabee, D. (2005). *Rethinking rehabilitation: Why we can't reform our criminals.* Washington, DC: AEI Press.

Fazel, S., & Danesh, J. (2002). Serious mental disorder in 23 000 prisoners: A systematic review of 62 surveys. *Lancet, 359*(9306), 545-550.

Fletcher, B.W., Lehman, W.E.K., Wexler, H.K., & Melnick, G. (2007). Who participates in the Criminal Justice Drug Abuse Treatment Studies (CJ-DATS)? *The Prison Journal, 87*(1), 1-33.

French, M.T., McCollister, K.E., Sacks, S., McKendrick, K., & De Leon, G. (2002). Benefit-cost analysis of a modified TC for mentally ill chemical abusers. *Evaluation and Program Planning, 25*(2), 137-148.

French, M.T., Sacks, S., De Leon, G., Staines, G., & McKendrick, K. (1999). Modified therapeutic community for mentally ill chemical abusers: Outcomes and costs. *Evaluation and the Health Professions, 22*(1), 60-85.

Harrison, P.M., & Beck, A.J. (2005). *Prison and jail inmates at midyear 2004.* Washington, DC: U.S. Department of Justice, *Office of Justice Programs.*

Hartwell, S. (2004). Triple stigma: Persons with mental illness and substance abuse problems in the criminal justice system. *Criminal Justice Policy Review, 15*(1), 84-99.

Hiller, M.L., Knight, K., & Simpson, D.D. (1999). Prison-based substance abuse treatment, residential aftercare and recidivism. *Addiction, 94*(6), 833-842.

James, D.J., & Glaze, L.E. (2006). *Mental health problems of prison and jail inmates.* Washington, DC: Office of Justice Programs.

Kleinsasser, L.D., & Michaud J. (2002). *Identifying and Tracking Mentally Ill Offenders in the Colorado Department of Corrections.* Presentation to Mental Health Corrections Consortium Conference, May 2002, Kansas City, MO.

Lang, M.A., & Belenko, S.R. (2001). A cluster analysis of HIV risk among felony drug offenders. *Criminal Justice and Behavior, 28*, 24-61.

Martinson, R. (1974). What works? Questions and answers about prison reform. *The Public Interest, Spring,* 22-54.

McGeary, K.A., French, M.T., Sacks, S., McKendrick, K., & De Leon, G. (2000). Service use and cost by MICAs: Differences by retention in a TC. *Journal of Substance Abuse, 11*(2), 1-15.

Melnick, G., Sacks, S., & Banks, S. (2006). Use of the COVR in violence risk assessment. Letter to the editor. *Psychiatric Services, 57*(1), 142.

Monahan, J. (1993). Mental disorder and violence: Another look. In S. Hodgins (Ed.), *Mental disorder and crime* (pp. 287-302). Newbury Park, CA: Sage Publications.

Monahan, J., Steadman H.J., Robbins, P.C., Appelbaum, P., Banks, S., Grisso, T., Heilbrun, K., Mulvey, E.P., Roth, L., & Silver, E. (2005). An actuarial model of violence risk assessment for persons with mental disorders. *Psychiatric Services, 56*(7), 810-815.

Monahan, J., Steadman, H.J., Robbins, P.C., Silver, E., Appelbaum, P., Grisso, T., Mulvey, E.P., & Roth, L. (2000). Developing a clinically useful actuarial tool for assessing violence risk. *British Journal of Psychiatry, 176,* 312.

Morgan, D.W., Edwards, A.C., & Faulkner, L.R. (1993). The adaptation to prison by individuals with schizophrenia. *Bulletin of the American Academy of Psychiatry Law, 21,* 427-433.

Mumola, C. (1999). *Substance abuse and treatment, state, and federal prisoners,* 1997 (NCJ Publication No. 172871). Washington, DC: U.S. Department of Justice.

National Center on Addiction and Substance Abuse (CASA) (1998). *Behind bars: Substance abuse and America's prison population.* National CASA, Columbia University, 633 Third Ave, 19th Fl, New York, NY 10017-6707.

National Institute of Justice (1997). *Drug use forecasting–1996.* Washington, DC: U.S. National Institute of Justice.

O'Brien, M., Mortimer, L., Singleton, N., & Meltzer, H. (2003). Psychiatric morbidity among women prisoners in England and Wales. *International Review of Psychiatry, 15,* 153-57.

Petersilia, J. (2000). *When prisoners return to the community: Political, economic, and social consequences.* Washington, DC: Office of Justice Programs.

Robins, L., Cottler, L., Bucholz, K., & Compton, W. (1995). *Diagnostic Interview Schedule for DSM-IV (DIS-IV).* Bethesda, MD: National Institute on Mental Health (NIMH).

Sacks, S., & Pearson, F. (2003). Co-occurring substance use and mental disorders in offenders. *Federal Probation, 67*(2), 32-39.

Sacks, S., Sacks. J.Y., & De Leon, G. (1999). Treatment for MICAs: Design and implementation of the modified TC. *Journal of Psychoactive Drugs* (special edition), *31*(1), 19-30.

Sacks, S., Sacks, J.Y., & Stommel, J. (2003). Modified TC for MICA inmates in correctional settings: A program description. *Corrections Today,* Oct., 90-99.

Sacks, S., Banks, S., McKendrick, K., & Sacks, J.Y. (in press). Modified therapeutic community for co-occurring disorders: A review of four studies. *Journal of Substance Abuse Treatment,* special edition.

Sacks, S., De Leon, G., Bernhardt, A.I., & Sacks, J.Y. (1997). A modified therapeutic community for homeless MICA clients. In G. De Leon (Ed.), *Community-as-method:*

Therapeutic communities for special populations and special settings. Westport, CT: Greenwood Publishing Group, Inc.

Sacks, S., De Leon, G., Bernhardt. A.I., Sacks, J.Y., Staines, G., Balistreri, E., & McKendrick, K. (1998). Modified therapeutic community for homeless MICAs: Socio-demographic and psychological profiles. *Journal of Substance Abuse, 15*(6), 545-554.

Sacks, S., McKendrick, K., Sacks, J.Y., Banks, S., & Harle, M. (in press). Enhanced outpatient treatment for co-occurring disorders: Main outcomes. *Journal of Substance Abuse Treatment.*

Sacks, S., Sacks, J.Y., McKendrick, K., Banks, S., & Stommel, J. (2004). Modified TC for MICA offenders: Crime outcomes. *Behavioral Sciences & The Law, 22,* 477-501.

Steadman, H.J., Mulvey, E.P., Monahan, J., Robbins, P.C., Appelbaum, P.S., Grisso, T., Roth, L.H., & Silver, E. (1998). Violence by people discharged from acute psychiatric inpatient facilities and by others in the same neighborhoods. *Arch Gen Psychiatry, 55*(5), 393-401.

Stommel, J. (2006). Personal communication, November 20, 2006.

Sullivan, C.J., McKendrick, K., Sacks, S., & Banks, S.M. (2006). *Modified TC for MICA offenders: Substance use outcomes.* Manuscript submitted for publication.

Taxman, F.S., Young, D., & Byrne, J.M. (2002). *Targeting for reentry: Matching needs and services to maximize public safety.* Washington, DC: National Institute of Justice.

Taylor, J.A. (1953). A personality scale of manifest anxiety. *Journal of Abnormal and Social Psychology, 48,* 285-290.

Ventura, J., Green, M.F., Shaner, A., & Liberman, R.P. (1993). Training and quality assurance with the brief psychiatric rating scale: "The drift buster." *International Journal of Methods in Psychiatric Research, 3*(4), 221-224.

Visher, C., LaVigne, N., & Travis, J. (2004). *Returning home: Understanding the challenges of prisoner reentry.* Washington, DC: The Urban Institute.

AUTHORS' NOTES

Christopher J. Sullivan, PhD, is Assistant Professor, Department of Criminology, University of South Florida, 4204 E. Fowler Avenue, SOC326, Tampa, FL 33620-8100 (E-mail: csullivan@cas.usf.edu).

Stanley Sacks, PhD, is Director, Center for the Integration of Research & Practice (CIRP), National Development & Research Institutes, Inc. (NDRI), New York, NY (E-mail: sacks@ndri.org).

Karen McKendrick, MPH, is Project Director, Center for the Integration of Research & Practice (CIRP), National Development & Research Institutes, Inc. (NDRI), 71 W. 23 Street, 8th Floor, New York, NY 10010 (E-mail: mckendrick@ndri.org).

Steven Banks, PhD, is Research Associate Professor of Psychiatry, University of Massachusetts Medical School , 55 Lake Ave. North, Worcester, MA 01655 (E-mail: tbosteve@aol.com).

JoAnn Y. Sacks, PhD, is Deputy Director, Center for the Integration of Research & Practice (CIRP), National Development & Research Institutes, Inc. (NDRI), 71 W. 23 Street, 8th Floor, New York, NY 10010 (E-mail: sacks@ndri.org).

Joseph Stommel, MS, is Chief of Rehabilitation Programs, Colorado Department of Corrections, Clinical Services, 2862 South Circle Drive, Colorado Springs, CO 80906 (E-mail: joe.stommel@doc.state.co.us).

Dr. Sullivan was on staff at NDRI while this manuscript was developed; he has since assumed his current role at the University of South Florida.

Address correspondence to: Stanley Sacks, PhD, Director, CIRP/NDRI, 71 W. 23 Street, 8th Floor, New York, NY 10010 (E-mail: stansacks@mac.com).

doi:10.1300/J076v45n01_15

Mental Health Issues in the Criminal Justice System. Pp. 249-256.

Available online at http://jor.haworthpress.com

© 2007 by The Haworth Press, Inc. All rights reserved.

doi:10.1300/J076v45n01_16

Recidivism Among Child Molesters:
A Brief Overview

KEITH F. DURKIN

ALLISON L. DIGIANANTONIO

ABSTRACT The sexual abuse of children has received a tremendous amount of attention in recent years. Accordingly, both the criminal justice and mental health systems deal with child molesters. Since much of the public concerns revolve around the potential dangerousness of any given child molester, practitioners are frequently responsible for making assessments regarding these risks. Ideally, this should be based on the research on recidivism. However, studies on this topic frequently produce conflicting and confusing results. This paper reviews the relevant literature to summarize the problems facing many recidivism studies. Considering these limitations, estimates of baseline recidivism rates and risk factors for recidivism are discussed. doi:10.1300/J076v45n01_16 *[Article copies available for a fee . from The Haworth Document Delivery Service: 1-800-HAWORTH. E-mail address: <docdelivery@haworthpress.com> Website: <http://www.HaworthPress. com> © 2007 by The Haworth Press, Inc. All rights reserved.]*

KEYWORDS Sex offender, recidivism, children

INTRODUCTION

The sexual abuse of children is currently considered a major social problem (Hanson, Steffy, & Gauthier, 1993). This constitutes a high profile topic of public discourse that has often assumed a political dimension, resulting in legislation such as the Wetterling Act, Megan's Law, and Jessica's Law. There is ample cause for concern, given the extensive body of empirical literature that indicates that children who are molested suffer a vast array of problems due to their victimization (see Becker & Reilly, 1999; Browne & Finkelhor, 1986; Conte & Berliner, 1988; Firestone et al., 2000; Lurigio, Jones, & Smith, 1995). For instance, victims may suffer physical injuries and damage. Children who are molested frequently experience psychological problems such as fear, anxiety, depression, and low self-esteem. Other problems may include behavioral issues such as poor academic performance, social maladjustment, aggressive behavior, and sexual acting out.

Because of the great societal concern regarding the sexual abuse of children, it is important to ascertain the risk that a specific offender may pose. This is usually based upon their likelihood of re-offending (i.e., recidivism). Mental health professionals are increasingly called upon to make assessments regarding the dangerousness of these individuals. This information may serve as the basis of sentencing and parole recommendations, as well as offender classification. New civil commitment laws also call for mental health professionals to make risk assessments (Doren, 1998). Information on recidivism can also be useful to legislators and policymakers who need to understand the risk posed by individuals who have molested children (Song & Lieb, 1994). Also, investigative workers, such as child protective service workers and police detectives, would also benefit from having an adequate understanding of these risks (Levenson & Morin, 2006). Additionally, public health professionals are increasingly called upon to become involved in treatment and prevention efforts (Becker & Reilly, 1999; McMahon, 2000).

The purpose of this paper is to provide a brief overview of the research on recidivism among individuals who sexually abuse children (i.e., child molesters). Despite the tremendous importance of research on recidivism, these studies have produced some of the most convoluted findings in all of the behavioral sciences. This is probably attributable to the fact that many of these studies are plagued by a variety of methodological difficulties. The current undertaking discusses these methodological considerations in detail. Even though many of these studies have methodological weaknesses, several correlates of recidivism by child molesters have been identified. These will be presented in the following discussion. Finally, the baseline estimates of recidivism that were derived from large-scale, long-term studies will also be presented.

METHODOLOGICAL ISSUES

In a recent text, two criminal psychologists mused that with all of the problems associated with the measurement of recidivism rates for child molesters, one has to wonder how large the number truly is (Bartol & Bartol, 2008). In fact, there is a clear lack of consistency in the use of the term recidivism (Barnes et al., 1994; Falshaw, Bates, Patel, Corbett, & Friendship, 2003; Langevin et al., 2004; Sample & Bray, 2006). First, some studies measure recidivism as the offender being arrested again. However, this could be an arrest for any offense or an arrest for a sex crime specifically. Second, other studies define recidivism as being reconvicted (again it could be for any offense or for a sex crime specifically). Third, this may be classified as any subsequent sexual offense whether or not it came to the attention of law enforcement.

A large number of studies rely on official statistics to measure recidivism. However, these official numbers are likely to be a gross underrepresentation of the actual number of offenses that occur (Firestone et al., 2000). For instance, in their scathing critique of official measures, Groth, Longo and McFadin (1982) administered an anonymous survey to sex offenders. They found that these individuals reported committing at least twice as many offenses as they were apprehended for. This is because most sex offenses are never reported to law enforcement (Becker & Reilly, 1999; Doren, 1998; Maletzky & Steinhauser, 2002; Sample & Bray, 2006). Reconviction is the standard outcome measure for many of the recidivism studies conducted in the United Kingdom (Falshaw et al., 2003). Yet even fewer offenses result in conviction (Hanson et al., 1993). Furthermore, plea bargaining and other negotiations can result in a conviction on lesser charges rather than a sex offense (Barnes et al., 1994; Firestone et al., 2000).

Another methodological issue is the fact that different recidivism studies use different follow-up periods. Some studies track offenders for five years or less, while a few other studies have used 25-year follow-ups. In general, five years or less is simply too short of a period to accurately measure recidivism (Barnes et al., 1994; Doren, 1998; Langevin et al., 2004; Soothill, Harman, Francis, & Kirby, 2005). This is a major problem since studies have found the highest risk of re-offending is between five and 10 years out from their arrest (Hanson et al., 1993). Also, long-term studies tend to report higher recidivism rates (Langevin et al., 2004). This wide variation in follow-up periods among the various recidivism studies makes comparison between these various studies nearly impossible (Barnes et al., 1994).

There are other problems aside from the use of official statistics and inadequate follow-up periods. For instance, some researchers have used self-reports of re-offending to avoid the problems that are typically associated with the use of official statistics. However, self-reports are prone to dishonesty and misrepresentation (Bogaerts, Delclerca, Veheule, & Palmans, 2005; Hanson & Bussiere, 1998). Additionally, some studies of recidivism by child molesters have been criticized for using sample sizes that are considered to be too small (Song & Lieb, 1994).

ESTIMATING AND PREDICTING RECIDIVISM

Despite the limitations inherent in this type of research, there is a compelling need to attempt to estimate the true recidivism rate for child molesters. Doren (1998) conducted an exceptionally thorough review of the research on this topic. His conclusion was that 52% was an acceptable conservative estimate for the base rate for long-term recidivism among extra-familial child molesters (those who target children who are not a member of their extended family or stepfamily). Also, Langevin et al. (2004) conducted a 25-year follow-up study of child molesters. They estimated the recidivism rate for extra-familial offenders at approximately 70%. The same research estimated the long-term recidivism rate among incest offenders at approximately 50%.

Researchers have identified a number of factors that seem to be associated with recidivism among child molesters. The first set of variables are sometimes called "static" or "historical" factors because they cannot be changed. The first is the victim-offender relationship. It is well-established that child molesters who target extra-familial victims have higher recidivism rates (Bartol & Bartol, 2008; Doren, 1998; Hanson, 2002; Hanson & Bussiere, 1998). On the other hand, incest offenders have notably lower rates (Doren, 1998; Friendship & Beech, 2005; Hanson, 2002; Song & Lieb, 1994). In fact, offenders who only victimize female relatives generally have particularly low recidivism rates (Hanson et al., 1993). Child molesters who have previous offenses have higher recidivism rates than those who do not (Barbaree & Marshall, 1998; Craig, Browne, Stringer, & Beech, 2005; Hanson & Bussiere, 1998; Hanson et al., 1993; Maletzky & Steinhauser, 2002; Song & Lieb, 1994). An early onset of sexual offending is also associated with recidivism (Hanson & Bussiere, 1998; Levenson & Morin, 2006). Offenders who victimize boys have a higher rate of recidivism than those who target girls (Bartol & Bartol, 2008; Friendship & Beech, 2005; Hanson & Bussiere, 1998; Hanson et al., 1993; Maletzky & Steinhauser, 2002; Song & Lieb, 1994). Child molesters who have never been married are a higher recidivism risk than other offenders (Hanson et al., 1993; Levenson & Morin, 2006). Finally, offenders who target very young children (Soothill et al., 2005), as well as those who used force during the crimes (Barbaree & Marshall, 1988), are at a higher risk for re-offending.

A second set of associated variables are called "dynamic" factors since clinicians believe that these can be changed. A pattern of deviant sexual arousal is a particularly strong predictor of recidivism among child molesters (Firestone et al., 2000; Hanson & Bussiere, 1998; Levenson and Morin, 2006; Roberts, Doren, & Thorton, 2002). In fact, Seto and Lalumiere (2001, p. 16) asserted that a "relative sexual interest in children was the single best predictor of sexual recidivism." Psychopathology is also a predictor of re-offending (Bogaerts et al., 2005; Firestone et al., 1999; Roberts et al., 2002). Recidivism has also been found to be related to personality disorder (Craig et al., 2005), impulsivity (Hanson, 2002; Soothill et al., 2005) and lack of empathy toward victims (Craig et al., 2005). Offenders who utilize cognitive distortions have a higher recidivism rate than those who do not (Craig et al., 2005; Roberts et al., 2002). Cognitive distortions "are attitudes and beliefs which offenders use to deny, minimize, and rationalize their behavior" (Blumenthal, Gudjonsson, & Burns, 1999, p. 129). Child molesters who are alcohol abusers present a greater recidivism risk than those who are not (Firestone et al., 1999, 2000). Finally, offenders with a low IQ or a learning disability have higher recidivism rates (Barbaree & Marshall, 1988; Craig et al., 2005; Craig & Hutchinson, 2005).

One strategy to reduce recidivism among child molesters is through treatment. Witt and Greenfield (2001) argued that treatment can reduce recidivism rates for child sexual abusers by as much as 30%. This assertion is based upon studies which find that treated child molesters have lower re-offending rates that those who did not receive treatment (Levenson & Morin, 2006; Looman, Abracen, & Nicholaichuk, 2000). While the results of the research on the effectiveness of the cognitive-behavioral treatments for child molesters are encouraging, these techniques only seem to work with subjects who understand that their sexual urges involving children are not appropriate (Arehart-Treichel,

2006). Offenders who comply with the treatment program, accept responsibility, and express remorse are thought to be lower recidivism risks (Hanson & Bussiere, 1998). However, short-term treatment is not considered an effective strategy, and treatment must be a long-term process (Hanson et al., 1993). Even so, failure rates appear to increase with the passage of time (Maletzky & Steinhauser, 2002). Finally, dropping out of treatment is positively associated with re-offending (Bartol & Bartol, 2008; Craig et al., 2005; Hanson & Bussiere, 1998).

DISCUSSION

The sexual abuse of children is considered a major social problem. Legislators, law enforcement personnel, and mental health professionals all have to deal with the challenges posed by individuals who sexually abuse children. A major issue is the likelihood that a child molester will re-offend. Ideally, this information would be the product of the large corpus of research on recidivism among child molesters. Unfortunately, many of these studies are plagued by a variety of methodological shortcomings. Accordingly, there are a wide range of estimates of the recidivism rate for child molesters. However, some of the better designed research on the subject suggests a conservative estimate of long-term recidivism to be 50% or higher, depending on the type of offender.

However, researchers seem to have been more successful in identifying individual factors that are associated with recidivism. Offenders who target children they are not related to (i.e., extra-familial offenders) are recidivism risks. Child molesters who have a deviant pattern of sexual arousal are more likely to re-offend. High risk offenders include those who have sexually abused children in the past. Other risk factors include targeting boys, impulsivity, using cognitive distortions, and psychopathology. There is surely a need for well-designed studies of recidivism among child molesters. In the meantime, when assessing the risks posed by an individual offender, one needs to take into consideration both the static and dynamic risk factors for that individual.

REFERENCES

Arehart-Treichel, J. (2006, May 19). Pedophilia often in headlines, but not in research labs. *Psychiatric News, 41*, 37.
Barbaree, H.E. & Marshall, W.L. (1988). Deviant sexual arousal, offense history, and demographic variables as predictors of reoffense among child molesters. *Behavioral Sciences and the Law, 6*, 267-280.

Barnes, A.R., Baca, M., Dix, M., Flahr, S., Gaal, C., Whitaker, M. et al. (1994). *Sex Offender treatment project: Literature review.* Anchorage, AK: Justice Center.

Bartol, C.R. & Bartol, A.M. (2008). *Criminal behavior: A psycholosocial approach* (8th ed.). Upper Saddle River, NJ: Pearson/Prentice-Hall.

Becker, J.V. & Reilly, D.W. (1999). Preventing sexual abuse and assault. *Sexual Abuse: A Journal of Research and Treatment, 11*, 267-278.

Bogaerts, S., Delclerca, F., Vaheule, S. & Palmans, V. (2005). Interpersonal factors and personality disorders as discriminators between inter-familial and extra-familial child molesters. *International Journal of Offender Therapy and Comparative Criminology, 49*, 48-62.

Browne, A. & Finkelhor, D. (1986). Impact of child sexual abuse: A review of the literature. *Psychological Bulletin, 99*, 66-77.

Conte, J.R. & Berliner, R. (1988). The impact of sexual abuse on children: Empirical findings. In L. Walker (Ed.), *Handbook of sexual abuse on children* (pp. 72-93). New York: Springer.

Craig, L., Browne, K.D., Stringer, I. & Beech, A. (2005). Sexual recidivism: A review of static, dynamic, and actuarial predictions. *Journal of Sexual Aggression, 11*, 65-84.

Craig, L. & Hutchinson, R.B. (2005). Sexual offenders with learning disabilities: Risk, recidivism, and treatment. *Journal of Sexual Aggression, 11*, 289-304.

Doren, D.M. (1998). Recidivism base rates, predictors of sex offender recidivism, and the sexual predator commitment laws. *Behavioral Sciences and the Law, 16*, 97-114.

Falshaw, L., Bates, A., Patel, V., Corbett, C. & Friendship, C. (2003). Assessing reconviction, reoffending, and recidivism in a sample of UK sexual offenders. *Legal and Criminological Psychology, 8*, 207-215.

Firestone, P., Bradford, J.M., McCoy, M., Greenberg, D.M., Curry, S. & Larose, M.R. (2000). Prediction of recidivism in extrafamilial child molesters based on court related assessments. *Sexual Abuse: A Journal of Research and Treatment, 12*, 203-221.

Firestone, P., Bradford, J.M., McCoy, M., Greenberg, D.M., Larose, M.R. & Curry, S. (1999). Prediction of recidivism in incest offenders. *Journal of Interpersonal Violence, 14*, 511-531.

Friendship, C. & Beech, A. (2005). Reconviction of sexual offenders in England and Wales: An overview of research. *Journal of Sexual Aggression, 11*, 209-223.

Groth, A.N., Longo, R.E. & McFadin, J.B. (1982). Undetected recidivism among rapist and child molestors. *Crime & Delinquency, 28*, 450-458.

Hanson, R.K. (2002). Recidivism and age: Follow-up data from 4,673 sexual offenders. *Journal of Interpersonal Violence, 17*, 1046-1062.

Hanson, R.K. & Bussiere, M.T. (1998). Predicting relapse: A meta-analysis of sexual offender recidivism studies. *Journal of Consulting and Clinical Psychology, 66*, 348-362.

Hanson, R.K., Steffy, R.A. & Gauthier, R. (1993). Long-term recidivism of child molesters. *Journal of Consulting and Clinical Psychology, 61*, 646-652.

Langevin, R., Curnoe, S., Fedoroff, P., Bennett, R., Langevin, M., Peever, C. et al. (2004). Lifetime sex offender recidivism: A 25-year follow up study. *Canadian Journal of Criminology & Criminal Justice, 46*, 531-552.

Levenson, J.S. & Morin, J.W. (2006). Risk assessment in child sexual abuse cases. *Child Welfare 85*, 59-82.

Looman, J., Abracen, J. & Nicholaichuk, T.P. (2000). Recidivism among treated sexual offenders and matched controls. *Journal of Interpersonal Violence, 15*, 279-290.

Lurigio, A.J., Jones, M. & Smith, B.E. (1995). Child sexual abuse: Its causes, consequences, and implications for probation practice. *Federal Probation, 59*(3), 69-76.

Maletzky, B.M. & Steinhauser, C. (2002). A 25-year follow up of cognitive/behavioral therapy with 7,275 sexual offenders. *Behavior Modification, 26*, 123-147.

McMahon, P.M. (2000). The public health approach to the prevention of sexual violence. *Sexual Abuse: A Journal of Research and Treatment, 12*, 27-36.

Roberts, C.F., Doren, D.M. & Thorton, D. (2002). Dimensions associated with assessments of sex offender recidivism risk. *Criminal Justice and Behavior, 29*, 569-589.

Sample, L.L. & Bray, T.M. (2006). Are sex offenders different? An examination of rearrest patterns. *Criminal Justice Policy Review, 17*, 83-102.

Seto, M.C. & Lalumiere, M.L. (2001). A brief screening scale to identify pedophiliac interests among child molesters. *Sexual Abuse: A Journal of Research and Treatment, 13*, 15-25.

Song, L. & Lieb, R. (1994). *Adult sex offender recidivism: A review of the studies.* Olympia, WA: Washington State Institute for Public Policy.

Soothill, K., Herman, J., Francis, B. & Kirby, S. (2005). Identifying future repeat danger from sexual offenders against children: A focus on those convicted and those strongly suspected of such crime. *The Journal of Forensic Psychiatry and Psychology, 16*, 225-247.

Witt, P.H. & Greenfield, D. (2001). Pedophilia. In C.D. Bryant (Ed.), *Encyclopedia of criminology and deviant behavior, Vol. III: Sexual deviance*. Philadelphia: Brunner-Routledge.

AUTHORS' NOTES

Keith F. Durkin, PhD, and Allison L. Digianantonio are affiliated with Department of Psychology and Sociology, Ohio Northern University, Ada, OH.

Address correspondence to: Keith F. Durkin, PhD, Department of Psychology and Sociology, 105 Hill Hall, Ohio Northern University, Ada, OH 45810 (E-mail: k-durkin@onu.edu).

doi:10.1300/J076v45n01_16

Mental Health Issues in the Criminal Justice System. Pp. 257-273.
Available online at http://jor.haworthpress.com
© 2007 by The Haworth Press, Inc. All rights reserved.
doi:10.1300/J076v45n01_17

Designing a Classification System for Internet Offenders: Doing Cognitive Distortions

STEVEN F. HUNDERSMARCK
KEITH F. DURKIN
RONALD L. DELONG

ABSTRACT Televised features such as NBC's *To Catch a Predator* have highlighted the growing problem posed by Internet sexual predators. This paper reports on the authors' attempts in designing a classification system for Internet offenders. The classification system was designed based on existing theory, understanding the nature of Internet offenders and the needs of police officers in the field. Designing the classification system was an inductive process that involved reviewing videotapes of offender interviews and reviewing existing literature on offender typologies and cognitive distortions. This paper describes the first step in designing a classification system that will be used to classify Internet offender typologies, identify cognitive distortions and recommend interview techniques for confronting distortions for criminal justice personnel. doi:10.1300/J076v45n01_17 *[Article copies available for a fee from The Haworth Document Delivery Service: 1-800-HAWORTH. E-mail address: <docdelivery@haworthpress.com> Website: <http://www. HaworthPress.com> © 2007 by The Haworth Press, Inc. All rights reserved.]*

KEYWORDS Cognitive distortion, situational offender, preferential offender

INTRODUCTION

Currently, the victimization of children online by sexual predators is considered a serious social problem. For instance, there have been a number of *To Catch a Predator* features on the *Dateline NBC* television program, where adult men are arrested after arriving for what they believe will be a sexual encounter with a young teen they met online. Fortunately, the "teen" was a decoy working in conjunction with a law ·enforcement sting operation. These types of offenders are typically called "travelers," men who attempt to solicit children online to eventually meet in person for sexual purposes (Alexy, Burgess, & Baker, 2005). The phrase Internet crimes against children (ICAC) has been recently introduced to describe "any computer-facilitated sexual exploitation of children including online solicitation and child pornography" (Alexy et al., 2005, p. 804). The results of a recent survey on adolescent Internet experiences conducted by researchers at the University of New Hampshire give us a glimpse into the extent of this phenomenon. They found that one in seven young people reported receiving unwanted sexual solicitations while online, while one in three were unwittingly exposed to pornographic material (sometimes via chat or e-mail) (Wolak, Mitchell, & Finkelhor, 2006).

Consequently, police are increasing their efforts to combat this problem. A very common strategy is the proactive investigation. In this context, the officer poses as a minor and goes online to attempt to identify adults who are soliciting minors for sex or who are sending them pornographic material. Proactive investigations generally begin in chat rooms and tend to develop very quickly (Mitchell, Wolak, & Finkelhor, 2005). Some practitioners (e.g., McLaughlin, 2004) have provided recommendations on how investigators could develop online personas that will appeal to offenders. The limited body of literature on the effectiveness of proactive Internet investigations is promising. For instance, Mitchell et al. (2005) found that about 90% of the arrests from these investigations result in guilty pleas. However, lawyers are developing various defense arguments (e.g., entrapment or fantasy role play) that are now used in court proceedings.

Internet crimes against children are considered a serious social problem that law enforcement is called upon to deal with. The problem continues to expand despite the efforts of law enforcement and the publicity of televised stings. Accordingly, academic research that can enhance our understanding of these offenders is sorely needed. The purpose of this paper is to discuss a new study called the Internet Sex Offender Research

Project. We are in the initial stage of data collection. The data are based on videotaped police interrogations of men arrested for Internet crimes against children. Thus far we have been able to obtain 18 videotapes taken by two different police agencies of arrested Internet offenders. One set of videotapes are normal interview tapes recorded by a metropolitan police agency in Ohio as part of their interrogation and arrest policy. The second sets of tapes involving another police agency in Ohio are more comprehensive and include footage of the offenders taken by NBC during an Internet sting. These tapes include television interviews, arrest and police interrogation footage. The offenders in all the tapes had plead guilty and their cases were no longer active. The cases are recent and range from 2003 to 2006. Generally the interviews are between 25-30 minutes in length. The shortest interview is approximately 10 minutes in length, the longest is almost two hours long.

One of the major aims is to develop a classification scheme for these offenders. This will be helpful to police who are charged with the identification and apprehension of these offenders. The typology should also be useful for police interrogations. Also, probation and parole officers, who are responsible for the management of these individuals, should find it helpful as well. Finally, this research could be useful for mental health professionals who are responsible for the assessment of these offenders.

CLASSIFICATION OF OFFENDERS

The problem at the onset in coding sexual offenders is the fact that sex offenders are recognized as one of the most heterogeneous group of offenders in all of criminology (CSOM, 2001). Within the literature focused solely on child sexual abuse one can find different categorizations in theories, etiology, typologies and recommended treatment for child offenders (Terry & Tallon, 2004). There is even considerable debate in how to define sexual offenders (see Geffner, 2004). Lanning (2001) notes that there is a great deal of confusion in the literature in simply defining the difference between pedophiles and child molesters. The literature is varied and difficult to make sense of when looking for commonality. It helps to overcome this confusion by focusing on a particular typology such as the Internet predator. However, even with Internet predators there is a great deal of variance between offenders. It is possible to generalize when coding to remove some of the variance; however, the obvious cost is accuracy. Another problem in coding results because most classification categories are static while the offender may develop across categories and quite often the nature of the offense is context variant.

When formatting an offender typology there are a number of considerations. The first consideration is to understand the context in which the typology will be used. The typology will be used in the field by police officer practitioners who do not have an abundance of time to weight or score a typology. The typology should be user friendly and not overly complex. At the same time a degree of accuracy is necessary. Thus the second consideration is in designing a typology that is empirically and theoretically sound. The final consideration involves taking into account the nature of the Internet predator. It would be a mistake to map existing typologies onto Internet predators; the Internet predator differs to some degree with existing typologies of child molesters. A related mistake would be classifying Internet predators as fitting into one typology. Deciding on a typology involves a process of give and take with the various considerations.

Thus, designing a typology is in reality a process that is grounded in practice and theory. We used a grounded approach similar to what Suri (1999) calls a lines-of-argument synthesis. In a lines-of-argument synthesis, data is gleaned from individual sources (video, written reports etc.) and constantly compared and contrasted with other sources being synthesized. Understanding of the entire phenomenon results through an understanding of each report being synthesized and comparing it to theory.

As previously indicated, the first step in deciding which typology to use is to understand the context in which it will be used. Police officers do not have the luxury of long interviews with the offender and his family. As such, the typology has to be designed with practicality in mind versus technically-based psychological criteria. Typologies for police officers should include material that they have at their disposal. A good guide for police officers in the initial stage of classifying an offender should include material that can be accessed electronically such as an individual's criminal history, driving record and the offender's place of residence. Other information used for categorizing offenders can be gained through initial observations such as physical appearance, dress, availability of transportation and other criteria that are directly accessible through the senses.

The typology should also include information obtained through the online discussions with the offender. This will include the degree of organization and sophistication as well as impulsivity or compulsivity apparent during the online chats with the suspect. Police officers may also gather information on the offender's typology through the initial information gathering phase of an interview. During the initial phase the police officer may gather information directly about the offender's past relationships, employment, residence history, etc. It is also possible to gather information indirectly by listening to how the offender answers the questions. The police interviewer will be able to judge how an individual responds to the interview; is he calm and collected, or highly emotive as evidenced by anger, fear or sadness. The officer can also quickly determine how organized the offender is based on his response to interview questions. Finally, information for the typology can be gained by determining the degree of sophistication as noted by the offender's level of schooling, use of grammar, etc. Thus information gathering is a multifaceted process that informs itself. The best part about the information gathering process is that it can be done quickly and is fairly reliable.

The second consideration facing us was determining which typological behavioral problem should be adopted to use as a theoretical overview. This consideration was balanced against the first consideration, the context of the situation and the last consideration, the typology of the Internet predator. A number of behavioral typologies were considered as part of the decision process. Terry and Tallon (2004) identified seven different typologies used since the 1970s. The most widely used of the typologies include Groth's original Fixated-Regressed Typology, Lanning's original FBI Typology and the Massachusetts Treatment Center's MTC:CM3 Typology.

Groth's classification model is based on whether or not the offender has been attracted to children on a continual basis since adolescence. If so, they are most likely a fixated offender (Terry & Tallon, 2004). If on the other hand the offender sexually abuses children as a result of a stressor or a blow to his self-esteem, he is considered a regressed offender (Bartol & Bartol, 2005). The fixated offender is the most dangerous type of offender as he is focused solely on children or adolescents. As such, he is the type who is more organized and spends time planning the offense and grooming the victim before committing his crime. The regressed offender may have adult relationships and the need to offend comes from an outside stressor such as divorce or the loss of employment. Groth's classification system works on a continuum overcoming most of the developmental and contextual problems inherit in the categorical classification systems.

However, Groth's classification does not map onto the context in which police officers work with online sexual predators. Groth's typology requires a sophisticated grading instrument to score an offender's psychological needs. A police officer doesn't have the time or tools to score psychological needs. The Groth typology also does not map as well onto the information a police officer has at his or her disposal in the field to classify an offender. Lastly, Groth's classification does not encompass the online predator typology as well as other classification systems. Groth's fixated–regressed typology is beneficial as it paved the way for a classification system that was modified in part by Lanning for use by law enforcement personnel.

The Massachusetts Treatment Center (MTC) uses a four dimensional typology for classifying pedophiles called the MTC:CM3. Within the four dimensions are two different axis levels, five dimension levels and 10 types (Bartol & Bartol, 2005). While this typology is very thorough and can be used on a clinical level, its biggest drawback is that it is very unwieldy for practitioners who cannot use it as a field guide. However, the degree of fixation (Axis 1) is a useful typology construct for use in coding and is also somewhat consistent with Groth's typology and Lanning's Situational-Preferential typology.

The Lanning typology has developed and changed since its inception in the mid 1980s. Lanning's original typology has two broad categories first identified by Dietz as preferential and situational (2001). Within the two broad categories were seven subordinate typologies. The original typology was designed to fit the needs of law enforcement officials as opposed to clinicians by using descriptive terms instead of diagnostic terminology. However, the original typology with its seven subcategories was too unwieldy as it was difficult for law enforcement officers to categorize human behavior into "neat little boxes" (Lanning, 2001, p. 22). To compensate for this weakness Lanning devised a new typology based on a continuum from situational to preferential. The situational–preferential continuum in the new typology makes it more amenable for classifying human behavior.

Lanning writes that situational offenders tend to be less intelligent, are more likely to be impulsive, make sloppy mistakes, are more spontaneous, are more emotive and are of a lower SES. Situational offenders are less apt to be driven by a psychological need to victimize children. However, they may commit acts of abuse due to divorce, loss of employment or other situational factors (2001). Preferential offenders on the other hand generally are more intelligent, are of a higher SES, are fantasy driven and are more compulsive in nature. Unlike situational offenders, preferential offenders are driven by sexual needs that compel them to victimize children (2001). The situational-fixated continuum also takes into account the degree of development or change that may occur with the violator over time or in different contexts.

By using this scale it can also be inferred that the organized-disorganized dichotomy fits in well with the typology. The organized-disorganized typology was designed by the Behavioral Science Unit of the FBI in part to facilitate police officers in the field (Turvey, 2003). Use of the organized-disorganized typology during the interrogation process has been used in law enforcement before (Holmes & Holmes, 2002). The organized-disorganized classification system in this case is the best typology for police officers to use as a quick guide to classify Internet offender behavior. However, we also designed our classification system with notable behavioral traits above and beyond the organized-disorganized dichotomy.

The behavioral traits exhibited by offenders and observed by police officers conform to Lanning's typology. Psychological constructs are unseen but apparent in the typology and reflect the degree of control and organization that is apparent in the crime. Since Lanning's typology was designed for law enforcement personnel it is an excellent classification system for our coding process. The typology had to be designed so that it could be applied in a non-clinical setting. It is understood that a degree in accuracy would be lost as the typology becomes more generalized and dimensions or layers of coding are removed.

Lanning (2001) also uses his preferential-situational typology to generally describe online offenders. Situational offenders do not specifically target children purposely, but may target a child due to random opportunity. Situational offenders include two offender subtypes. The first subtype contains offenders who are impulsive or curious and offend against a child. The second subtype is a morally indiscriminate power/anger offender with a history of violent offenses who offends against a child through opportunity. Preferential offenders specifically and purposely target children in their online activity. Preferential offenders also include two subtypes of offenders. The first subtype is the diverse offender who engages in a wide variety of deviant activities involving children. The second subtype is the latent offender who has recently begun to act out previously latent sexual behavior against children.

Lanning writes that in the past most online predators fit into the preferential typology and were generally more intelligent and affluent individuals. However, since the Internet has become more commonplace there is a wider range of violators including more situational offenders who come from a lower SES and are less intelligent (2001). The wide range of violators is evident with the offenders in our database. The offenders we observed thus far have ranged from an individual who was almost destitute and used a library computer, to a practicing medical doctor who bragged about his sports car and flourishing practice. On the continuum between the doctor and homeless individual were individuals who lived in trailer parks and some currently enrolled as college students. Although our database is not large, nonetheless there is a great deal of variance between the offenders.

Although heterogeneous in nature, the Internet offender does merit special recognition that will enable the police investigator. In a study conducted by the Crimes against Children Research Center, University of New Hampshire (Wolak, Mitchell, & Finkelhor, 2003), the following Internet offender traits were found among arrestees. The violator was almost always a Caucasian male who was 26 years-of-age or older (86%). Almost all acted alone (97%) and a majority possessed child pornography of some type (67%). Most had been arrested for online crimes against an identified child (45%), whereas a smaller percentage had been arrested as a result of a police sting (27%). Despite the work of groups like Perverted-Justice and stings broadcasted nationally on NBC's *To Catch a Predator*, predators continue to proliferate the web. Truly a large proportion of offenders are getting away with their crime.

The Internet provides an ideal tool to facilitate the goals of the sexual offender wherever they may fall on the fixated-situational continuum. The computer provides a degree of anonymity and protection not afforded in face-to-face encounters. It is well-established in the psychological literature that child molesters often suffer from loneliness, personal distress, a lack of confidence, and low self-esteem (Fisher, Beech, & Browne, 1999; Hudson & Ward, 2000; Marshall, Serran, & Cortini, 2000). Furthermore, research has shown that sexually troubled individuals, such as child molesters, use the Internet to avoid negative affective states such as anxiety and boredom (Quayle, Vaughan, & Taylor, 2006).

Using the Internet, offenders can troll for young victims with relatively little risk of being detected (Lanning, 2001). The victims of most online predators are unsupervised and alone on the computer. This facilitates both types of offenders, as the situational offender does not have to cull the victim from a larger group of individuals publicly which requires social competence. The preferential offender uses the opportunity to search for vulnerable victims which may include children who are pre-adolescent, come from a broken family, are latch-key children or suffer from emotional and/or physical abuse due to parental neglect. Moreover, the Internet allows for some degree of focused targeting.

Chat rooms set up for teens, pre-teens or younger children are prime hunting grounds for predators. There are also rooms dedicated to special interests such as cheerleading, figure skating, tennis, or soccer. Whereas predators may have been out of place in public or private areas where these groups congregated, they may now remain stealthily in the background preying for ideal victims who enter a chat room or respond to their instant message. Our experience also suggests that predators sometimes troll social networking sites such as Myspace while on the prowl for potential victims.

DESIGNING A CODING SHEET

Our first task was to design a coding sheet for our purpose of determining an offender typology, then identifying and documenting the use of cognitive distortions by offender type or classification. The situational-preferential classification system works well at this preliminary stage with the offenders we have seen on video. However, a more detailed analysis involving coding will further clarify the classification criteria. It is a grounded process that will inform itself as data is gathered. This typology will be a first step in helping police officers form a strategy to recognize and overcome cognitive distortions used by Internet offenders. Designing a classification form requires that coders use the same information sources available to police officers through normal investigative techniques and observation. Since we are viewing videotapes of interviews we are in essence experiencing the same coding context that officers will eventually be using. As such, it is a projective device, in that it allows us to use the same information in coding that a police officer will use. The coding form as conceived is one page in length. It consists of two sections. The first section defines the offender typology using the situational-preferential scale. The second section is a cognitive distortion/defense typology that is used to count the number of distortion/defenses and will be discussed later.

The typology section uses nine different projective areas of measurement. Each area as measured uses a continuum scale that doesn't bind the coder to an artificial typology. The areas as defined are behavioral indicators derived from Lanning's offender typology. The behavioral indicators we will use to code are purposely consistent to the different sources of information available to police officers. The first area is projective and is in part dependent on the coding process. The scale as measured looks at public order offenses (drunkenness, disorderly conduct etc.) measured against no arrest record. This measure is experimental as it would seem that an individual that is arrested for more public order offenses would be a more situational offender. However, the research findings in this area are varied (Simon, 1997) or cannot be used due to poor classification and not properly defining in detail the different typologies of "sex offenders."

Intelligence, the third area, can be measured by the investigator through the interview process and possibly through the online chat record. Intelligence can be measured by the offender's achievements, employment, success and other available indicators. Lanning notes that preferential offenders most often have more intelligence than the situational offenders. This will have an impact in the type of distortion/defense mechanism they use. The next area is socioeconomic status (SES) and is measured on a low/high scale. As noted by Lanning (2001) situational offenders generally have a lower SES than preferential offenders. SES is measured through interview and observation and includes employment data, home ownership, clothing worn and vehicle ownership. The next area measured in emotional control. Lanning notes that situational offenders are more often emotive than preferential offenders. Lanning notes that situational offenders will be more emotional throughout the process. Their emotions may range from anger to fear. Preferential offenders throughout the process will show less emotion. It is imperative that emotions are not measured at one point in time (such as at arrest) but throughout the process of arrest and interview.

The fifth area measures offender organization through the subcategories of planning, control and verbal organization. As noted by Lanning (2001) situational offenders are more likely to have poor organizational skills. The lack of such skills is usually displayed through their lack of planning throughout the investigation which includes their online chats. Likewise, verbal organization is measured throughout the investigation process. It is measured by looking at the online discussions and the interview process. The investigator should note during the interview process if the offender follows an organized thought pattern, or is random and difficult to follow. The sub-category listed as control is a projective area that may be too subjective to code. This area looks at the degree of control the offender attempts to solicit during his online chats. Since preferential offenders more often rely on script and fantasy they will exert more control in the process. The investigator will have to infer control from the online dialogue.

The next area, impulsive versus compulsive, is rated on a continuum from opportunistic to need driven. Lanning (2001) describes the situational offender as being more opportunistic in nature versus the compulsive need-driven preferential offender. The investigator will have to glean evidence for this area from the online chat log. The situational offender may suddenly propose to meet after a quick discussion or make sudden suggestions or statements in an impulsive manner. Whereas the preferential offender will require a grooming process complete with scripted dialogue, then act in a compulsive manner once those requirements are met (Lanning, 2001). Both violators will make mistakes. However, the situational offender will make impulsive, sloppy mistakes versus the need-driven mistakes of the preferential offender (Lanning, 2001).

The eighth measurement area is the result of our observations of Internet predators coupled with police officer reports. This is another projective area, but is easily and quickly measured by police officers. Generally, most situational offenders tend to be more asocial (Lanning, 2001). As such, their appearance is more unkempt versus preferential offenders who may dress for a date. Investigators can observe and at times smell (as noted by officers in a number of our tapes) offenders based on their appearance at the time of arrest.

The last area of measurement is relationships with others. Since the situational offender is more asocial they will more often have a history of poor or no relationships (Lanning, 2001). During the interview process investigators will discern the offender's relationship history with particular attention paid to friends, family and members of the opposite gender. An area of concern is the organized antisocial preferential offender who may also have a history of failed relationships. In our dataset we had one possible antisocial preferential offender who had a long-term failed relationship. The difference with this offender was that his relationship was more long-term versus a number of short-term relationships.

While there is a fair degree of generality and projection built into the offender typology, it should be noted that the device is structured so that each of the nine areas is used in a deductive manner by the coder and, eventually, police officer to determine a likely offender typology. Each area should be related to the others before a typology can be determined. In some cases, when the continuum is continuously weighted in the middle, no distinct classification will be possible (see Table 1). Hopefully, based on the results of our research an officer will be able to determine the offender type, understand the common distortions/defenses used by that offender and proceed with the interview knowing in general how to confront the distortions/defenses raised by the offender.

☐ **Table 1: Coding Sheet**

Name	
Behavioral Scale	Situational Preferential Low ●————————————————————● High
Criminal History	VARIED OFFENSES, public order, etc. None ●————————————————————●
Intelligence	●————————————————————●
SES	●————————————————————●
Emotional Control	More anger/fear/crying lack/no emotion ●————————————————————●
Organization	Mistakes/poor planning Planning/alibi ●————————————————————● Uncontrolled Control ●————————————————————● Poor verbal organization Good verbal skills, logical ●————————————————————●
Impulsive/compulsive	Opportunistic Need driven ●————————————————————●
Appearance	Dirty/unkempt appearance Clean/tidy appearance ●————————————————————●
Relationships w/others	unstable relations w/family friends more stable ●————————————————————●
	Count	Total
Cognitive distortions		
Refutation		
Minimization		
Justification/ Rationalization		
Depersonalization		
Admittance		
	Total Coded	

CLASSIFYING COGNITIVE DISTORTIONS

Cognitive distortions are beliefs and attitudes that offenders use to rationalize, deny, and minimize their behavior (Blumenthal, Gudjonsson, & Burns, 1999; Hayashino, Wurtele, & Klebe, 1995). These are statements that reflect a distorted sense of reality, and allow offenders to construct their conduct as morally permissible (Feelgood, Cortini, & Thompson, 2005; Ward, Hudson, Johnston, & Marshall, 1997). For instance, child molesters may assert that children are not harmed by sex with adults, or even that children may enjoy the experience (Hall & Hirschman, 1992; Ward et al., 1997). Others may attribute their misconduct to situational factors such as stress or intoxication (Pollack & Hashmall, 1991). Cognitive distortions are thought to reduce the guilt and shame associated with offending (Feelgood et al., 2005; Lawson, 2003). Furthermore, they can play an important role in the initiation and maintenance of offending (Blumenthal et al., 1999; Ward et al., 1997). More specifically, when an opportunity for offending presents itself, these cognitive distortions may allow individuals to capitalize on that chance (Marshall & Marshall, 2000).

When choosing a typology to classify cognitive distortions it is imperative to use the same considerations as those involved in determining an offender typology. The first thing to remember is the context in which the typology will be used. Since it will be used in the field by police officers it is imperative that the typology not be category heavy. Schneider and Wright (2004) identified 12 different typologies, a number of which identified six or more types of cognitive distortions. Many of the categories have discrete differences and are difficult for a practitioner without clinical training. The key again is to find a typology that is theoretically sound yet allows for ease of use. At this point there is little information that relates Internet offenders with cognitive distortions. As such, this research will further serve to inform the research community on the types of cognitive distortions used by Internet offenders.

After reviewing the literature on the use of cognitive distortions by child sexual abusers, Schneider and Wright (2004) suggest three broad classification categories that overlap the more numerous typologies they reported on. The categories as recommended are refutation, minimization and depersonalization. The categories run on a continuum from complete denial to partial admittance. Schneider and Wright (2004, p. 8) define refutation as "complete denial that an offense occurred, coupled with claims that nothing harmful happened to the alleged victim." Minimization is defined as a partial admittance on the part of the offender that something inappropriate happened, but denial of active participation and responsibility for the offense. Schneider and Wright conclude that minimization often includes blaming the victim and justifying their activity as a form of partial denial. Depersonalization is defined as admittance of responsibility of an offense but denial of any type of sexual deviancy or pattern of activity. Schneider and Wright focus on distorted thinking as a defense mechanism for offenders who come to justify their action and come to believe in their own distortions.

Lanning (2001) uses a typology based on pedophile defenses. Unlike Schneider and Wright, Lanning seems to infer that offenders are actively defending themselves, which seems to point to a typology that focuses on deception as opposed to distorted thinking. The defenses are listed as denial, minimization, justification and fabrication. The scale used by Lanning does overlap in the areas of denial and minimization with Schneider and Wright's typology. However, Lanning's addition of justification and fabrication is a break from Schneider and Wright's typology. Justification and rationalization defenses are used by individuals who see themselves as helping children learn about sex, who blame stress or the victim for their own behavior. Fabrication according to Lanning is used by more intelligent offenders who use ingenious stories to explain their behavior.

For purposes of choosing a typology to use we went back and viewed the offenders we had on video. It appeared that almost all used different forms of distortion or defenses to justify their actions (a few offenders did admit their guilt). It was also apparent that the offenders used distortions or defenses for different reasons. Some appeared to buy into what they were saying while others were using defense strategies to avoid implicating themselves in a crime. As a result we compiled a typology that combines elements of Schneider and Wright's denial typology and Lanning's defense mechanisms. We felt that both typologies covered the range of Internet predators we had in our database.

The following is our classification system we use for coding cognitive distortions. It consists of four identified types of distortions or defenses. They run on a continuum from full denial to full admittance. The first type of distortion/defense is defined as refutation. A refutation is full denial of all aspects of the offense. The second area is defined as minimization. Minimization is partial admittance, but denial of accountability. Minimization often includes placing the blame on outside circumstances such as alcohol use or actions of the victim. The third type is identified as rationalization/justification which includes acknowledgement of the act but denial that behavior is deviant or, in the case of rationalization, devising self-satisfying but incorrect reasons for one's behavior. An example we witnessed included the offender who rationalized that he was meeting an underage female but he was only going to take her to a movie or dinner.

Related to this is the individual who justifies his behavior as acceptable because he provides an education in love to children. The fourth identified distortion is defined as depersonalization. In depersonalization the offender admits the act, but denies the extent of his deviant behavior. An example of a statement made by an individual using depersonalization would be, "I usually don't chase teenagers around like this, it just happened this once." The last typology is full admittance of the act and their deviant behavior. The typology we designed carries components of both typologies as discussed yet still fits on a continuum. The typology works for a different range of offenders and was tested against a subset of Internet offenders in our database (see Table 1).

CONCLUSION

The formation of the coding system we use will hopefully mirror the process that police officers will use when they approach an interview with an offender who has been arrested for Internet crimes against children. To our knowledge this is the first attempt to accomplish this task. The difficulty in designing a classification system is to combine the practical needs of the police officer in the field with the research-based classification system. The classification system must be practically-based and at the same time must be theoretically sound. We hope that by associating the coding process as closely as possible to the process that police officers go through during an investigation will bring both processes together. As such, we also expect the coding process to inform our classification system.

This goal of this project primarily is assisting law enforcement officers and other criminal justice personnel in their investigations. We also hope to inform theory and existing research in the field by reporting on trends we see between offender classification and cognitive distortions. Finally, we will establish interview strategies for confronting and overcoming cognitive distortions with established interview techniques by using classification of offender and cognitive distortion typology.

REFERENCES

Alexy, E.M., Burgess, A.W., & Baker, T. (2005). Internet offenders: Traders, travelers, and combination trader-travelers. *Journal of Interpersonal Violence, 20*, 804-812.

Bartol, C.R., & Bartol, A.M. (2005). *Criminal Behavior: A Psychosocial Approach* (7th ed.). Upper Saddle River, NJ: Prentice Hall.

Blumenthal, S., Gudjonsson, G., & Burns, J. (1999). Cognitive distortions and blame attribution in sex offenders against adults and children. *Child Abuse and Neglect, 23*, 129-143.

Center for Sex Offender Management (2001). U.S. Department of Justice, Office of Justice Program. *Recidivism of sex offenders*. Accessed on 02-24-07 at http://www.csom.org/pubs/recidsexof.html

Feelgood, S., Cortini, F., & Thompson, A. (2005). Sexual coping, general coping, and cognitive distortions in incarcerated rapists and child molesters. *Journal of Sexual Aggression, 11*, 157-170.

Fisher, D., Beech, A., & Browne, K. (1999). Comparison of sex offenders to non-offenders on selected psychological measures. *International Journal of Offender Therapy and Comparative Criminology, 43*, 473-491.

Geffner, R., Crumpton-Franey, K., Geffner, T., & Falconer, R. (2004). *Identifying and Treating Sex Offenders*. Binghamton, NY: The Haworth Press, Inc.

Hall, G.C.N., & Hirschman, R. (1992). Sex aggression against children: A conception of etiology. *Criminal Justice and Behavior, 19*, 8-23.

Hayashino, D.S., Wurtele, S.K., & Klebe, K.J. (1995). Child molesters: An examination of cognitive factors. *Journal of Interpersonal Violence, 10*, 106-116.

Holmes, R.T., & Holmes, S.T. (2002). *Profiling Violent Crimes. An Investigative Tool* (3rd ed.). Thousand Oaks, CA: Sage.

Hudson, S.M., & Ward, T. (2000). Interpersonal competency in sex offenders. *Behavior Modification, 24*, 494-527.

Lanning, K.V. (2001). *Child Molesters: A Behavioral Analysis* (4th ed.). Washington, DC: National Center for Missing & Exploited Children.

Lawson, L. (2003). Isolation, gratification, justification: Offenders' explanations of child molesting. *Issues in Mental Health Nursing, 24*, 695-705.

Marshall, W.L., & Marshall, L.E. (2000). The origins of sexual offending. *Trauma, Violence, and Abuse, 1*, 250-263.

Marshall, W.L. Serran, G.A., & Cortini, F.A. (2000). Childhood attachments, sexual abuse, and their relationship to adult coping in child molesters. *Sexual Abuse: A Journal of Research and Treatment, 12*, 17-26.

McLaughlin, J.F. (2004). Characteristics of a fictitious child victim: Turning a sex offenders' dreams into his worst nightmare. *International Journal of Communications Law & Policy, 9*, 1-27.

Mitchell, K.J., Wolak, J., & Finelhor, D. (2005). Police posing as juveniles to catch sex offenders: Is it working? *Sexual Abuse: A Journal of Research and Treatment, 17*, 241-267.

Quayle, E., Vaughan, M., & Taylor, M. (2006). Sex offenders, Internet child abuse images and emotional avoidance: The importance of values. *Aggression and Violent Behavior, 11*, 1-11.

Simon, L.M. (1997). Do criminal offenders specialize in crime types? *Applied and Preventive Psychology, 6*, 35-53.

Suri, H. (1998). *A critique of contemporary methods of research synthesis.* Paper Retrieved October 31, 2003 from http://www.aare.edu.au/98pap/sur98250.htm

Terry, K.J., & Tallon, J. (2004). *Child Sexual Abuse: A Review of the Literature.* New York, NY: John Jay College.

Turvey, Brent (2003). *Criminal Profiling: An Introduction to Behavioral Evidence Analysis* (2nd ed.). New York, NY: Academic Press.

Ward, T., Hudson, S.M., Johnston, L., & Marshall, W.L. (1997). Cognitive distortions in sex offenders: An integrative approach. *Clinical Psychology Review, 17*, 479-507.

Wolak, J., Mitchell, K., & Finkelhor, D. (2003). *Internet Sex Crimes Against Minors: The Response of Law Enforcement.* Durham, NH: University of New Hampshire Crimes Against Children Research Center.

__. (2006). *Online Victimization of Youth: Five Years Later.* Washington, DC: National Center for Missing & Exploited Children.

AUTHORS' NOTES

Steven F. Hundersmarck, PhD, is Assistant Professor of Psychology and Criminal Justice, 200 Dukes Memorial, Ohio Northern University, Ada, OH 45810.

Keith F. Durkin, PhD, is Associate Professor and Chair, Department of Psychology and Sociology, 105 Hill Hall, Ohio Northern University, Ada, OH 45810.

Ronald L. Delong, MS, LPC, CCJS, is affiliated with Mid West Ohio Forensic Services, LLC, P.O. Box 612, Celina, OH 45822.

doi:10.1300/J076v45n01_17

Index

Page numbers in *italic* designate figures; page numbers followed by "t" designate tables.

278 MENTAL HEALTH ISSUES IN THE CRIMINAL JUSTICE SYSTEM